WRITE TO BE READ

WRITE TO BE READ

Informed Methods for Engaging Students as Writers

Barbara J. Smith and Hope Blecher

ROWMAN & LITTLEFIELD
Lanham • Boulder • New York • London

Published by Rowman & Littlefield
An imprint of The Rowman & Littlefield Publishing Group, Inc.
4501 Forbes Boulevard, Suite 200, Lanham, Maryland 20706
www.rowman.com

86-90 Paul Street, London EC2A 4NE

British Library Cataloguing in Publication Information Available

Library of Congress Cataloging-in-Publication Data

Names: Smith, Barbara J., 1956– author. | Blecher-Sass, Hope, 1962– author.
Title: Write to be read : informed methods for engaging students as writers / Barbara J. Smith and Hope Blecher.
Description: Lanham : Rowman & Littlefield, [2021] | Includes bibliographical references. | Summary: "Write to Be Read is for designers of engaging curriculum interested in improving the teaching of writing in schools today. Assumptions are challenged with reference to traditional models for teaching writing. Examples of students writing and activities are presented with self and teacher models of assessment to engage the writing lives of students"—Provided by publisher.
Identifiers: LCCN 2023026172 (print) | LCCN 2023026173 (ebook) | ISBN 9781475873061 (cloth) | ISBN 9781475873078 (paperback) | ISBN 9781475873085 (epub)
Subjects: LCSH: English language—Composition and exercises—Study and Teaching—United States.
Classification: LCC PE1405.U6 S645 2021 (print) | LCC PE1405.U6 (ebook) | DDC 808/.042071—dc23/eng/20230816
LC record available at https://lccn.loc.gov/2023026172
LC ebook record available at https://lccn.loc.gov/2023026173

We dedicate this book to everyone in education committed to breaking through the boxes that shape the fixed ways of teaching English language arts.

CONTENTS

Acknowledgments ix

Introduction: A Work in Progress xi

PART I: MAKING CONNECTIONS 1

1 Thinking Through Writing 3

2 Doing the Write Thing 11

3 Writing With Others 29

4 Disciplinary and Interdisciplinary Writing 35

PART II: NEW APPROACHES TO TEACHING WRITING 49

5 Poetry as a Gateway to Prose 51

6 Prompts for Writing Prose 68

7 Planning to Write Prose 73

8 Producing a First (Prose) Draft 77

9 Polishing Written Work 80

10 Presenting Written Work 90

11 Purpose-Based (PB) Writing Model 93

PART III: WRITING FOR A PURPOSE, ONE GRADE AT A TIME 97

12 Primary Writing Classroom 99

13 Grades 3 Through 5 Writing 105

14 Middle School Writing in an Upper Elementary School Setting 128

15 Middle School Writing in a High School Setting 152

16 Upper High School Writing 161

PART IV: DEEP DIVE INTO WRITING FORCES 173

17 Differentiating Writing Instruction 175

18 Feedback and Assessment of Writing 186

19 Handheld Devices 195

20 Parent Role in Student Writing 204

21 Challenges to Changing Writing Instruction 209

Conclusion: From Student to Writer 219

References 225

About the Authors 235

ACKNOWLEDGMENTS

Write to Be Read has been ten years in the making so we would like to thank our families for giving us the time and space to complete this work.

Thank you to our relatives, friends, and colleagues who believe us when we say that we enjoy teaching and being creative. This text became possible because our complementary styles and experiences have been supported by so many people throughout our careers.

Many thanks to Mike Crowley, Lisa M. Parry, Diana Sefchik, and Larry Swartz for taking time to endorse these ideas in *Write to Be Read*. We wish to thank our publisher, Rowman & Littlefield, specifically the insights of Tom Koerner, Carlie Wall, Jasmine Holman, and Kira Hall for seeing the need for new approaches for writing instruction.

Our educational journey has blossomed because key people in our lives were receptive to our voice and passion for education. We would like to acknowledge the support and voices of Douglas Barnes (posthumously), Helen D. Blecher, Libbie Blecher (posthumously), David Booth (posthumously), Steve Caley, Carol Cochi, Luke Coles, Ray Croney, Jenny Ellison, Oren Farhi, Gertrude Gilman (posthumously), Wayne Jones, Delphie Joy, Bena Kallick, Chemagne Kania, Lori M. Krivda, Diane Manica, Kris Masson, Valerie Miller, Molly Nelson, Ghazala Nomani, Nichole Nuzzi, Sharon Russell-Fowler, Loren I. Sass, Colin J. Sass,

Bev Scudamore, Sandra Scudamore, Simon Smith, Martin Smith, Sarah Smith, Tony Upson, Blossom, Flossie, Viola, and Tigger.

Many thanks to our former and current students and families, our mentees and mentors, and all educators bold enough to support meaningful change in schools.

Your futures are bright.

INTRODUCTION

A Work in Progress

Disneyland will never be completed, as long as there is imagination left in the world.

—Walt Disney[1]

Yes, this is another book about teaching writing, another work in progress, cut with a slice of imagination to further spark student engagement and capacity. *Write to Be Read: Informed Methods for Engaging Students as Writers* is a culminating project blending experiences from two careers reflecting on decades of searching for meaningful ways to engage and empower students to write well.

COVID may be subsiding, but writing remains a mystery, a stirring quest that requires a constant commitment to adaptation and innovation. The solution for teaching all students to write does not already exist. It is not on a single page, a chapter, or elaborated in manuscripts of funded research projects. Increasing the critical mass of confident learners, eager to write, is a worthy goal in schools.

Teachers can be more than implementers of others' ideas. They can be designers and innovators of new approaches to support young writers.

Reading, writing, speaking, listening, and nonverbal communications should not be competing forces; developing exceptional literacy skills can emerge from a balanced focus. This book outlines how students can use their own writing as a source for reading, speaking, listening, and responding to nonverbal and visible clues.

Much insight was gained when examining the possibilities for teaching writing in public, charter, independent, and international schools in Canada, the United States, and Belgium. Together Barbara Smith and Hope Blecher have more than 80 years of experience as teachers, teacher leaders, academic leaders, and authors. They have examined curriculum and developed resources aligned with expectations for many states in the United States, including Alabama, California, Florida, Georgia, Michigan, New York, Pennsylvania, New Jersey, and Virginia.

Reading what others write seems to be the predominant course of study for most mainstream English language arts (ELA) programs. The following teaching and learning story is a tired one, ready for a new beginning, middle, and ending:

> Someone in the school purchases a "ready to mix" ELA curriculum where teachers give students short fiction and informational passages to read. Some texts may even graze a variety of contexts, including science and social studies subject matter. After reading the passage, students answer trick questions aimed at determining if they can distinguish between the right answer and the distractor option. More progressive tests may include an open-ended essay or short-answer questions. In most cases, it is reading comprehension that is assessed through writing options. The quality of the writing tends to be overlooked, as changes to outlines or rough drafts are rarely considered in the analysis of such tests. Writing takes a back seat, when the emphasis in ELA is firmly fixed on the big test at the end of the year.

But the writing story in elementary or secondary schools does not need to lead to such a shallow life; it can be revived to support learning and engagement. Educators just need to be granted permission to do things differently. *Write to Be Read* was written to bring more balance to the "communications" ship that seems to be missing its keel, tipping over from the pressure to define language arts as a narrow set of reading skills.

This book is divided into four parts. Part I focuses on "making connections" with the current literature and research related to teaching writing. Chapter 1, "Thinking Through Writing," emphasizes just that, thinking through writing, and the volume of research supporting the need for quality writing curriculum and instruction.

The second chapter, "Doing the Write Thing," contrasts traditional writing methods with more engaging options. Examples of curriculum guides that link content, skills, and understandings within the context of authentic activities highlight the interconnectedness of meaningful learning tasks and the application of understandings to solve real-world problems.

"Writing With Others," chapter 3, does as the title of the chapter says, focuses on writing with others. Connecting with the research on the value of learning in blended social and individual contexts is hailed as a progressive consideration for writing instruction.

The fourth chapter in part I, "Disciplinary and Interdisciplinary Writing," features a deep dive into disciplinary and interdisciplinary writing. This chapter uses research and concrete examples to promote an emphasis on writing in individual subject areas, as well as the value of project-based work that integrates different disciplines to enhance and engage students as writers.

Part II shares new approaches for fine-tuning the teaching of writing that support a purpose-based (PB) approach to writing. This section outlines the beginning of a PB writing model, citing in chapter 5 how poetry can be a gateway to prose and how it can be more than a context for reading and an inspiration for writing. Chapters 6, 7, 8, 9, and 10 detail how prompts, plans, first drafts, polishing and revising, and the presentation of writing can help guide and enhance student engagement.

Chapter 11 reveals an emerging model for writing practice that celebrates key stages in the process while, at the same time, recommending authentic contexts for writing. No matter how technically sound a piece of writing might be, if it lacks substance and the commitment of the writer, the experience is superficial; a single model alone cannot guarantee transformational writing.

In part III, more practical writing ideas for teaching writing are revealed one grade at a time. Examples of writing for a purpose are broken down into ideas that span primary, grades 3 through 5, and middle school divisions in an elementary school and middle and senior high school divisions in a secondary school (chapters 12 to 16). Concrete examples are offered so the writer can decompose and further construct new options for infusing expectations with potentially meaningful activities into the depth and breadth of classroom writing instruction. According to Dr. Darrow:

> Think about what it means when we don't teach children to write authentically and profusely and critically: What does that do for democratic education? What does it do as far as facilitating voice? To structure an argument? I would like programs to think about writing as more than just a subject but as a way of fostering democracy.[2]

Part IV, "Deep Dive Into Writing Forces," addresses such important issues as differentiation, assessment, technology, parent role, and systematic barriers to writing mastery. Chapter 17, "Differentiating Writing Instruction," features a discussion of the importance of meeting students where they are. Many students need more time to grasp and apply complex skills and understandings; some students require accommodations and modifications; English-language learners need time to assimilate and make meaning of the connections with their first language.

"Feedback and Assessment of Writing," chapter 18, addresses feedback and assessment as an integral part of curriculum, not separate from it. The current approaches to assessing writing tend to keep the bell curve in place, with a few at the top end being "exceptional," a few at the bottom end giving up, and a large chunk in the middle churning out substandard work. Examples of assessment are featured throughout the book; this chapter specifically examines the force of feedback and its impact as a guide for young writers.

Chapter 19, "Handheld Devices," acknowledges handheld devices as physical and digital resources for supporting your writers. This chapter addresses the advantages and disadvantages of tools developed to support student writing.

"Parent Role in Student Writing," chapter 20, is a discussion of proactive conditions that may be helpful in the overall development of student writing. Parents can play a variety of roles, but some are more productive and supportive than others. Parents are a significant force potentially impacting all areas of curriculum and instruction.

Chapter 21, "Challenges to Changing Writing Instruction," reveals the many challenges that can be unearthed when considering changing the current path of writing instruction. Ideas for how to navigate around the barriers are featured, as well as a resounding call for change.

Write to Be Read concludes with a summary and description of what education can do to move identities from students to writers, accepting the notion that progress is ongoing, never completed, but in a constant state of improvement. We are not there yet, but we are firmly committed to what could happen next in tomorrow's classrooms. As Donald Graves noted: "Every study of young writers I've done for the last twenty years has underestimated what they can do. In fact, we know very little about the human potential for writing."[3] It's time to dig in and continue the quest to learn more about improving writing instruction.

Each chapter begins with "professional conversation starters" in the form of questions, statements, or quotes. Positioning these conversations at the beginning of each chapter, rather than at the end, was deliberate. The ideas and experiences of the reader matter. This resource was written to scaffold to the reader's understandings, recognizing that no one utopian solution exists for improving student writing.

Many chapters include mini lessons that emphasize a change from delivery of content to a customizing of needs. This book contains a range of sample mini lessons, not emphasized every year, but strategically, progressively, and vertically designed for a PK to 12 curriculum. It can be an opportune way to make room for students to craft their writing, not simply do lots of it. The ~ symbol introduces each mini lesson throughout this text.

To meet the disconnected targets of teaching an objective a day, many schools have morphed the practice of teaching writing into a lengthy advertisement that dulls creativity and takes away much-needed time for students to craft their writing. The idea of mini lessons enables teachers and writers to use conferencing times as teaching time.

Mini lessons are not any less rigorous than what the traditional teacher-directed approach can offer. When the student's writing becomes the focal point for learning, the teacher can introduce language tools and literary devices to individuals, small groups, or the entire class as a 10-minute teaching moment. Different from Atwell's "mini lessons,"[4] given to the entire class at a time, the mini lessons in this book are customized for when students are ready to apply them. Ideally, teachers should teach the mini lessons to one or two students at one time.

Write to Be Read aims to encourage teachers to try fresh ways of teaching writing to improve reading, writing, and critical thinking capacities of young people in many distinct classroom settings. The question "How can writing be a valued process if it is not read?" fuels this read, not the conventional practice of the teacher reading it to rank students for a score but writing so that people will read it, be moved by it, and act on it.

Just as Disneyland may never have its final "spike," the writing process should continue to be the focus of research and discussion. Having more alternatives to support writing instruction can't be a bad thing.

> *If you focus on what you left behind, you will never be able to see what lies ahead.*
>
> —Gusteau, *Ratatouille* (the movie)[5]

NOTES

1. Heaton, D. (August 30, 2021). Disneyland will never be completed. Tomorrow Society, https://tomorrowsociety.com/disneyland-will-never-completed/.
2. Paulick, J. H., Myers, J., Quinn, A., Couch, L., & Dunkerly-Bean, J. (Winter/Spring 2019). Examining practice: Examining elementary writing methods instruction. *Teaching/Writing: The Journal of Writing Teacher Education,* 6(1), 73.
3. Graves, D. (1994). *A fresh look at writing*. Portsmouth, NH: Heinemann, 99.
4. Atwell, N. (2015). *In the middle: A lifetime of learning about writing, reading, and adolescents.* Portsmouth, NH: Heinemann.
5. *Ratatouille*, dir. Brad Bird and Jan Pinkava. Walt Disney and Pixar, 2007.

Part I

MAKING CONNECTIONS

Good writing does not succeed or fail on the strength of its ability to persuade. It succeeds or fails on the strength of its ability to engage you, to make you think, to give you a glimpse into someone else's head.

—Malcolm Gladwell

1

THINKING THROUGH WRITING

PROFESSIONAL CONVERSATION STARTERS

1. Describe how you think writing relates to thinking.
2. Which experts and researchers inform you or your district's academic leaders?
3. What does it mean to ground practice in theory?
4. What do you think about the idea of advancing theory by grounding it in practice?

This chapter focuses on contributions that link to the notion that thinking can be enhanced through writing. Much has been examined in the past half century that informs not only our current practice, but also instruction yet to become more commonplace. How does research inform how students learn how to write; how can such understandings provide a foundation for further examination of the reciprocal relationship between writing and thinking; and how can both advance each other?

A rich foundation for supporting a school-wide emphasis on student writing has been shaped by the National Reading and Writing Project (NRWP)[1] and the National Council of Teachers of English (NCTE).[2] Such work provided valuable starting points for writing instruction.

Many researchers see writing as synonymous with thinking.[3] Writing tasks can be constructive, meaning-making activities. The first assets for fueling engaging school-wide writing cultures are the student and teacher writers who accept the role as constructivists. Students and teachers can take part in meaning-making activities using writing as a tool for thinking and innovation. Eighteenth-century philosopher Giambattista Vico captured the essence of constructivism with the words "The only way of 'knowing' a thing is to have made it."[4]

Dewey claimed: "Education is not an affair of 'telling' and being told, but an active and constructive process."[5] The notion that the learner needs to be an active participant in the shaping of knowledge is also fueled by the work of Kelly,[6] Bruner,[7] Piaget,[8] Bloom,[9] and Krathwohl and Anderson,[10] who claim to value creativity over evaluation.

Students need teachers to model how writing contributes to thinking. Ritchhart and Perkins wrote about principles of "cultural thinking," noting: "Schools must be cultures of thinking for teachers."[11] When students take part in activities that involve constructing understandings, they are indeed engaged in a culture of thinking.

The influence of constructivism supports new approaches to writing instruction. Britton promoted writing as a "tool of self-expression,"[12] and Emig claimed that writing was a "significant tool for advancing understanding."[13] Langer and Applebee concluded: "The greatest variety of reasoning operations occur during essay writing," adding, "This type of activity provides time for students to think most flexibly as they develop their ideas."[14] It may be an assumption, however, that the act of crafting a piece of writing inevitably would lead to a mind-challenging experience.

Without a commitment to the ideas and the process of reshaping them, students and teachers could go through the motions to "get it done" to meet a requirement developed beyond the personal reach of the writer. When authors are invested in their constructions, they take ownership of the learning. As Lemke noted: "Passion for something leads to the commitment of time and energy needed to learn about it deeply and comprehensively."[15]

Langer claimed that literacy "gives importance to individuals and the oral and written texts they create and encounter, and calls upon as well as fosters the kinds of language and thought that mark good and sharp thinking."[16] The central features of a constructivist approach, according to Naylor and Keogh, are that learners "can only make sense of new situations in terms of their existing understanding. . . . Learning involves an active process in which learners construct meaning by linking new ideas with their existing knowledge."[17]

Lemke recommended that educators consider creating new schools where more time is spent in the real world, "in internships, apprenticeships, and service learning. Doing. And then coming back to small groups with experienced adults (not necessarily always trained teachers) to reflect on and critique what they've done and seen other people doing."[18] Using real tools and reaching outside the walls of a school is what digital natives do on a regular basis, but as Lemke suggested, the disconnect between school and learning is growing.

An authentic writing piece should be much more than a written assignment turned in on a regular basis, reviewed by a teacher, graded or not, and returned, rarely read again or linked to future writing or other readers. What kinds of writing assignments do teachers use that lead students to reread their own writing? Creating a class or school newspaper is an activity that moves well beyond a narrow teacher audience. Lidvall noted: "I have heard from various parents how the kids love sharing their newspaper at home and usually ask to keep the weekly papers in special boxes."[19]

When young authors write material they want to read, they not only apply rigorous reading and editing to their own work, and work with the teachers or mentors as guides, but they also target a real audience who ideally will respond to their message. Duke and Hall focused their research on the role that an audience can play when influencing a sense of authenticity:

> Audience is generally agreed to be a critical aspect of writing process and product . . . outside of instructional context, literate people almost always write only if there is a reader for their writing, even if (in the case of journal or personal memo writing) the reader is the writer.[20]

Behizadeh explains: "Teachers can perceive their assessment tasks as being authentic writing projects (not knowing that their students think quite differently)! So whether a writing project is authentic clearly depends on who is being asked."[21] Surveying students to find out how they respond to writing tasks is worth the investment of time. Such information should inform curriculum improvement efforts.

Purcell-Gates, Duke, and Martineau claim: "A project is authentic if the genre exists in the world outside of school and the purpose for writing is the same as it would be if the child was writing it outside of school."[22] Linking with community service activities and addressing social justice issues are examples of potential authentic opportunities in the community.

All writers in a school context have the potential to become co-constructivists. The notion that learning is a social process has gained much worthy attention. Vygotsky's ideas on the social construction of learning[23] suggest that students need to go back and forth between individual and social settings.

A socially constructed writing process includes the expectation that student and teacher writers go back and forth between stages to edit their outlines and drafts based on both inner speech, a dialogue with themselves, and ongoing conferencing with each other. The teacher, as the more mature writer at first, helps guide the student during conferencing sessions to move through the "zone of proximal development."[24] By interacting with more expert writers, students have more opportunities to move from the role of novice to apprentice by learning to use the tools like experts. Further, when writers have opportunities to co-construct texts with others, powerful learning opportunities can emerge.

Educators have much to gain as co-constructivists as writing can be the activity that helps students appropriate the language of expert writers. According to the Dartmouth Writing Institute: "Collaboration encourages students to talk about their writing. In peer review sessions, students have to field questions about their writing. They have to explain and sometimes defend their writing strategies."[25] Levels of classroom engagement can be elevated when meaning making happens in a constructivist learning culture.

If a general agreement is that writing can enhance thinking, then it makes sense to focus attention on improving writing in school and in the workplace. Many researchers have documented such gains and conditions that can be barriers to writing.

The frequency of poor writing practices is more commonplace in schools that do not have sustainable and enriching writing cultures.[26] Many educators may think that they have established ideal conditions for teaching writing, but as Behizadeh suggests, "writing too often resides within a task or text chosen by the teacher, rather than residing with the student themselves."[27]

Wray et al. noted that some students can be discouraged from writing because, for example, they

- feel they have nothing to say;
- feel they do not write well and become discouraged by their final product; and/or
- get tired of doing the same old task over and over again.

Students feel that after all their efforts, no one notices what they have done anyway.[28]

Graham and Perin were commissioned by the Carnegie Corporation of New York to report on effective writing strategies. They listed 27 practices, including ones in which the teacher

- is enthusiastic about writing;
- adapts to meet the needs of individual writers; and
- organizes the writing program for productive collaborations when students help each other as they plan, draft, revise, edit, and/or publish their work.[29]

The National Literacy Trust states: "Seven times as many children and young people who enjoy writing write above the expected level for their age compared with those who don't enjoy writing."[30] Surveying students to find out which tasks are more engaging than others could help guide curriculum revision that should respond to the needs of students. Schools can enrich "writing lives" in ways that contribute to deeper understandings. Interest is growing in authentic writing instruction.[31] Behizadeh defined authentic writing as "a child's judgement of the connection between a writing project and their life."[32]

How a writing task can align with a student's life tends to take a secondary position when teachers feel pressure to follow a one-size-fits-all curriculum. According to Lidvall: "Students must see this real, human reason behind their writing if they are going to engage in the writing process."[33] Just because a teacher assigns a task, that cannot be assumed to be enough of a reason to fully commit to writing.

According to Behizadeh: "Both genre and purpose need to have real-world relevance and be valued outside of school," adding that writing activities that connect to the students' lives should be "meaningful to them." She also claimed that student engagement and achievement are enhanced by the "authenticity of the task."[34]

According to Gilbert and Graham, 60% of teachers in grades 4 through 6 indicated that they felt ill-equipped to teach writing.[35] Even though many educators realize the importance of writing, teachers admit to being underprepared for the task.[36] With the volume of literature in high school English language arts (ELA) programs, little time is left for writing[37] beyond tasks to complete to receive a grade or finish an assignment.

The idea of developing a cultural theory of writing, embedded within a larger view of research into student and teacher learning, might help guide students and staff to lead more passionate, persuasive, and innovative writing lives.

NOTES

1. National Reading and Writing Project (NRWP). https://readingandwritingproject.org.
2. National Council of Teachers of English (NCTE). https://ncte.org.
3. Hillocks, G. (2010). Teaching argument for critical thinking and writing: An introduction. *English Journal,* 99(6), 24–32; Shepard, L. S. (2008). A brief history of accountability testing, 1965–2007. In K. E. Ryan & L. S. Shepard (Eds.), *The future of test-based educational accountability* (pp. 25–46). New York: Routledge; Spandel, V. (2013). *Creating writers: Six traits, process, workshop, and literature*. Boston: Allyn & Bacon.
4. "Giambattista Vico." Wikipedia. https://en.wikipedia.org/wiki/Giambattista_Vico.
5. Dewey, J. (1915/2015). *The school and society and the child and the curriculum.* Chicago: University of Chicago Press, 38.
6. Kelly, G. A. (1955). *The psychology of personal constructs. Vol. 1, A theory of personality. Vol. 2, Clinical diagnosis and psychotherapy.* New York: Norton.
7. Bruner, J. (1960). *The process of education*. Cambridge, MA: Harvard University Press.
8. Piaget, J. (1952). *The origins of intelligence in children.* New York: International Universities Press.
9. Bloom, B. S. (1956). *Taxonomy of educational objectives handbook: The cognitive domain*. New York: David McKay.
10. Anderson, L. W., & Krathwohl, D. R. (2001). *A taxonomy for learning, teaching, and assessing: A revision of Bloom's taxonomy of educational objectives.* New York: Longman.
11. Ritchhart, R., & Perkins, D. N. (2005). Learning to think: The challenges of teaching thinking. In K. J. Holyoak & R. G. Morrison (Eds.), *The Cambridge handbook of thinking and reasoning* (pp. 775–802). Cambridge: Cambridge University Press.
12. Britton, J. N. (1970). *Language and learning*. Coral Gables, FL: University of Miami.
13. Emig, J. A. (1971). *The composing processes of twelfth graders*. Urbana, IL: National Council of Teachers of English.
14. Langer J. A., & Applebee, A. N. (1987). *How writing shapes thinking: A study of teaching and learning.* Urbana, IL: National Council of Teachers of English, 100.
15. Lemke, J. L. (March 2010). Lessons from Whyville: A hermeneutics for our mixed reality. In *Games and Culture.* New York: Sage, 155.
16. Langer, J. A. *Envisioning Literature: Literary understanding and literature instruction.* New York: Teachers College Press, 1.
17. Naylor, S., & Keogh, B. (1999). Constructivism in classroom: Theory into practice. *Journal of Science Teacher Education, 10*(2), 93–106, esp. 93.

18. Lemke, J. L. (March 31, 2010). After schools what comes next? http://www.jaylemke.com/imported-20110501025959/tag/school-reform.

19. Lidvall, C. D. (Spring 2008). *Get real: Instructional implications for authentic writing activities capstone experience*. Vanderbilt University's Peabody College of Education. https://ir.vanderbilt.edu/bitstream/handle/1803/789/CarlyLidvallCapstone.pdf?sequence=1&isAllowed=y.

20. Duke, N. K., & Hall, L. A. (2006/2007). Authentic literacy activities for developing comprehension and writing. *Reading Teacher, 60*(4), 344–355.

21. Behizadeh, N. (January 2014). Adolescent perspectives on authentic writing instruction. *Journal of Language & Literacy Education, 10*(1), 27–44.

22. Purcell-Gates, V., Duke, N. K., & Martineau, J. A. (2007). Learning to read and write genre-specific text: Roles of authentic experience and explicit teaching. *Reading Research Quarterly, 42*(1), 8–45. https://doi.org/10.1598/RRQ.42.1.1.

23. Vygotsky, L. (1978). *Mind in society*. London: MIT Press.

24. Vygotsky (1978).

25. Dartmouth Writing Institute. http://dartmouth.edu/writing-speech/teaching/first-year-writing-pedagogies-methods-design/collaborative-learninglearning-peers.

26. Graham, S., Gillespie, A., & McKeown, D. (June 29, 2012). Writing, importance, development, instruction. *Reading and Writing, 26*, 1–15.

27. Behizadeh (January 2014).

28. Wray, D., Beard, R., Raban, B., Hall, N., Bloom, W., Robinson, A., Potter, F., Sands, H., & Yates, I. (1988). *Developing Children's Writing.* Leamington Spa: Scholastic.

29. Graham, S., & Perin, D. (2007). *Writing next: Effective strategies to improve writing of adolescents in middle and high schools*. New York: Carnegie Corporation of New York.

30. National Literacy Trust. (2017). https://literacytrust.org.uk.

31. Dombey/UKLA. (2013). *Teaching writing: What the evidence says UKLA argues for an evidence-informed approach to teaching and testing young children's writing.* UKLA: London; Gadd, M. (2014). *What is critical in the effective teaching of writing? A study of the classroom practice of some year 5–8 teachers in the New Zealand context*. Unpublished doctoral thesis. Auckland: University of Auckland; Goouch, K., Cremin, T., & Lambirth, A. (2009). *Writing is primary: Final research report*. London: Esmee Fairbairn Foundation; Graham & Perin (2007).

32. Behizadeh (January 2014).

33. Lidvall, C. D. (Spring 2008). Get real: Instructional implications for authentic writing activities capstone experience. Vanderbilt University's Peabody College of Education. https://ir.vanderbilt.edu/bitstream/handle/1803/789/CarlyLidvallCapstone.pdf?sequence=1&isAllowed=y.

34. Behizadeh, (January 2014).

35. Gilbert, J., & Graham, S. (2010). Teaching writing to elementary students in grades 4–6: A national survey. *Elementary School Journal, 110*, 494–518.

36. Brimi, H. (Fall, 2012). Teaching writing in the shadow of standardized writing assessment: An exploratory study. *American Secondary Education, 41*(1); Gilbert & Graham (2010); Juzwik, M. M. (2010). Negotiating moral stance in classroom discussion about litera-

ture: Entextualization and contextualization processes in a narrative spell. In P. A. Prior & J. A. Hengst (Eds.), *Exploring semiotic remediation as discourse practice*. London: Palgrave Macmillan. https://doi.org/10.1057/9780230250628_4; McQuitty, V. (2012). Emerging possibilities: A complex account of learning to teach writing. *Research in the Teaching of English, 46*, 358–389; Rowsell, J., & Lapp, D. (2011). New literacies in literacy instruction. In L. M. Morrow & L. B. Gambrell (Eds.), *Best practices in literacy instruction* (pp. 395–411). New York: Guilford; Smagorinsky, P. (2011). Vygotsky's stage theory: The psychology of art and the actor under the direction of Perezhivanie. *Mind, Culture, and Activity, 18*(4), 319–341. https://doi.org/10.1080/10749039.2010.518300.

37. Smagorinsky (2011); Tremmel, R. (2001). Seeking a balanced discipline: Writing teacher education in first-year composition and English education. *English Education, 34*(1), 6–30.

2

DOING THE WRITE THING

PROFESSIONAL CONVERSATION STARTERS

1. What would an ELA curriculum look like if writing, rather than reading, were the main driver?
2. Why do you think there is a need for so much repetition of expectations in each grade?
3. How can you tweak a disengaging practice and make it more memorable and engaging?
4. In your experience, what contrasting engaging and disengaging experiences in classrooms can you share?

The notion of engagement is central to building a vibrant writing culture in a classroom and school. All schools can do more "write things," not simply check off a writing box in an English language arts (ELA) curriculum. School practitioners can make room for more critical and creative thinkers and leaders. If many students are having difficulty after 12 years of education, then perhaps the way we do it needs to change.

It is not enough to tell young people to write so that the teacher will grade it. Teachers need to select tasks that have meaning and purpose for young writers. Inspiring writing prompts can make a difference for a student who must turn a blank page into an extraordinary piece of writing.

The teacher, as writing coach, can design a learning setting that primes the student "well" of possibilities. Informed teachers do not pour knowledge, like water, into the head of the learner; rather, the teacher uses prompts and customized instruction to enable students to bring their own resources and creative work to the surface.

Asking the "so what?" question is usually a litmus test of engagement potency. The echo from college professors and employers that many young scholars struggle to write should make educators dive deeply into how young people are being taught to master this critical craft, as well as what we are asking them to write.

Calkins emphasizes: "Children should generate their own texts, using material from their own lives." Her website affirms that her approach to literacy "reviles" direct teaching, "where the teacher stands in front of the room and lectures, preferring instead that children work in small groups and consult each other as much as possible," adding that teachers need to "routinely engage in conferences with each individual child about his or her writing and reading experiences."[1]

At the heart of Calkins's philosophy is the need for children to use and develop their voice, to be "encouraged to discover and refine their own personal writing style," as they compose "stories that matter."[2] Similarly, the notion of a purpose-based (PB) curriculum is grounded in student engagement and interaction with teachers and learning materials that matter.

Engagement in any writing task should spiral through definitive stages of a process, ideally emphasizing in final stages a link or a connection to an authentic audience. Work that matters often becomes a piece of writing for others to view and read. The will to write and invest time in the process of constructing written work, however, requires that teachers know and understand their students, what makes them excited and moves them to action.

What kinds of activities move students to inspired writing? Writing tasks in a PB curriculum can be modified in many ways.

- Reading short texts and writing a scripted response for a test or the teacher could be . . . reading short texts of interest and writing a review online.
- Responding to questions after each chapter in a novel study could be . . . writing a review of a novel on Amazon/other online book ordering companies; rewriting the ending in a novel; rewriting a novel into a script.

- Writing a biography about people you have never met could be . . . interviewing seniors, service providers, artists . . . and writing biographies of real people—to be read by others.
- Writing about literary terms found in poetry or other texts could be . . . using literary terms to add richness to your own writing.
- Writing five paragraphs could be . . . writing a five-paragraph school newspaper article.
- Writing a pretend application could be . . . writing an actual application.
- Writing about the history of the school could be . . . writing about the design or renovation of the school.
- Writing about other people's theories could be . . . creating your own theories.
- Responding to questions with prose could be . . . creating tables, making lists, drawing and labeling images, creating instructions for how to make things, play games, or follow directions.
- Writing by yourself could be . . . writing with others and for others.
- Revising your own writing could be . . . peer editing (younger students in writing buddy scenarios).

Dewey described curriculum as

> a map, a summary, an arranged and orderly view of previous experiences, that serves as a guide to future experience; it gives direction; it facilitates control; it economizes effort, preventing wasted wandering, and pointing out the paths which lead most quickly and most certainly to a desired result.[3]

Informed schools follow curriculum plans that have both grade and vertical alignment. Table 2.1 reveals the expectations of the Common Core State Standards (CCSS) writing portion for grades 11 and 12 ELA.

What is a vertical alignment of curriculum, and what does it look like when focusing on the mastery of writing skills at a basic level? Simply put, quality alignment happens when what is learned in one grade builds on what was mastered in the previous grade.

How are curriculum maps at the board, state, national, or other levels part of a continuous improvement cycle? The CCSS in the United States were intended to provide comprehensive guidelines for establishing identified "nonnegotiables" for learning ELA and mathematics.

Teachers have roughly 175 days to ensure that their students have mastered 76 concepts of varying complexities. Table 2.1 details 27 expectations

Table 2.1. CCSS Writing Expectations for Grades 11 and 12

CCSS.ELA-LITERACY.WHST.11-12.1 Write arguments focused on *discipline-specific content.*
CCSS.ELA-LITERACY.W.11-12.1.A Introduce precise, knowledgeable claim(s), establish significance of claim(s), distinguish from alternate or opposing claims, create organization that logically sequences claim(s), counterclaims, reasons, and evidence.
CCSS.ELA-LITERACY.W.11-12.1.B Develop claim(s) and counterclaims fairly and thoroughly, supplying most relevant evidence pointing out strengths and limitations in manner that anticipates audience's knowledge, concerns, values, and possible biases.
CCSS.ELA-LITERACY.W.11-12.1.C Use words, phrases, clauses, and syntax to link major sections of text, create cohesion, clarify relationships between claim(s) and reasons, between reasons and evidence, and between claim(s) and counterclaims.
CCSS.ELA-LITERACY.W.11-12.1.D Establish and maintain a formal style and objective tone while attending to norms and conventions of the discipline in which they are writing.
CCSS.ELA-LITERACY.W.11-12.1.E Provide concluding statement or section that follows and supports argument presented.
CCSS.ELA-LITERACY.WHST.11-12.2 Write informative/explanatory texts, including narration of historical events, scientific procedures/experiments, or technical processes.
CCSS.ELA-LITERACY.W.11-12.2.A Introduce topic; organize complex ideas, concepts, and information so new element builds on what precedes it to create unified whole; include formatting, graphics, and multimedia when useful to aiding comprehension.
CCSS.ELA-LITERACY.W.11-12.2.B Develop topic thoroughly by selecting most significant and relevant facts, extended definitions, concrete details, quotations, or other information and examples appropriate to audience's knowledge of topic.
CCSS.ELA-LITERACY.W.11-12.2.C Use appropriate and varied transitions and syntax to link major sections of text, create cohesion, and clarify relationships among complex ideas and concepts.
CCSS.ELA-LITERACY.W.11-12.2.D Use precise language, domain-specific vocabulary, and techniques such as metaphor, simile, and analogy to manage the complexity of topic.
CCSS.ELA-LITERACY.W.11-12.2.E Establish and maintain a formal style and objective tone while attending to norms and conventions of discipline in which they are writing.
CCSS.ELA-LITERACY.W.11-12.2.F Provide a concluding statement or section that follows from and supports the information or explanation presented.
CCSS.ELA-LITERACY.W.11-12.3 Write narratives to develop real or imagined experiences or events using effective technique, well-chosen details, and well-structured event sequences.
CCSS.ELA-LITERACY.W.11-12.3.A Engage and orient reader by setting out problem, situation, or observation and its significance, establishing 1 or multiple point(s) of view, and introducing narrator/characters; create smooth progression of experiences or events.
CCSS.ELA-LITERACY.W.11-12.3.B Use narrative techniques, such as dialogue, pacing, description, reflection, and multiple plot lines, to develop experiences, events, and/or characters.

CCSS.ELA-LITERACY.W.11-12.3.C Use a variety of techniques to sequence events so that they build on one another to create a coherent whole and build toward a particular tone and outcome.
CCSS.ELA-LITERACY.W.11-12.3.D Use precise words and phrases, telling details, and sensory language to convey a vivid picture of the experiences, events, setting, and/or characters.
CCSS.ELA-LITERACY.W.11-12.3.E Provide a conclusion that follows from and reflects on what is experienced, observed, or resolved over the course of the narrative.
CCSS.ELA-LITERACY.W.11-12.4 Produce clear and coherent writing in which the development, organization, and style are appropriate to task, purpose, and audience.
CCSS.ELA-LITERACY.W.11-12.5 Develop and strengthen writing as needed by planning, revising, editing, rewriting, or trying a new approach, focusing on addressing what is most significant for a specific purpose and audience.
CCSS.ELA-LITERACY.W.11-12.6 Use technology, including the Internet, to produce, publish, and update individual or shared writing products in response to ongoing feedback, including new arguments or information.
CCSS.ELA-LITERACY.W.11-12.7 Conduct short and sustained research projects to answer question/solve problem; narrow/broaden inquiry when appropriate; synthesize multiple sources, demonstrating understanding of subject under investigation.
CCSS.ELA-LITERACY.W.11-12.8 Gather relevant information from multiple authoritative print and digital sources, use advanced searches effectively; assess strengths and limitations of sources in terms of task, purpose, and audience; integrate info into text selectively to maintain flow of ideas, avoid plagiarism and overreliance on 1 source, following standard citation format.
CCSS.ELA-LITERACY.W.11-12.9.A Apply grades 11–12 Reading standards to literature.
CCSS.ELA-LITERACY.W.11-12.9.B Apply grades 11–12 Reading standards to literary nonfiction.
CCSS.ELA-LITERACY.W.11-12.10 Write routinely over extended time frames (time for research, reflection, and revision) and shorter time frames (a single sitting or a day or two) for a range of tasks, purposes, and audiences.

Source: Common Core State Standards (ELA Literacy Grade 11–12 Writing), http://www.corestandards.org/ELA-Literacy/WHST/11-12/.

listed in the CCSS for grades 11 and 12 writing. It could be argued that the volume of expectations for each grade contributed to the lack of mastery of key concepts in each subject area.

Absent from the list is specific reference to media literacy, a powerful context that students do need to examine in preparation for college, life, and the world of work. Through the backward design lens, imagine what it would be like for a teacher in grade 12 to design lessons and units for English, given the following expectations:

- 27 for writing
- 17 for language
- 22 for reading literature and informational texts
- 10 for speaking and listening

Even if teachers spread such expectations over two years, they would have just shy of five days to make sure their students met each standard. Such a volume of objectives leaves little time to review or link expectations to each other or build in project-based activities to apply understandings and promote the kind of deep learning that makes learning stick.

Often alignment is assumed when schools use curriculum maps. If no deliberate attention is paid to what is unique in each grade, it is possible that maps can house repeated experiences or poor practices. Having a curriculum map does not guarantee that a school has a quality program. Without someone responsible for overseeing how the big picture (K through college) will unfold, gaps can be inherent.

Rosenshine recommended that teachers should not "overwhelm their students by presenting too much new material at once. Rather, the most effective teachers only present small amounts of new material at any time, and then assist the students as they practice this material."[4] The notion of "less is more" is a common theme in more general curriculum discussions, but it has significant implications for teaching effective writing habits.

Schools have competing disciplines competing for time, yet more time is required for quality writing instruction. Specifically, the volume of specific kinds of writing should be the focus of discussion and curriculum design.

On the one hand, regular informal writing in the form of journaling, blogging, and using graphic organizers such as webs, charts, and graphs has tremendous value. Rather than more formal writing tasks, it makes sense to reduce these numbers to build in more room for expert support and focused attention to emulating process behaviors of career authors. Rubin, Abrego, and Sutterby noted: "Students need to be given opportunities to revise and edit their writing and do peer editing. This may mean that they write fewer texts, but they will have a better understanding of the writing process."[5]

Reducing the number of written assignments give students more time to think through word choices, sentence order, and use a host of tools to shift and enhance the quality of their work. Writing can be a process that supports thinking, but when educators use it to "cover" the curriculum, the potential benefits from crafting and recrafting ideas can be lost.

The concern is that students must "follow the same curriculum, one that urges coverage of a blizzard of specific 'expectations'—almost 4,000 for students from grades 1 to 8, an average of 500 per year." Further, McAdie and Leithwood warn: "Students are learning a little bit about a lot of different subject areas—it is curriculum that promotes memory work and rote learning, emphasizing coverage rather than understanding."[6]

It seems logical that writing often increases one's confidence in feeling like a writer. However, deliberately reducing the amount of writing a student is assigned can lead to significant improvement. Graves's[7] message about writing daily does not mean that students should be writing without instructional support.

Experts agree that most writing assignments require time to gather ideas in various outline forms (e.g., words, images, charts), draft initial sentences, revise sentences, craft a published work, and in some cases, display images in illustrative and/or digital forms. A piece of writing can take upwards of several weeks, months, or years when students engage in various writing projects. To emulate novel writers, students can take several years to research, draft, and complete their novel.

A formal piece of writing in any subject area, such as a response to literature, an assignment in history, or a report in science, should be given ample time to permit the development of each phase of a writing process. The practice of scribbling a first response without the opportunity to think through choices at each stage of a writing process not only limits the overall intellectual return, but it can contribute to the consolidation of poor writing habits, void of thoroughly developed outlines and revisions to the initial draft.

The sheer quantity of questions that students answer in prose form each day may be perpetuating a culture of sloppy writing practices. Rather than oversubscribing to hastily constructed sentences, students could opt to respond to some questions by submitting words or phrases within tables or other graphic organizers. Without having novice writers apprentice with more expert writers, students can easily acquire weak habits, such as run-on sentences, lack of clarity, and redundancy.

The volume of writing a student is expected to complete should be in proportion to the time the teacher can invest in conferencing and providing direct support. How often does the image of the teacher overwhelmed by piles of ungraded papers show up on social media sites? Not only do emergent writers need immediate feedback, but they also should have ongoing input throughout the process. If the writing mentor cannot keep up with supporting each assignment, the number of tasks needs to be revisited.

Typically, the CCSS and most commercial resources flood the annual curriculum expectations with all genres, all story elements, the "mother lode" of literary devices, and a random use of grammatical and punctuation applications. It is rare for schools, districts, or state curriculum guides to identify a focus beyond the "teach everything every year" approach.

Pinterest, Kickstarter, and Teachers-Pay-Teachers feature grassroots educational innovation that can be overjoying, yet, at the same time, overwhelming for teachers. The downside to such abundance, however, is the lack of filtering to decipher which resources are more engaging for students than others.

It makes sense that such a jam-packed core curriculum would not engage students or teachers. Rather than make decisions about what is essential, it appears that the writers of the CCSS and other state, provincial, or national curricula provide a smorgasbord of unrealistic expectations, which can contribute to less interest in entering the teaching field and more current teachers considering their exit.

Students need to be in schools where the curriculum is aligned, so that what is mastered in one grade will support the learning in the next grade. When teachers and students have too much on their plate, there is little guarantee that the foundation for learning is being built on each year. Too many expectations can contribute to a random application of the curriculum.

An ELA curriculum often revolves around the reading choices for the school year. When this happens, key writing expectations can be lost in the weeds. Curriculum guidelines and standards often fall short of clearly designating what might be recommended to be taught and when best to teach it. Overengineering expectations challenges educators to decipher which understandings and skills should be mastered by all students. Table 2.2 lists the first core standard for writing literacy for grades 4 and 5 with subtle adjustments.

The designers of the CCSS curriculum for ELA suggest that grade 4 students should group but not be expected to "logically" group ideas; that

Table 2.2. CCSS for Grades 4 and 5 Writing

4.1 Write opinion pieces on topics or texts, supporting a point of view with reasons and information.	5.1 Write opinion pieces on topics or texts, supporting a point of view with reasons and information.
CCSS.ELA-LITERACY.W.4.1.A Introduce a topic or text clearly, state an opinion, and create an organizational structure in which related ideas are grouped to support the writer's purpose.	CCSS.ELA-LITERACY.W.5.1.A Introduce a topic or text clearly, state an opinion, and create an organizational structure in which ideas are logically grouped to support the writer's purpose.
CCSS.ELA-LITERACY.W.4.1.B Provide reasons supported by facts and details.	CCSS.ELA-LITERACY.W.5.1.B Provide logically ordered reasons supported by facts and details.
CCSS.ELA-LITERACY.W.4.1.C Link opinion and reasons using words and phrases (e.g., for instance, to, in addition).	CCSS.ELA-LITERACY.W.5.1.C Link opinion and reasons using words, phrases, and clauses (e.g., consequently, specifically).
CCSS.ELA-LITERACY.W.4.1.D Provide a concluding statement or section related to the opinion presented.	CCSS.ELA-LITERACY.W.5.1.D Provide a concluding statement or section related to the opinion presented.

Source: Common Core State Standards (ELA-Literacy, Grade 5), http://www.corestandards.org/ELA-Literacy/W/5/.

grade 4s do not need to provide "logical reasons" and should understand phrases but not clauses. If any task requires reasoning, it should be logical. Further, the expectation that all grade 5s have a solid understanding of grammatical clauses is a concern. A listed expectation should be one that all students in the age/grade level should be able to master.

Teachers tend to view curriculum by focusing on what is determined at the governmental levels for a particular grade level. It's important, however, for teachers to work with vertical teams to identify which expectations are new and which expectations are identified for review. Further, it is necessary to determine which expectations are more essential than others.

Gardner recognized that a "one-size-fits-all" approach to teaching does not give all students equal opportunities for learning, noting: "I think that we teach way too many subjects, and we cover way too much material, and the end result is that students have a very superficial knowledge, as we often say, a mile wide and an inch deep."[8]

In Fratt's article "Less is More: Trimming the Overstuffed Curriculum," she notes:

> Overstuffed and under-nourishing is the way many experts describe the science curriculum. The Third International Math Study characterizes U.S.

> math and science curricula as "a mile wide and an inch deep." Instead of forcing students to digest more and more content and vocabulary as science continues to advance, experts recommend a science curriculum "diet" to help take a bite out of the nation's current science achievement woes. . . . Less is more.[9]

With so much information readily available in the 21st century, it is easy to see how textbooks in all subject areas continue to expand. It could be argued that in many ELA classes, the sheer volume of writing in response to the add-on of more literature and informational texts may be contributing to a growing mass of reluctant, stressed learners and teachers.

The CCSS lists 84 expectations for grade 4 ELA and 73 for grade 5 ELA. Many states adopted the CCSS. A few, including Virginia, kept their own standards. Overall, the state of Virginia lists 69 ELA expectations for grade 4 and 75 for grade 5. Even though standards may be written differently, what remains is much repetition between grades and frankly, too many overall expectations for teachers and students to ensure mastery of and any sense of deep learning.

Writing standards for grades 4 and 5 in Virginia include 11 duplicate expectations, some rewording very similar expectations to appear as distinct. For instance, in grade 4, "The student will write in a variety of forms to include narrative, descriptive, opinion, and expository (4.7)"; and in grade 5, "The student will write in a variety of forms to include narrative, descriptive, expository, and persuasive (5.7)," making the difference a matter of opinion and persuasion.

In grade 4, students are expected to "write related paragraphs on the same topic." And in grade 5, students are expected to "write multi-paragraph compositions." How are such expectations really distinct? Commas are expected to be mastered in grade 4: "Use commas in series, dates, and addresses"; and again, in grade 5: "Use commas to indicate interrupters, items in a series, and to indicate direct address." Isn't the function of commas to interrupt?

The time dedicated to making arbitrary distinctions among standards that, it could be argued, are not as essential as other standards makes it confusing for teachers to plan for writing instruction. The test-making companies can filter the standards to generate questions that focus on what distinguishes grade 5 expectations from grade 4, namely, in the case of Virginia:

- Use precise and descriptive vocabulary to create tone and voice.
- Use plural possessives.
- Use interjections.
- Use prepositional phrases.
- Edit for fragments and run-on sentences.
- Use coordinating conjunctions.
- Use a hyphen to divide words at the end of a line.

Should such understandings be considered essential for students in grade 5, and what research and rationale exist to support such determinations?

It is difficult to view curriculum in its entirety for a grade or compare between grades when so many expectations are listed. The province of Ontario in Canada lists 75 expectations for grade 4 and 75 for grade 5.[10] How is it possible in 175-plus school days for students to master all these expectations? They cannot possibly all be essential.

Now, consider the students facing the added load of mastering expectations listed for all subject areas. It is a miracle that so many students continue to tolerate the unrealistic burden of expectations from all their studies. The lessons learned about reduced levels of student engagement seem to be falling on the deaf ears of many curriculum mappers.

There is no need to teach fables every year, or Shakespeare, or adjectives, or advertising. If students have time to delve into these critical areas without the superficial plan to teach everything every year, they will have more room for learning that sticks. There is no need whatsoever to test for a student's knowledge of adverbs in grade 2 or expect grade 3s to identify metaphors on a multiple-choice test.

If all students could apply language conventions, figurative language, and punctuation in their writing, then it would be fair game for testing. Without a progressive curriculum that identifies when the adjective might best be introduced for all student writing, then it makes sense that such a piecemeal approach to teaching ELA will have limited lasting effects.

Table 2.3 provides a big picture idea of how a scope and sequence can be designed to address a sample depth and breadth of writing expectations. A school's academic leader needs to be in a room for a few days with the language arts teachers to examine how the ELA curriculum can be aligned. Relying on a textbook to do the design work minimizes the depth of experience the teacher brings to the table.

The tendency to push unrealistic expectations to lower grades can also be a deterrent to learning. If a standard is listed, all students should have the developmental capacity to be proficient or demonstrate exemplary understanding and skills. The idea that all kindergarten or grade 1 students should be able to write paragraphs or read chapter books makes no sense at all. Yes, some students will read more and write more than others at an earlier age, but such experiences should be deemed exceptional, not be an arbitrary ceiling that rushes the curriculum and limits deep learning.

The sample K–12 writing curriculum (table 2.3) provides fewer distinct writing targets for each grade, based on two key understandings:

- There is much to learn in language arts in 13 years.
- ELA expectations do not have to be random.

Note: PK refers to pre-kindergarten, which can include junior kindergarten in some jurisdictions and SK refers to senior kindergarten.

When students move from grade to grade, their writing instruction can be disjointed without a clear, comprehensive school-wide approach to teaching writing. The injections outlined in this book can serve to begin further discussions about what can fuel an effective writing process and how an engaged writing culture can evolve from deliberately attending to building an exceptional school-wide approach to writing.

If teachers do not study the expectations from the previous grade, they have no way of knowing what parts of textbooks and curriculum expectations are repeated. Therefore, the gap can widen when students are not given enough time and exposure to what's new in each grade. Teachers have a wealth of ideas for breathing life into expectations; their insight and wisdom are equally important when determining how the curriculum fits together.

Many resources rarely distinguish what skills, habits, and understandings could be mastered at each grade. Students need to be in schools where the curriculum is aligned, so that what is mastered in one grade will support the learning in the next grade. Examining the overlap in the standards from grade to grade illustrates the lack of clarity to guide teachers, textbooks, and other resources.

At the college/university level, students can be offered writing labs that focus on learning how to write abstracts, executive summaries, op-eds, grant proposals, and poster papers. When colleges need to establish in-

Table 2.3. Sample PK to Grade 12 Writing Curriculum

Fiction Reading Themes	*Words*	*Language/ Grammar Focus*	*Sentence Structure and Punctuation*	*Fiction Poetry*	*Fiction Focused Writing*	*Nonfiction (NF); Poetry*	*NF Focused Writing*
Nursery Rhymes (PK)	identify and record uppercase letters; two-letter words	hard letter sounds	listen and respond to questions	gestures in key words in nursery rhymes	draw and dictate order of events in nursery rhymes	dictate poems about family members	dictate and illustrate stories about family members
Fairy Tales (SK)	uppercase and lowercase letters; three-letter words	hard and soft letter sounds	listen and respond to one-step directions	acrostic poems (fairy-tale characters)	dictate own fairy tale . . . "Once upon a time . . ."	dictate ABC poems about school	dictate and illustrate stories about people at school
Fables (Grade 1)	simple consonant and vowels; four-letter simple words	simple action verbs	record sentences using period and question mark	rhyming poem about fable	sentences about lessons in fables	shape poems (global city landmarks)	sentences that compare houses in different cities
Folklore (Grade 2)	complex vowel; compound and blended letter words; alliteration	noun and pronoun use (common, proper)	capital use, titles, point form notes, label maps, short answers	haiku poems; tanka poems	write new endings to folklores	found poems about nature	create media messages advertising country
Comedy (Grade 3)	synonyms, similes, puns	adjective use	single-paragraph composition, exclamations	limerick poems	character makeover paragraph	looped poems	friendly email letter to a global e-pal
Adventure/ Mystery (Grade 4)	antonyms, hyperbole, satire	adverb use	three-paragraph compositions; hyphens, dash, comma use	cinquain poems	write a fictional book review	diamante—comparing past and present	descriptive writing (Middle Ages)

(continued)

Table 2.3. *Continued*

Fiction Reading Themes	*Words*	*Language/ Grammar Focus*	*Sentence Structure and Punctuation*	*Fiction Poetry*	*Fiction Focused Writing*	*Nonfiction (NF); Poetry*	*NF Focused Writing*
Myths (Grade 5)	homonyms, onomatopoeia, assonance	phrases, prepositions	five-paragraph compositions, apostrophe use	mythical poems	compare three myths	color poems	compare three ancient civilizations
Fantasy (Grade 6)	metaphor, symbolism, idioms	subject and predicate; adverbial clause; conjunctions	article writing, novel writing, outline	fantasy poems	new worlds for fantasy setting	current event poetry	newspaper article about current event
Science Fiction (Grade 7)	personification, allusion, flashback	adjectival clause	creative writing; speech writing; novel writing draft; colon use	palindrome poems	science fiction writing	technology poetry	STEM and research writing; speech writing
Social Justice (Grade 8)	irony, allegory, foreshadowing	objects; noun clause	persuasive essay; publish novel; brackets and parentheses	blank verse poems	comparing books by same author	social justice poetry; song writing	business letter writing/letter to the editor; abstract
Media, Mentors, Models (Grades 9–10)	euphemism; analogy; colloquialism	referencing; quotations; interjections; footnoting	journal writing; cover letter and résumé; semicolon use; slash	iambic pentameter poems	script writing; film and concert review	poet in the poems	biographical writing; blog writing
World of Work and Life (Grades 11–12)	juxtaposition, oxymoron, paradox, motif, soliloquy	text and tools; make a website	documentary writing; debate writing; ellipses	sonnets, ballads, epic poem	comparing authors and messages	writing personal poems	autobiography; annotated bibliography; lit review

person or online writing tutorials or labs to help students develop writing skills, this is evidence that current approaches taken in elementary and secondary education do not seem to stick.

Duke University's Thompson Writing Program provides a series of comprehensive writing tools to support the development of this critical skill for college-level success. According to the Duke website: "We use the term genres to describe categories of written texts that have recognizable patterns, syntax, techniques, and/or conventions."[11] Princeton and other colleges offer similar supports:

- Princeton: http://www.princeton.edu/writing/center/
- http://www.princeton.edu/writing/files/PWPOutcomesStatement WritingSeminar.pdf

It makes sense for curriculum designers to ensure that a solid foundation of writing, including research writing, has been mastered in preparation for writing expectations at college and university. Rather than present all kinds of writing as a 12th grade "bucket list," a concerted effort is needed to synthesize a curriculum that truly prepares students for writing demands in higher education and the workplace.

In addition to determining what should be emphasized in which grade, teachers can ensure that activities are not repeated in each grade. Students do not need to write to soldiers three years in a row or write Amazon or Barnes and Noble reviews every time they read a novel. When activities are repeated, they lose their potency.

A well-tuned curriculum will give students a chance to learn how to read and write different literary genres, as well as styles of varied subject disciplines. Pulling together poetry, sentences in a paragraph, or multiple paragraph prose requires understanding a framework that can best suit the purpose for writing.

Teachers need guides for determining what to focus on during the year. The notion of "language across the curriculum" emerged from Barnes,[12] Graves,[13] and a host of experts who realized decades ago that teaching to read and write every genre each year would not be effective. Nearly half a century later and knee-deep in a host of new technological genres, it is now even more ridiculous to claim that each genre must be "covered" each year.

Key considerations for enhancing school writing programs include:

- Authentic writing requires an audience.
- Project-based writing increases student engagement.
- Authentic writing pieces can be about real-world issues.
- Authentic writing is not limited to social justice themes.
- Students need to experience writing about social justice issues as well as other genres.
- Writing for environmental sustainability promotes forward thinking.
- Teaching writing is a tall order.

Students should not have to interrupt their learning each year to adapt to different ways of learning a writing process. A common language for teaching grade-specific writing expectations and activities can be established by teacher teams from each grade.

When a staff can pool ideas and be open to new findings from experts, then students can benefit from a long-term, coordinated approach to teaching writing. After collaborative dialogue, the academic leader can synthesize and formalize a common writing process.

While a comprehensive ELA curriculum involves speaking, listening, reading, and in some jurisdictions, media literacy, it is important to integrate the reading of what students write with such expectations. Writing should not be a struggle in all subject areas if students have been explicitly taught the genre of the discipline writing style in advance.

A quality writing experience should include student written texts that can be read by the writer and other readers. Many ELA experiences center around fictional texts, which can limit the emphasis on informational text and nonfiction writing and reading. What would a curriculum look like if writing, rather than reading, were the main driver?

Though the contents of the CCSS, alternative state curricula, or the Ontario curriculum differ to a degree, they have more in common with each other: they all have too many expectations. Students do not appear to be more engaged when schools abide by such standards, so a change in writing and ELA curriculum should be seriously considered.

Decisions must be made about what writing can be mastered within the designated ELA curriculum and how writing can be addressed in integrated and interdisciplinary ways. These conversations about what should be taught in which grade are happening in separate corners of the education world, distant often from the input of teachers or voices of students.

Ideally, after the scope and sequence of writing expectations are laid out, it is important to speak about which authentic activities can fit the best with specific expectations. Professional conversations need to have more than a sharing goal in mind. If teachers can learn to co-construct curriculum, then they are better equipped to help and support students co-construct new understandings and evidence of their learning.

The CCSS[14] in the United States or the provincial departments of education in Canada do not claim to provide "curriculum"; rather, government documents serve a guiding function. Publishing companies pay attention to such guidelines, and by searching for authors who span a broad range of backgrounds, they do their best to provide many options.

The sheer volume of activities that district, state, and provincial documents recommend makes it difficult for teachers to know what to select as most critical and how to design pacing guides and lesson plans that study anything in-depth. By identifying essential or "power standards," teachers can view activities through a lens that can help them filter in or out activities that fit what's essential to learn.

When someone asks what curriculum a school is using, the response should never be a textbook series. Rather, a curriculum should be designed from a combination of current research, government expectations, college graduation requisites, and employability skills. Such a curriculum cocktail would not be complete without teacher input and student evidence of learning.

Holding a customized curriculum accountable is not a simple matter of comparing rankings of test scores and solely quantifiable data. Accreditation agencies, government authorizers, blue-ribbon designations, or other honors hold schools accountable to standards that link to qualitative and quantitative college-level research and study.

Even when resources support expectations, the curriculum of choice for many schools is working backwards from the local or regional standardized tests—in other words, a "teach-to-the-test" curriculum. Resources that can support student learning such as textbooks (secondary sources) or expert interviews (primary sources) should be welcome tools when crafting a customized curriculum.

A curriculum of best practice is comprehensive and constantly evolving through school and classroom-level professional growth. A curriculum of informed practice must be flexible enough to adjust quickly when one or more factors change (research, government curriculum, college expectations, workplace needs). A school, therefore, should not rely on one text series to be the "curriculum."

Finding a way to motivate and inspire students so they have the will to write takes time and an openness to admit what might be disengaging and what is not. Sometimes all it takes to transform a boring task is tweaking it, but sometimes the task requires a significant makeover.

NOTES

1. Calkins, L. The Lucy Calkins project. Education Next. http://educationnext.org/the-lucy-calkins-project/.
2. Calkins, The Lucy Calkins project.
3. Dewey, J. (1915/2015). *The school and society and the child and the curriculum.* Chicago: University of Chicago Press.
4. Rosenshine, B. (2012). Principles of instruction: Research-based strategies that all teachers should know. *American Educator, 36*(1), 12.
5. Rubin, R., Abrego, M. H., & Sutterby, J. A. (2015). What are the best strategies for streamlining your curriculum? Teach Thought. http://www.teachthought.com/uncategorized/less-is-more-4-strategies-to-streamline-your-curriculum/.
6. McAdie, P., & Leithwood, K. (2005). Less is more: Teaching for deep understanding. *Voice: Elementary Teachers Federation of Ontario,* 7(2), 8.
7. Graves, D. (1994). *A fresh look at writing*. Portsmouth, NH: Heinemann; Calkins, L. (1986). *The art of teaching writing.* Portsmouth, NH: Heinemann.
8. Borovoy, A. E. (April 1, 2009). Big thinkers: Howard Gardner on multiple intelligences. Edutopia. http://www.edutopia.org/multiple-intelligences-howard-gardner-video#graph5.
9. Fratt, L. (2002). Less is more: Trimming the overstuffed curriculum. Advancing Science, Serving Society. http://www.project2061.org/publications/articles/articles/da.htm?txtRef=https%3A%2F%2Fwww.google.com&txtURIOld=%2Fresearch%2Farticles%2Fda.htm.
10. Language. Ontario English Curriculum. (2006). http://www.edu.gov.on.ca/eng/curriculum/elementary/language18currb.pdf.
11. Genres of Writing. Duke University, Thompson Writing Program. https://twp.duke.edu/twp-writing-studio/resources-students/genres.
12. Barnes, D. (1976). *From communication to curriculum.* Thousand Oaks, CA: Sage.
13. Graves (1994).
14. Common Core State Standards. https://learning.ccsso.org/common-core-state-standards-initiative.

3

WRITING WITH OTHERS

PROFESSIONAL CONVERSATION STARTERS

1. When do you think writing should be independent and when do you think it is value-added for writing to be a collaborative venture?
2. How does collaborative writing emulate what can happen in the world of work?
3. How can teachers model writing for students?
4. How can administrators model writing for teachers and students?

Should writing be an independent action? In many classrooms, the writing process tends to be isolated, but writing does not have to be such an independent activity. Many teachers do encourage students to discuss their outlines and drafts with their classmates. In some schools, teachers build in collaboration between students in the form of peer editing and peer assessment. Internal classroom blogs can also provide feedback forums for classmates to share their reviews.

Writing is also collaborative when the teacher conferences with students throughout the process. For such collaborative activity to be effective, conferences require sustained amounts of time. Calkins's in-depth look at conferencing incorporates the need for a social milieu in writing. Her work provides explicit ideas for cultivating rich conferencing experiences.

She suggests that teachers give students at least two compliments at the beginning and end of writing conferences.[1]

Students feel things matter when the teacher keeps notes about their conversations and demonstrated mastery. A piece of writing is a powerful human construct, rendered as value-added or not, by socially agreed-upon norms. Teachers need to provide substantive feedback that can contribute to enhancing a piece of writing, at the same time formalizing stronger writing habits. Teachers who subscribe to writing conferences become more involved as social meaning makers with their students.

Ensuring that writers interact with experts can "shrink" the zone of proximal development (ZPD).[2] The quality of writing evolves when students can appropriate the more mature language of expert writers through social interaction. Experts have the capacity to understand varied perspectives, so when novice writers interact through talk with more expert others, they can acquire more expanded worldviews. Teachers can also model writing and share how their writing transformed throughout the writing process.

VanDerHeide studied the interactions of students using an online writing platform for peer feedback. The teachers in this study became coauthors as they edited the students' writing. As a result of this experience, she found that the writing was "longer, more explicit" and that peers provided "more directive online comments" for each other. The study recommended that teachers "provide scaffolding for students that includes different types of peer feedback."[3]

Writing approaches should add the collaborative action of students reading aloud their work and listening to others read aloud their work. A writer who can hear how writing sounds, from her own voice and others, can catch where words are left out and when word endings are missing. This polishing step can be a powerful collaborative feature and practice for supporting the development of strong writers.

Students can also construct writing pieces together. Students can co-develop writing by drawing illustrations, preparing outlines, writing drafts, and revising texts together. The social interaction can render creative ideas throughout the "storming" and crafting phases of writing. In one school, pairs of grade 4 students created fractured fairy tales to share with their reading buddies. The talk about which words, ideas, and illustrations to use for these written projects demonstrated how students could work well together.

Paired work is a powerful form of interaction; when one person speaks, the expectation is that the other person will respond. A larger group gives students more opportunities to opt out of contributing; and without entering into a conversation, thinking, engagement, and growth are limited.

Most students can go through elementary, secondary, and college education without writing with others; yet in the workforce, this can be common practice. Collaborative writing opportunities help students understand that writing is a process; at the same time, they can become more aware that mastery of such a complex task is not easy. The students also learn that working with the support of others can be beneficial for both parties and that such efforts can be collaborative rather than competitive.

Katie Wood Ray's circle of voices activity involves the teacher standing in a circle while each student reads aloud one metaphor from their "journal jots." Later, this list is turned into a *ladder poem* and published in an end-of-the-year literary magazine. Samples of metaphors that students generated that completed the prompt "An abandoned barn on the prairie is . . ." are included in the following list:

. . . a weathered old rancher who is living his last days in a nursing home
. . . a bag lady sitting on a park bench with nowhere to go
. . . the kid who sits by himself at lunch[4]

Peer teaching is also a powerful collaborative strategy that can benefit both seasoned and less-seasoned writers. Some teachers recognize the learning potential when older students work with younger writing buddies. When instructing their peers, students learn how to improve their own prose. According to one teacher, Terence Rodgers, the mentoring opportunities in a multiage classroom make for a "magical" learning context:

> This is the essence of the multiage classroom: Older students model good behavior and, through continual peer mentoring, stretch their teaching muscles and solidify their own knowledge. And the younger students learn that teachers aren't the only ones who know a thing or two. I haven't had a student yet who, even six years later, didn't remember whom they helped and who helped them.[5]

Peer teaching in multiage contexts can have a significant impact on the writing lives of students in a school. This gem of a strategy is somewhat rare but when implemented presents memorable and meaningful learning experiences.

When students are aware that their teachers are also writers, this can help them understand that writing is not simply an exercise to endure but a craft for cultivating thinking and innovative action. According to Graves and Kittle:

> When teachers compose texts of their own—texts they care about—during writing workshop, precious time is saved. Teachers reveal to their students the decisions all writers must make about every aspect of writing and demonstrate the skills that make writing clear and meaningful.[6]

Writing for teachers can be a somewhat lonely process if their narrow audience is a professor of a graduate or continuing education course, outside the context of their own schools. DuFour's recognition of professional learning communities stopped short of helping teachers become deeper thinkers through the process of writing:

> The professional learning community model . . . profoundly affects the practices of schooling. But initiating and sustaining the concept requires hard work. It requires the school staff to focus on learning rather than teaching, work collaboratively on matters related to learning, and hold itself accountable for the kind of results that fuel continual improvement.[7]

Just as students need authenticity for engagement, teachers need to know that their participation in professional meetings can lead to something tangible in both the short and long term. Building professional communities where teachers develop writing resources, then conduct action research to revise and improve the curriculum based on evidence of student learning, can help teachers see and influence the practices of schooling.

Professional learning communities represent ideal opportunities for starting conversations about writing, but if teachers meet and only talk about classroom management and single lesson activities, it is less likely to have an overall school impact.

Universities can also play a role in cultivating habits of teacher writers. To meet course requirements, student teachers or educators enrolled in further education could benefit from having their work featured in education journals or magazines. It could be beneficial for colleges of education and journal publishers to consider expanding the number of practitioner-type journals available for teachers to develop their professionalism in more authentic ways.

It is rare for the direct voice of teacher practitioners to be heard in academic journals. Many college professors, whose tenure depends on publishing, will interview, analyze, and interpret what teachers say, but teachers' ideas, like students in school, can be muted. Professor David Booth at the University of Toronto, a maverick in a way, invited teachers to write with him for more than three decades.

Booth's work on the *Talk Project*[8] in the early nineties involved collecting and publishing teachers' action research. Seeing the worth of such a transforming experience, Booth continued to publish his graduate student and mentees' work in a series of practitioner books, including *It's Critical*,[9] *Caught in the Middle*,[10] and most recently, *Exploding the Reading*.[11] Booth, in his editorial role, met with teacher writers throughout the process and then celebrated with them when their collaborative work was published.

Building a staff of writers, people who can write fiction, documentaries, or establish a school-wide writing curriculum, is at the core of building a writing culture. Establishing environments conducive to supporting the growth of teachers as writers may help determine how a school can coordinate a culture of thriving student writers.

As challenging as it can seem for a student to envision being an author, it can be even more of a stretch for a teacher to identify as a writer. Teachers need to be involved in making meaning, and through the process of writing curriculum for their students, and each other, their voices can be heard.

Unfortunately, many teachers are stuck in cultures that instruct them to follow lessons as repetitive scripts. Such fixed patterns focus teaching on individual tasks, assess only products, keep control of the talk in classrooms, reward right answers on multiple-choice tests, and trust that writing skills evolve through reading alone.

Becoming a writer not only demonstrates to students that they have writing models in their lives who craft lessons and material for them daily, but it also gives teachers a voice in collaboratively shaping the vision of the school. Professionals are empowered when they are encouraged to write about what works in their classrooms, how to revise activities from the Web or print resources to make them more authentic, and/or how to establish a common language in a school for teaching any subject matter.

When teachers are expected to work on a team to think through and define what is most essential, reduce the number of assignments, or coordinate an aligned curriculum between grades, they are more invested in the plan and therefore, have ownership over the direction of teaching and learning.

Ultimately, bringing teachers into the world of expertise through writing can have far-reaching effects for students. When teachers realize that their ideas can be honored and trusted, they can be open to giving students more autonomy as well. If more teachers can embrace their role as authentic meaning makers, education cultures can be more inclined to adopt more research-based practices, making them more mainstream.

Cooperative learning, peer teaching, and learning buddies are deliberate authentic programs that celebrate learning with others. Authentic learning experiences for teachers and students help reduce busy work and increase the volume of purposeful, authentic writing. In an empathetic sense, teachers might be more inclined to support reducing the volume of written texts if they were active members of a writing community.

At the school level, systematic collaborative action research is rare or considered optional as a personal professional development action. For administrators to understand the value of such professional practice, they, too, would need to model it for their teachers.

Few principals engage in or publish their own work that could contribute to school improvement or strategic planning. Collaboration for students, teachers, and administrators should be more than an option or elective activity. For students to construct deeper understandings and demonstrate the capacity to transform their writing, they need to experience writing in a social context with adult role models showing them the way.

NOTES

1. Calkins, L. http://educationnext.org/the-lucy-calkins-project/.
2. Vygotsky, L. (1986). *Thought and language.* London: MIT Press.
3. VanDerHeide, J. (2018). Classroom talk as writing instruction for learning to make writing moves in literary arguments. *Reading Research Quarterly, 53*, 323–344.
4. Wood Ray, K., & Laminack, L. (2001). *The writing workshop: Working through the hard parts (and they're all hard parts).* Urbana, IL: National Council of Teachers of English, 21.
5. Jackel, M. (June 5, 2008). Wisdom of the multi-ages: Students learn by teaching. Edutopia. https://www.edutopia.org/multiage-classroom-looping-peer-mentoring.
6. Graves, D. H., & Kittle, P. (2005). *Inside writing: How to teach the details of craft.* Portsmouth, NH: Heinemann, 1.
7. DuFour, R. (2004). What is a "professional learning community"? *Educational Leadership, 61*, 6.
8. Booth, D., & Thornley-Hall, C. (1991). *Classroom talk*. Portsmouth, NH: Heinemann.
9. Booth, D. (2008). *It's critical: Classroom strategies for deepening and extending comprehension*. Portsmouth, NH: Heinemann.
10. Booth, D. (2011). *Caught in the middle: Reading and writing in the transition years*. Portsmouth, NH: Heinemann.
11. Booth, D. (2014). *Exploding the reading.* Portsmouth, NH: Stenhouse.

4

DISCIPLINARY AND INTERDISCIPLINARY WRITING

PROFESSIONAL CONVERSATION STARTERS

1. How often have you witnessed a dance, an art exhibit, a dramatic adaptation, or a musical rendition as a mode of presenting a written piece of work?
2. Fewer assignments can enable the expectations for all subjects to thrive in an interdisciplinary project setting. Teachers need time to develop project ideas. Discuss the advantages and disadvantages of interdisciplinary project work, given your current school conditions.
3. From your experience, describe some projects that engage students.
4. How can project-based learning help students become more aware of global issues?

The purpose of sharing distinct and hopefully memorable language arts experiences, where reading is coupled with writing, is to convey that there are many ways to design an engaging and progressive curriculum that invites subject-based, project-based, or integrated course work.

Part of apprenticing in the world of historians, sociologists, biologists, or astronauts, for instance, is for writers to understand and be able to emulate the distinct features of various subject matter genre, so someday they can build on existing theories and be accepted authentically as part of distinct learning cultures.

Language and culture are interdependent. A common language for teaching writing in different subject areas could help all students improve their writing skills. A writing curriculum, therefore, should involve teachers from all subject areas. If writing is accepted as an expression of thinking, all educators can not only embed these features within each distinct curriculum, but they can take more ownership in developing the process itself.

It was unfortunate that the school-wide notion of "writing across the curriculum" in the early seventies lost momentum and was short-lived. The ideals of collaboratively creating a writing curriculum were lost when many educators simply reduced writing to a quick check of grammar and spelling in course work beyond the walls of English language arts (ELA).

Teaching multiple genres each year in each grade, rather than concentrating on one at a time per grade, is often commonplace. A focus on one genre per year, allowing for a few comparisons from genres addressed in previous years, can give learners time to examine the nuances of genre in a more concentrated way. At the end of grade 12, it is possible that students have not even explored some genres, especially if the curriculum has not been coordinated.

Too often a rubric for a history essay is established in isolation of language arts writing expectations. Student writing can be augmented when educators look for ways to assess the application of writing in other subjects, and more authentically, to develop projects together. Students can also give more effort and attention to detail with fewer written projects hanging over their heads each term.

Interdisciplinary projects should link with an overall grade theme, one that makes the grade stand out from others. Table 4.1 illustrates sample general themes that demonstrate how an ELA experience can be linked to overall grade themes, as well as other disciplines.

The context of project-based learning usually supports an integrated approach that includes literacy mastery. It can also link directly to one or more specific disciplines. This can mean that a subject area as complex as ELA can be more intentional about coordinating more integrated experiences among writing, language, reading, speaking, and listening.

The idea of designing three-year cycles of themes among multiple grades worked well at the Middleburg Community Charter School in

Table 4.1. ELA Links with General Themes and Other Disciplines

Gr.	*Sample General Grade Themes*	*Nonfiction Focus*	*Fictional Themes*	*Potential Disciplinary Links*
PK	Family	alphabet, family poems	nursery rhymes	linguistics
SK	School	acrostic poems	fairy tales	education
1	Communities	shape poem (global structures/homes); sentence	fables	social studies
2	Nations	nature (land, water, air); found poems; advertising	folklore	geography
3	Modern Ages	looped poems; single paragraph	comedy (limericks, puns)—focus on character	anthropology
4	Middle Ages	three-paragraph descriptive composition; scientific writing (lab reports)	mystery/adventure (book review)—focus on plot	biology and chemistry
5	Ancient Times	color poems; five-paragraph essay comparing ancient civilizations	myths—focus on conflict	history
6	Imagination: novel writing outline	news article and media	fantasy (new world settings)	fine arts; archeology
7	Innovation: first novel draft	STEM research; speech writing	science fiction; technology poetry	physics, engineering
8	Culture: edit and publish novel	current local and global issues (war and peace); persuasive writing; letter to the editor	social justice; blank verse poetry; song writing	law
9	Wellness	footnoting and referencing in research projects; journal writing	plays and scripts (soliloquy)	psychology
10	Models and Mentors	biography; cover letter, résumé	reviews, blogs	philosophy
11	Work	autobiography; debate writing; annotated bibliography	comparing works from same author	political science
12	Life	documentary; website construction; literature review	comparing different authors' message on same theme	sociology

Virginia. Students in grades 3 through 5, for instance, studied three topics in science and social studies one year at a time.

The tasks were differentiated so that students, regardless of their actual grade, could be permitted to work on foundational skills if they required more support or enriched activities if they were ready to demonstrate their understandings at a more complex level.

Students in grades 7 through 12 at the Crefeld School in Philadelphia studied the same topics in humanities and science each year when their teachers designed a three-year curriculum cycle. Headmaster Michael Patron noted:

> When you focus the attention of so many adults and students on the same theme at once, everyone contributes the resources they have to the task. Even math and science teachers, and others not directly involved in the project, might try to focus something around the theme. And because individual teachers don't have four or five preps for different subject matters, they can go more deeply into both content and pedagogy.[1]

He added, "Last year all our humanities classes studied a common theme in ancient civilizations; this year everyone does Western Civ; next year is American studies."[2]

Learning how to research in terms of developing research questions; gathering evidence and data; referencing; using quotations; making footnotes; and writing abstracts, annotated bibliographies, and literature reviews can all be important skills to prepare for the next century. As well, embedding ways to present findings using social media can involve learning how to make and manage a website and generate customized software.

The GEMnasium Project[3] is a test lab for transdisciplinary learning. It explores what it might be like to step beyond what a college class looks like:

- https://www.youtube.com/watch?v=uns65hnH7-A

What if elementary and secondary schools could design their own GEMnasium?

* * *

Integrating the arts within interdisciplinary project work is not a matter of drawing a picture and slapping it on the canvas of the learned experience. Eisner claimed that the arts "are important because of the ways in which they engage and develop human intellectual ability . . . to judge, to assess, to experience a range of meanings that exceed what we are able to say in words."[4]

The *Flat Stanley* book series[5] sparked a new connection that transported a small (stuffed) eagle to many cities around the world. When the symbolic visitor arrived in a soft envelope in Toronto, the students read and spoke about where the eagle had been and where it might go to learn about Toronto.

On their own time students, with parent support, had their pictures taken with the eagle at the CN Tower, in the mayor's office, at the matinee theater taking in *Les Misérables*, the Eaton Centre, and many more memorable places. The students used those pictures for the front side of a postcard. In their ELA class, students wrote the postcard, sharing key details about the school and each landmark. At the end of the week, each postcard was placed in the soft envelope and mailed to Seoul, South Korea.

Referring to the power of a pen pal experience, Transformational Leadership Coach Elena Aguilar from Oakland, California, noted:

> Just before the Iraq War started in the winter of 2003, my middle school students had English-speaking pen pals in an international high school in Iraq. My students were very concerned about the impending war and they wanted to hear different perspectives on the brewing conflict; they also wanted to impress their older pen pals with their writing skills so they wrote, re-wrote, and revised their email letters until they were polished. And after they got responses, they were even more motivated to write long, detailed letters full of explanation and description—and without a single grammar, spelling, or convention error.[6]

Aguilar also wrote about writing to inform others. Like many social studies or health classes, her students created brochures, but what made the experience authentic was the fact that the information about the Avian flu was translated into different languages and distributed throughout the community. The writing was part of a larger health promotion project. Their writing mattered.

Providing distinct and memorable language arts experiences, where reading is coupled with writing, can help shape an engaging and progressive curriculum that supports subject-based, project-based, or integrated coursework. Project-based learning allows for applications of writing expectations in a range of integrated subject areas. A strong interdisciplinary experience does not necessarily feature an application in as many subject areas as possible, which often leads to superficial interrupted slices of learning, limiting the potency for deep learning.

There are numerous examples of integrated projects that can support learning expectations in different subject areas. The following samples were featured in public, independent, and charter schools in elementary and secondary schools in Canada and the United States. Teachers should not be forced into coordinating integrated projects; rather, schools should support teachers to learn more about integrated project work. Co-planning and co-teaching with confident mentors can help orient teachers new to the approach while giving students opportunities to experience a connected curriculum.

To set the stage for unpacking the potential of project-based and interdisciplinary learning in classrooms, this LinkedIn contribution from Elaine Roberts[7] from Chicago describes how her students worked on a documentary project.

DOCUMENTARY PROJECT (GRADE 11)

I teach 11th grade English (part-timer) at a small private school. It's an interesting bunch of kids with a wide range of interests and capabilities, just like at any other school. Our students have been working on creating a documentary on the topic of their choice. They created storyboards, and now they are working on refining those with some scripting work. The project isn't due until the end of the school year when we'll have an 11th grade showcase.

Today I handed out some guidelines for a project they'll be working on. They have been allotted land and a specific number of shipping containers. They'll use these materials to design a community; then they'll be writing a flyer to advertise their community and a script for a radio spot for their community. If they like, they can create a commercial, too. Is it traditional? Nope. Is it working? We'll see, but students seem to be responding and seem to be engaged.

Paying attention to what teachers are doing to engage students is part of a curriculum improvement cycle. The next example of an engaging interdisciplinary experience is featured in the description of the Fitweek Project in Kitchener, Canada.

THE FITWEEK PROJECT (GRADE 7)

At Doon Public School, middle school students organized fitness activities for students, teachers, and families in their school community. The project involved much preparation in advance of Canada's Fitweek celebration. The students set up a point system, whereby each student and staff member would score a point for themselves and each family member they brought to the school for three evenings of fun.

Students on the "prizes team" wrote letters to local businesses to ask for donations to use for incentives to encourage participation in the after-school community event promoting National Fitness Week. They received more than 50 donated items including sought-after travel gift certificates, fitness and golf club memberships, and free massages.

The "registration team" kept track of all the students in the school of more than 400 and their running record of points. They posted them daily on a thermometer at the front entrance to the school. The "publicity team" took photographs and posted them daily to help promote the event.

On the first night, more than 120 participated in differentiated fitness classes (beginner, average, and advanced) in three sections of the gymnasium led by students on the "fitness leader team" who created routines to the same music but with varied levels of difficulty.

On the second evening, students, staff, and families came to play a modified version of baseball. Each team member at bat could continue to run around the bases scoring a point per base until the team in the outfield got the ball, lined up, and moved it over and under the full team in the outfield. Each member of the infield team often scored six or seven points at a time. When the team finished one round of "at bats," the teams switched places to see if the other team could accumulate a higher score. Both teams typically scored more than 100 points.

On the final evening, the community was organized to participate in a series of relays, ending in the shoe scramble. Everyone removed their shoes and placed them in a middle circle where they were mixed up by student "relay leaders." Participants started the relay sitting in team lines; on "go" they all rushed to the find their shoes, put them on, and returned to their line sitting cross-legged. Everyone moved safely so no one was hurt. (For such events, it might be prudent to include a student risk management team.)

The literacy embedded in such an interdisciplinary project was clear from the speaking opportunities, but many preparations during the grade 7

English class involved outlining, editing, and finalizing each plan. Further, thank-you letters required drafting and polishing so they could be sent to each donor with a picture of the recipients receiving their prizes.

Language arts, physical education, and school culture with a strong reach to families created a memory fit for sharing. Unpacking the learning in such experiences reveals the makings of treasured and engaging memories. How many English classrooms organize a school event as part of their curriculum programs? What can schools do to convert lessons into memories?

LETTERS TO THE PRESIDENT (GRADES 3 THROUGH 5)

In Middleburg, Virginia, a group of students wrote to Barack Obama when he was president of the United States. After the prompt of listening to *CNN Heroes*[8] and opting to vote digitally, or not, for the heroes that resonated with them the most, grades 3, 4, and 5 students selected a charity in need of government support.

One student wrote about Smashing Walnuts,[9] a group passionate about increasing funding for pediatric cancer medications. There had been no approvals for new experimental drugs in more than 40 years. The student planned, drafted, and edited her letter before sending the final copy of a letter to the president, with ample evidence to back her claims and recommendations. Obama took the time to respond and promised further funding, which made the writing and reading experience authentic and memorable.

LOCATION, LOCATION, LOCATION (GRADE 4)

Grade 4 students at The Sterling Hall School for boys in Toronto, Canada, decided to change the conventional approach to learning about the province of Ontario. Rather than label a map and read a textbook, each student selected a town or city that he believed might be a good place to relocate the school.

In the project titled "Location, Location, Location," students needed to research and become experts about other communities. Students wrote to city councilors, mayors, and people listed on websites who might have something interesting to share about their community. All email communications, for safety reasons, was filtered through the teacher's school email.

Crafting the letters took time, but all students received responses welcoming the idea of bringing a new school to town. The mayor of Barrie, 60 miles north of Toronto, asked to visit the class and make a pitch to the students about the prospect of the school moving or possibly making connections with a sister school. The students felt empowered when their written words had an audience and that their efforts made others take notice of their ideas. Students presented their proposals to the class, so all could learn about alternative communities in the province, shaped by the students as co-designers, in a way, of the curriculum.

Apart from this interdisciplinary experience that highlighted several different subject areas, the students contributed to building a positive school culture, one that embraced multiage learning opportunities. Chapter 3 featured other examples of collaborative writing opportunities within the context of peer teaching.

Engagement cannot simply happen with active or hands-on learning. The glue that makes learning stick is "minds on learning" as part of a purpose-based curriculum. How to design curriculum for minds and hands-on learning varies, but key resources exist to help both teacher teams and government standard writers. It's not enough that writing is authentic and has an audience; it needs to have a lasting impact on the mind. Writing is not an exercise or a data slice; it is a powerful learning tool.

Cutting back the number of tasks or assignments in all subject areas can leave room for students to engage in more concentrated, integrated experiences. Project-based learning enables students to read and write using many learning tools. For educators new to the notion of project-based inquiry, the Buck Institute[10] provides prescriptive ideas for pooling instructional practices and services for sustaining school-wide initiatives.

Purpose-based learning enables students to read and write using many learning tools. According to the Teachers College Reading and Writing Project (TCRWP): "Post-Its loom particularly large in the Calkins universe. . . . Indeed, project methods require a vast array of accoutrements: charts, matrixes, Venn diagrams, page numbers, graphs, reading marathons, bookmarks, book corners, book bags, book celebrations, jazzed up 'book talk.'"[11] For educators new to PB inquiry, such tools can stimulate the mind.

The Buck Institute provides prescriptive ideas for pooling instructional practices and services to sustain school-wide initiatives. The model for teaching of projects according to a systematic design involves skill at gaining key knowledge, understanding, and building a bank of success skills, a challenging problem or question, sustained inquiry, authenticity, student voice and choice, reflection, critique and revision, and a public product.[12]

The Rigor of Interdisciplinary Experiences

How does interdisciplinary activity stack up to rigorous expectations? Costa and Kallick's work on the *Habits of Mind*[13] brings to the forefront the comprehensive possibilities of critical and creative thinking. The context of interdisciplinary project work embraces deep learning.

Each sample interdisciplinary project addressed most if not all of Costa and Kallick's 16 habits:

- persisting
- thinking and communicating with clarity and precision
- managing impulsivity
- gathering data through all senses
- listening with understanding and empathy
- creating, imagining, innovating
- thinking flexibly
- responding with wonderment and awe
- thinking about thinking (metacognition)
- taking responsible risks
- striving for accuracy
- finding humor
- questioning and posing problems
- thinking interdependently
- applying past knowledge to new situations
- remaining open to continuous learning

The creative options for interdisciplinary writing know no limits. Giving students and teachers the autonomy to use their imagination can lead to so many incredible teaching and learning opportunities. What if you could rewrite stories sending a character to camp or sending local politicians or world leaders back or forward in time?

Many interdisciplinary possibilities can surface with themes of peace and the United Nations. Students can learn how to write resolutions: https://bestdelegate.com/model-un-made-easy-how-to-write-a-resolution/.[14]

Students may examine what it takes to write a resolution and propose changes to the structure of a resolution, making it more readable by the public. A comparison with other jargon-embedded documents can bring up other opportunities to decipher messages.

Students can view the UN's 17 sustainable goals[15] and build an argument around their constructive restructuring into different more manageable groupings. Conversely, students might rewrite the UN Charter of Rights[16] to link it directly with their school or community. Students could argue for revising decision-making systems that change the veto system, which may not function in the best interest of peace. Given what a third world war would cost, students need to not simply memorize what exists but write about what could be better.

It seems fitting to conclude this section with a description of student engagement in Model UN that Kyle Wagner shared on LinkedIn.[17] He proudly described how a former student ambassador representing the United Kingdom addressed the UN General Assembly about nuclear disarmament at a Model UN Conference in Rome:

At the time of the photo, he was 10 years old. He's reading a resolution to subvert nuclear proliferation signed by his 10- to 13-year-old peers from around the world, representing multiple nationalities, with multiple perspectives. This is the power of "Model United Nations." And this is power our youth have when we give them the chance to speak.

As the invasion of Ukraine intensifies, how might we use the same process in our classrooms to empower our students as global citizens, critical thinkers, and problem-solvers?

Yesterday, I had the great privilege of chatting with Robert Gold, the Model United Nations coordinator at the International School of Kuala Lumpur, on how to start the discussion in our classrooms. In our short interview, Rob teaches us how to:

- Help students understand the complexities of the conflict
- Seamlessly weave together history, geography, and language topics found in our curriculum
- Help students differentiate between "real" and "fake" news
- Organize our own Model United Nations conference with little to no experience
- Motivate students to give up entire weekends to the process of diplomacy

(continued)

Listen on Spotify: https://spoti.fi/3IKDkOk; listen on Apple: https://apple.co/3HIAIPP

Have you addressed the conflict with students? How have you started the discussion?

In solidarity for Ukraine.

In solidarity for global peace.

* * *

Such a project is steeped in purpose and authenticity. A purpose-based curriculum provides an ideal setting for inquiry and project-based learning.

Based on a five-month qualitative study in seven high schools, Marciano and Warren described students who used Google Docs and the GroupMe chat app to share their research findings. They concluded that "youth participatory action research projects engage students in purposeful writing through their own interests, multiple modes of writing, and opportunities to share ideas with an authentic audience."[18]

Although much emphasis is placed on the significance of audience and the potential authenticity of interdisciplinary work, not much research has been done on the value of using a common writing process across a school for integrated project work.

In a recent systematic review of 46 science studies, Gere et al. determined that "assignments incorporating four components (meaning-making writing tasks, interactive writing processes, clear writing expectations, and metacognition) could effectively foster conceptual learning of science."[19] Their research recommended "collaborations between science educators and writing specialists" to address the need for further research, particularly in response to "the variety of learning measures used in writing-to-learn scholarship." Schools that develop a common school-wide writing process may very well be on to something better.

When teachers use a common language to set expectations for writing between grades vertically and in different subject areas, it can make expectations more coherent for students. Although different genres for writing exist for various forms of fiction, students can also master nonfiction forms more suitable for other subject areas.

Writing a scientific experiment or a social studies essay will have distinctive elements. Using a clear common process for writing, however, that makes students think, rethink, craft, document, and reflect on findings in a variety of subject areas can be a progressive step forward in curriculum design.

Curriculum that supports writing between grades vertically, as well as between subjects horizontally, is not easy to develop. But given the complexity of teaching and learning, it is necessary to reduce the random and disconnected approaches to teaching writing. The next section of *Write to Be Read* includes an example of a writing process presented for educators to use or adapt to inspire their own writing process. After all, educators should model writing in many ways, including the crafting of curriculum.

NOTES

1. Patron, M. Crefeld School in Philadelphia. https://www.binghamsplace.com/less-is-more.html.
2. https://www.binghamsplace.com/less-is-more.html.
3. University of Dayton. The GEMnasium: A test lab for transdisciplinary learning. https://www.youtube.com/watch?v=uns65hnH7-A.
4. Eisner, E. (1985). *Beyond creating: The place for art in America's schools*. Los Angeles: Getty Center for Education in the Arts, 69.
5. Brown, J. (1964). *The Flat Stanley series*. San Francisco: Harper & Row.
6. Aguilar, E. Motivating students: Writing for an audience. http://www.edutopia.org/blog/motivating-student-writers-audience-elena-aguilar.
7. Roberts, E. (March 9, 2022). LinkedIn.
8. *CNN Heroes*. https://www.cnn.com/specials/cnn-heroes.
9. Smashing Walnuts. https://smashingwalnuts.org.
10. Buck Institute. http://bie.org/about/what_pbl.
11. Teachers College Reading and Writing Project (TCRWP). https://readingandwritingproject.org.
12. https://readingandwritingproject.org.
13. Costa, A., & Kallick, B. (2000). *Habits of mind*. Alexandria, VA: ASCD.
14. Best Delegate. https://bestdelegate.com/model-un-made-easy-how-to-write-a-resolution/.
15. Model United Nations. https://bestdelegate.com/model-un-made-easy-how-to-write-a-resolution/.
16. UN Charter of Rights. https://www.un.org/en/about-us/universal-declaration-of-human-rights.
17. Wagner, K. LinkedIn. https://spoti.fi/3IKDkOk; Listen on Apple, https://apple.co/3HIAIPP.
18. Marciano, J. E., & Warren, C. A. (2019). Writing toward change across youth participatory action research projects. *Journal of Adolescent & Adult Literacy*, 62, 485–494.
19. Gere, A. R., Limlamai, N., Wilson, E., MacDougall Saylor, K., & Pugh, R. (2019). Writing and conceptual learning in science: An analysis of assignments. *Written Communication, 36*, 99–135.

Part II

NEW APPROACHES TO TEACHING WRITING

When designing an authentic writing program, the teacher must in the beginning show students that what they write will be read. If a student is working on letter writing, he or she should actually produce a letter and mail it to complete the authentic process.

—Carly D. Lidvall

5

POETRY AS A GATEWAY TO PROSE

PROFESSIONAL CONVERSATION STARTERS

1. How is the teaching of poetry systematically organized in your school's English language arts (ELA) curriculum?
2. How can poetry be an important context for teaching key concepts in ELA?
3. How can poetry support interdisciplinary study?

James Britton suggested that to optimize student learning, we must balance reading and writing lessons among three modes: transactional, expressive, and poetic.[1] Donald Graves, a poet himself, encouraged students to bring their lives to school by writing poetry. Poetry is often disconnected from the teaching of prose writing, because it tends to be free of sentence conventions. Just as prose can be fitted into genre groupings, many poems can be crafted in popular and recognizable styles.

Some forms of poetry are formalized as art forms (e.g., haiku, free form, sonnet) and others are almost craft-like in their design (e.g., acrostic, shape, diamante). Students can read and write poems, just as they can read and write different genres of prose. There are many ways to make poetry a fun and creative activity. Lane described the "telephone poem" as offering students a creative way to summarize the theme of a text or share a personal connection. Students write their phone number down the left side of the page. The number indicates how many words can be used on that line to compose a poem:

1 Once
3 I carried you[2]

When poetry is taught in schools, it can be disconnected from other writing. Poetry units tend to last two to three weeks, and often poems the students read can seem distant from their lives. Typically, students read and analyze classical poetry; sometimes teachers link it to lyrics from modern music. Some students prepare poetry anthologies, but rarely is learning how to write poetry, edit it, perform it, and compare it with classical or other works part of what most students experience in ELA classes.

Unlike prose, the capacity to write poetry is not viewed as a requirement for college and the world of work. However, ignoring the potential of poetry to support the development of prose can be a missed classroom opportunity. Not only can the development of poetic writing enhance the writing of prose, but it can free up the writer's creativity to promote original work.

Rather than teaching poetry as a "unit," it can be considered a "season of study" as well as an integrated part of all subject areas. Poetry does not simply provide an expressive medium for applying understandings (e.g., create a rap about the Civil War). It should allow students opportunities to construct meanings between different contexts and promote the understanding of new perspectives.

In some English classes, for instance, students compare a classic poem to modern music, noting what is similar and what is different, while thinking about how both texts can enrich their interpretations of the purpose or point of both writings. By making meaning in this way, which forces a comparison between two distinct sources, the writers can build tools to support their own writing.

Poetry can also contribute to teaching students about literary devices used in both poetry and prose. Rather than read through pages of prose in the form of novels or plays, students first learn to identify examples of literary tools within the context of the less-dense poem.

The sample curriculum (table 2.3) outlined in chapter 2 details a sample scope and sequence for introducing various literary devices based on the idea that more seasoned students of poetry would be able to grapple with more complex tools. Alliteration, for instance, where the initial consonant letter of a word is repeated, is easier to identify than an oxymoron, which puts two contradictory words together, such as bittersweet.

It is fairly common for students to learn about imagery, similes, and metaphors. But without examining the depth of devices that can enhance writing, it is possible that students could engage in a K through 12 education without exposure and time to apply these important literary devices. These tools include applications of alliteration, assonance, hyperbole, onomatopoeia, personification, oxymoron, foreshadowing, irony, antithesis, euphemism, paradox, satire, zoomorphism, allegory, puns, anachronisms, and allusions. Many sites can be accessed by students and teachers to clarify meanings.

Teachers and students can take part in inquiries to evaluate the varied definitions and samples of literary devices. Any search engine can pull up multiple sites filled with examples to explore:

- https://blog.reedsy.com/literary-devices/#juxtaposition[3]
- https://www.masterclass.com/articles/22-essential-literary-devices[4]
- https://www.grammarly.com/blog/literary-devices/[5]

For a deep dive into tools for prose and poetry, try peeling back the layers of the thousands of devices listed in sites such as https://literarydevices.net.[6]

* * *

Exploring a few devices each year makes more sense than exposing students to an unruly number. Ideally, prior to college entry students should have a solid grasp of how to identify and use such literary devices in works of poetry and prose.

Learning how to appreciate poetry and write poems requires much more than a daily read aloud of classic poems. Rather than introducing poetry with T. S. Eliot's 1910 piece *The Love Song of J. Alfred Prufrock*,[7] it might be worthwhile to start with something a tad lighter. The teacher is a guide to support all students, recognizing that some materials and examples are more appealing than others.

Hooking students into reading and writing poetry is not simple. The curriculum may include a set plan of poems to introduce it, but it needs wiggle room for students to bring to the table poems that they discover, poems that move them in some way.

Many creative activities can breathe life into a poetry curriculum. Students can relate poems to a mystery or crime scene investigation. Teachers may share clues, but only the author knows the motive for writing a poem. Often students (and teachers) infer ideas about poems.

Rather than celebrate the students' original ideas and responses to poetic texts, their contributions are often compared with experts who typically have studied dead poets for years. Students learn early on to simply default to memorizing "right answers," forfeiting any desire to make their own meaning. Many writers of poetry and prose, however, neither want nor expect the reader to replicate literal interpretations from afar; rather, they prefer that their work lead to creative interpretation.

Cornell University's M. H. Abrams wrote many classic works, including the famous *Norton Anthology of English Literature*[8] and the comprehensive *A Glossary of Literary Terms*.[9] He identified four dimensions of a poem: the physical "appearance of the poem in print"; "the sounds of the words when they are read aloud"; "the meaning of the words that we read or hear"; and "the oral activity of enunciating the great variety of speech sounds that constitute the words of a poem." Abrams was convinced that the fourth dimension is "almost totally neglected in discussions of poetry."[10] He shared his perspective in a YouTube presentation:

- https://www.youtube.com/watch?v=d1Ofwljw4Y0[11]

Reading and discussing poetry written by poets is not enough. Students need to apply their understanding to create a variety of poetic texts and experiences. Among the experiences that can spark students to be writers of poetry is listening to poems. This use of one's auditory sense while closing one's eyes opens the listener to becoming enveloped by the sounds, words, and images of the poetry. The following TedTalk featuring Uri Hasson is particularly illuminating with respect to the "aural joy of poetry" and how the brain responds to communication:

- https://www.ted.com/talks/uri_hasson_this_is_your_brain_on_communication?language=en[12]

This interplay, the rhyme, rhythm, meter, and verse, are elements that define poetry. Add free verse, and the boundaries of what is poetry become deeper and wider. Then, as on a blank page or canvas, add the placement of the letter, the word, and the text, and that becomes the visual choreography of symbols with sounds. As noted in an online Purdue University course:

> The combination of sound and visual elements provides a poem's *structure*, the resultant sum of all sound and visual form in a poem. The craft of poetry traditionally has concerned itself only with the sounds of the words; but as a *written* thing, we cannot deny that a poem has a certain "paginess," and that the patterns developed in that visual field can't be overlooked if we concern ourselves with the full potential of the poem's structure.[13]

* * *

As writers move from poetry to prose, from the self-written to the read to self, to the read-aloud, and from the write for oneself to the write for an audience, the physical, auditory, and visual movements are moving toward prose. This path may not occur in a straight line, nor does one outgrow the benefits of read-alouds.

Although it may seem that becoming a silent reader is a goal of elementary school teaching, the benefits of the interplay of the auditory, physical, and visual have been noted in research. Walden University describes five benefits:

1. Reading to children improves comprehension.
2. Listening to books builds vocabulary.
3. Reading aloud reduces stress.
4. Reading aloud strengthens community in the classroom.
5. Reading aloud can help students succeed in life.[14]

By removing the mechanical conventions of prose writing, students are free to write and focus on "idea-rich" contributions. Project-based approaches that integrate literature can bridge the gap between poetry and prose for young people and, in doing so, allow literature to inspire creativity in writing.

It makes sense that readers of poetry become writers of poetry to enhance their capacity to analyze and examine their own and others' work. Project-based learning and inquiry activities stress critical and creative thinking, and poetry can be a meaningful integrated activity to include in a list of expectations. The Habitats: Missing in Action Project is an example of how the understanding and application of free verse poetry can be enhanced in an interdisciplinary learning context.

THE HABITATS: MISSING IN ACTION PROJECT (HMA)

Similar to other project-based learning opportunities, HMA required students to write poems in response to the loss of habitats for animals and other wildlife worldwide. The experience, however, diverged from the conventional when students took part in customized mini lessons, linking the outlining, drafting, editing, and presenting stages of writing with the construction of their poems.

Students worked in pairs to write a free poem about their concerns about the loss of animal habitats. The purpose of the activity was to support students to write freely without prose conventions to share eight-stanza free-form poems as responses to concerns raised about the encroachment of humankind into natural habitats.

Prompt

- Students began the project by comparing D. H. Lawrence's poem "Snake"[15] with the lyrics of a song of their choice. They discussed how the poems were the same and how they were different.

"Snake" is a classic free verse 16-stanza poem. It made sense to break up longer poems into sections for different students to practice reading aloud.

After hearing the poem shared aloud through various voices, the class discussed responses to a few questions, including "Should the boy have killed the snake and why?" A short discussion at the prompt stage should be enough to get things started. Too many questions can kill curiosity!

The teacher also encouraged the class to look for bias in the message. In the case of "Snake," when Lawrence said, "If you were a man you would take a stick and break him now, and finish him off," he was projecting a blatant gender bias. Given that the poem was written in the early 1920s, it portrays glimpses of a culture where killing a snake was accepted as a way men should behave in dangerous and threatening situations.

Many poems are rich with elaborate imagery. Students can scour the words used in "Snake" to build a bank of words for future writing tasks. To draw attention to more complex vocabulary, students compiled new words and arranged them in a creative way as a separate adapted or sub-poem.

In the case of "Snake," the following sub-poem emerged as a way to display a condensed meaning based on the organization of more complex words.

Adapted Snake Poem

pacified albatross, thrice a dream
mused
fissure, exile
perversity, accursed
undignified,
writhed, convulsed
paltry, pettiness, expiate

In pairs, students also examined the lyrics of a song of their choice. They discussed what "Snake" and their lyrical poem (song) had in common. The differences are easy to record—but finding the connections is where creative thinking helped to motivate students to think critically.

Creative teachers can come up with a variety of writing prompts that function as a hook to inspire student writing action. Teachers can also link reading activities as prompts. For instance, students might record ideas in a Venn diagram comparing settings or characters, how they are the same and different.

Rushing the prompting phase can lead to students going through the motions to complete the task on the teacher's agenda. Inspiring students to plan their poems requires patience and creativity.

Planning the Poem

Students can create plans that illustrate how they will turn words into poems and lyrics. Students can draw images, then use words/phrases to label the images. They can then edit the images by considering how characters, environments, actions, and conflicts can change or perhaps expand the original plans by adding new human or nonhuman protagonists and antagonists and/or new settings. In the case of concerns about the loss of animal habitats, the protagonist could very well be an animal.

Webbing and mind maps are also popular outlining tools, as are other digital tools such as Jamboard.[16] When the writer is ready to move the words to a first draft, the outline can be a guide and a medium for further illustrations and ideas. Moving back and forth between the outline and the draft should be commonplace in an engaging writing environment.

Producing a First Draft

Before students move to drafting and writing free-form poems, the teacher can share mini lessons to help them learn the language of poetry.

~ *Free Verse Mini Lesson*

To determine the format for writing a free verse poem, students need to clarify terms such as verse, stanza, meter, rhyming scheme, quatrain, and imagery.

The first draft can emerge when the young poet uses words and phrases from the illustration or other outlining tools. The words can be simple, the sentence structure does not need to be complex, and the spelling can be somewhat inventive at this stage. The purpose of the first draft is to build a foundation for the heavy lifting required to polish an early piece of poetry.

Students who hand in almost perfect drafts sooner than everyone else should not receive bonus points or prizes. Such a lesson is about speed, not quality. Further, handing in the longest poem can mean that the writer did not cut out anything, not seeing the wisdom in the guidance of moving from more to less.

Expert poets spend dedicated time crafting and recrafting their work. Emulating the work of experienced poets should be celebrated. Examples provided of poems from books, songs, and other sources can be rich resources for budding poets.

Finally, drafts should be written on every other line, double-spaced as digital works, or by hand. This gives the writer and reviewers ample room to polish the draft in the next stages of the work. Teachers can prepare support tools that shade every other line to prevent students from submitting single-spaced work.

Looking closely at the writing expectations, as presented on assessment and feedback tools, can lighten the student work to meet certain standards in a particular grade. For instance, a tool may contain criteria such as:

- Use words to create images.
- Use lines of varying lengths.
- Format in eight stanzas.
- Present a conflict or challenge.
- Write on every other line (make room for future edits).

Students can use the expectations to self-assess their first draft; as well, the teacher should use the criteria to make sure students have a solid foundation in place before polishing and revising their drafts. It's important to align the formative feedback at the beginning of the writing process with the specific writing instructions. Students can also create assessment tools using the criteria as a guide for revising. Teachers and peers can also focus on expectations in support conferences at the early stages of writing.

Polishing the Drafts

In the polishing stage, student writers need to pay particular attention to expectations; using a scoring or grading scheme to revise each draft can help shape the editing part of the writing process. Table 5.1 features the sample tool used for editing a free-form poem.

Such assessment tools can be formative without any overall scoring, or they can be summative as a way of documenting the mastery of a particular stage of writing. Rather than using A or S, teachers can use a numerical system with A = 2, S = 1, and NY (not yet) = 0. The larger the range of options (1, 2, 3, 4 or A, B, C, D, F), the more difficult it is for the student and teacher to be aligned on their judgments. Keeping it simple enables the writing to improve from below expectations, through meeting expectations, to exceeding them.

Implementing sound assessment practices, particularly when numerical scores may be assigned to work, is important. The tools can be used as both formative and summative resources. For instance, a teacher may conference

Table 5.1. Sample Feedback/Assessment Tool for Editing a Free-Form Poem

Feedback/Assessment Tool for Editing a Free-Form Poem		
Student Self-Score	*Quality of Writing* *(A) ample evidence, (S) some evidence, (NY) no evidence yet*	*Teacher Score*
	a creative title	
	a captivating starter line	
	words used to create mood/theme of poem fit with conflict/ challenge	
	interesting characters (human/nonhuman)	
	selected words create a compelling setting (time and spatial cues)	
	contains at least six powerful descriptive adjectives	
	contains at least three lines with alliteration	
	contains at least three examples of assonance	
	rarely uses rhyming words at the end of lines	
	an interesting final line that brings the poem to a strong close	
	ideas flow in a logical sequence	
	does not use stereotypes	
	changes made to draft when writers listened to poem read aloud	
	changes made to draft when writers read their own poem aloud	
	evidence of changes made to most lines in each stanza	
/30	Total	/30
Comments:		

with a student about the quality of the polishing phase, indicating that more attention to the piece is required to revise the scores.

The purpose of writing is to improve students' capacity to write, so regrading can be a powerful force to that end. The first score in a regrading situation is thus formative feedback. A summative score would then happen after the next set of revisions.

Given that professional writers go back and forth with their publishers on many drafts, it makes sense that the assessment is also game for revision. The goal of teaching writing is not to find out who gets it faster; the goal is to make sure all students "get it."

~ "The Sky Is Busy" Mini Lesson

It can help throughout the writing process to read and listen to poems as prompts. A simple poem by indigenous poet Pat Christie,[17] for instance, can provide additional examples to discuss along the way and potentially stimulate new perspectives about the draft crafted.

The Sky Is Busy
Pat Christie

I saw my first feather falling from the sky yesterday
separated from a bird's body flying somewhere,
but it was how it gently spiraled to Mother Earth and
then it landed on the concrete like it had been a part of the scenery forever.
How could such beauty, gentleness and serenity be a part of this fast,
honking, concrete Earth jungle?
The feather reminded me of a story a man once told me about his son watching
an eagle's feather float from the sky until he caught it between the tips of his fingers!
I saw but I didn't catch the glory of this moment.

Mini lesson discussions can emerge from a variety of questions including the following:

- How did the story make you feel?
- What did this piece of writing say to you?
- Which techniques did the poet use to tell this story?

Students can look at alternative poetry for similar themes to see if the discussions during mini lessons give the poets new perspectives and ideas for reshaping their drafts.

Notably absent from the list of expectations in the sample feedback/tool for editing (table 5.1) was reference to accurate spelling and punctuation. These types of revisions should happen at the final polishing stage, when the poem moves from the double-spaced draft to the form and shape of the final look (see table 5.2). It should be noted that the rules of punctuating prose may not apply in poetry.

A quality writing process should reveal how the writing transitioned from outline to first draft, to several polished drafts, and then the final work. Students learn the difference between writing and drafting as they emulate the practices of real poets.

Table 5.2. Assessment of the Final Copy of a Free-Form Poem

Self	*This final copy of this free-form poem has the following: (A) ample evidence, (S) some evidence, (NY) no evidence yet*	*Teacher*
	Accurate spelling or use of inaccurate spelling or inventive words for emphasis	
	Punctuation complements and supports the message of the poem	
	Font choice contributed to supporting message of poem	
	Organization of stanzas and line spacing (physical look contributes positively to the poem)	
	Has been reviewed by a teacher	
Comments:		

Presenting the Draft

The difference between writing poetry to hand in to a teacher and writing poetry for others to read is what distinguishes an authentic piece of work from assigned busy work. Arguably, the presentation of any work takes time; although some educators may worry about the time it can take away from other learning, it is, nevertheless, what can move students into a deeper, more memorable experience.

For decades, many schools have emphasized a smattering of disconnected objectives, and in doing so, educators have learned that such practice does not enhance learning, nor does it contribute to increasing the mass of passionate, engaged learners. It is time to do something else. Paying attention to authentic experiences that promote student engagement is a prime place to start.

Students can present their poetry in many ways, as the arts provide a powerful medium for supporting how a poem can be expressed. Students can present their poems at a recital or poetry celebration. They can form publishing teams to pull together classmates' poems in a collective anthology. Questions to consider when presenting poems include:

- Will the work be cataloged for the school library?
- Will the form of the poem by available digitally, in hard copy, or both?

- Will illustrations be included; if so, how will they be formatted with the text?
- If a collective work is to be published, what will the title page be?
- How will authors' names be presented on publicly shared materials to ensure safety and privacy?
- Will the poem be shared orally face-to-face, or virtually in a synchronous or asynchronous media setting?
- Will the book be sold to support a charity or service-learning activities?

Poems can come to life through the spoken word. Making time for poetry readings and recitals can be fun and a great way to hear the words of poets. Table 5.3 reveals simple criteria for providing such feedback.

If students read their poems to an audience, they can also be assessed on speaking. Poems can be presented in many ways. At one school students created visual images to represent stanzas in lengthy poems, took pictures of the images, and pooled them in a slide show about the poem. The slide show presentations of poems added further interpretations and interest. In this case, speaking, visual arts, and technology skills were assessed at the same time.

Many students are drawn to messages about social justice. Music can be a wonderful medium for exploring poetry moved by societal issues of concern. Before words become a song, they are poems. To make poetry

Table 5.3. Assessment of the Reciting of the Poem

Self-Assess	*Reciting of the poem: (A) ample evidence (2 points), (S) some evidence (1 point), (NY) no evidence yet*	*Teacher Assess*
	Stressed key words in poem	
	Volume good for audience to hear	
	Pace was good for all to follow	
	Costume/props/artifacts suited poem	
	Poem was memorized (you crushed it!)	
Comments:		

more appealing, teachers can encourage students to bring in lyrics to music. Songwriting and the reading of lyrics is a powerful language force that tends to exist outside the typical classroom. Poetry in the context of music can be a rich way into examining messages inspired by word combinations.

Students can rewrite poems as plays and put on dramatic productions. Video recording such productions can add value to a student's portfolio. Novels can be condensed into poems and presented in various artistic forms that work well in an interdisciplinary context.

Drama is also a meaningful medium for supporting writing. Kiger Lee et al. examined the impact of an eight-week improvisational drama program on the writing of grade 3 students. They found that "asset-oriented sociocultural theories of learning and imagination" contributed to improvements in writing performance.[18]

* * *

At the end of the school year, when students tend to willingly relinquish their notebooks to the abyss of trash cans, there was no sight of their poetry anthologies, a litmus test in a way of work that mattered. When teachers have the autonomy and time to create activities for students that can make memories, it is anticipated that student (and teacher) engagement will improve.

Engagement crosses grades and ages. The Lewis Carroll Project[19] designed by middle school teacher and administrator Hope Blecher reveals how units can weave together multidisciplinary expectations. She made sure that the project was a collaborative venture with the students and teachers. She collaborated with the Hebrew teachers to ensure that students would tackle the Jabberwocky task in an authentic, genuine matter.

Blecher's experience, as described in "The Lewis Carroll Project" that follows, confirmed that educators need more space to play at being kids. As she noted, "From pondering to pencil, from heads to hands, from digital to digits, this poetry to chess project included problem solving, peers teaching peers, multilingual and multigenerational aspects." Students learned to appreciate poetry and so much more. They learned to cooperate with others while ensuring a mutual respect for the classroom and others, not leaving messes for the school maintenance crew.

THE LEWIS CARROLL PROJECT

While choosing texts for the middle school, Hope Blecher had important decisions to make. The ponderings included the ages of the students, the availability of the book, the anticipated comments from parents, and buy in/engagement from the "tweens."

Coupled with drops of confidence and credibility, she chose *Alice in Wonderland* by Lewis Carroll. Among the reasons for this choice were

- initial expectations of comments that it's a children's story and/or already known;
- copies available from local libraries, bookstores, and online;
- fond recollections of the movie from the grownups;
- connections to historical events;
- author's craft;
- availability of illustrations to project via smartboards and overhead projectors; and
- two tricks she had up her sleeves that were yet to be revealed.

While making the text choice, Hope also spoke with other staff members. They agreed to support her in at least two ways: dedicating time within instructional lessons and sharing classroom space.

As the unit progressed, the teachers read *Alice in Wonderland* with the students in English and in Hebrew. As a yeshiva, this cross pollination reinforced literacy and interdisciplinary learning in addition to the transfer of experiences.

That transfer was important when the students were asked to step into the role of writers of poetry. Tasked with reading the poem "Jabberwocky," students were then asked to create their own Jabberwocky-like piece. At first students wanted to simply translate Carroll's creation. They grappled with the notion that Hebrew and English do not rhyme. This thinking challenge stretched their imagination; and reactions to the activity aroused applause, awes of silence, concluding the overall positive community response.

And as a result, they took creative license with their Jabberwocky iterations. Creativity spread when the students discovered Dinah, the Cheshire Cat, playing chess. Hope admitted that she did not know how to play but would become a co-learner of the game and an admirer, with the class, of the art

(*continued*)

forms of the chess boards and the pieces. Students were determined to make their own chess sets, which segued into connections with the art teacher. Students brought in materials and were given a choice of working with peers or individually. Teachers, administrators, and parents on school tours popped in throughout the project. And students were eager to clean up their creative chaos each day; no one complained about this month-long work in progress.

When families shared stories of their children playing chess at home and wanting to read more of Lewis Carroll's writings, Blecher smiled and reflected, "That's what passion and commitment feels like."

It is not advisable to teach all kinds of poetry each year. A focus on one kind of poetry makes more sense. Certain kinds of poetry can be recommended for different age groups, depending on whether a class is addressing integrated project-based work. For instance, if a primary class is studying Asia, the class might compare haikus with other Asian poetry.

Just as teaching every reading genre every year can dilute learning, so, too, can teaching multiple forms of poetry each school year. A progressive curriculum of poetry should provide opportunities for students to read and write poems to apply their understandings and promote deeper, more sustainable learning experiences.

NOTES

1. Britton, J. (1993). *Language and learning*. Portsmouth, NH: Heinemann; Graves, D. H. (1994). *A fresh look at writing*. Portsmouth, NH: Heinemann.
2. Lane, B. (2003). *Reviser's toolbox*. New York: Discovery Writing Press, 22.
3. Reedsy blog. https://blog.reedsy.com/literary-devices/#juxtaposition.
4. Master Class. (September 7, 2021). 22 essential literary devices and how to use them in your writing. https://www.masterclass.com/articles/22-essential-literary-devices.
5. Ellis, M. (August 17, 2021). 28 common literacy devices to know. https://www.grammarly.com/blog/literary-devices/.
6. Literacy devices. https://literarydevices.net.
7. Eliot, T. S. (1910). *The love song of J. Alfred Prufrock*. Bartleby. http://www.bartleby.com/198/1.html.
8. Greenblatt, S., & Abrams, M. H. (2006). *The Norton anthology of English literature* (eighth edition). New York: Norton.
9. Abrams, M. H., & Harpham, G. G. (1999). *A glossary of literary terms*. Cornell University. https://static.s123-cdn.com/uploads/3433317/normal_606f55ccdaf2b.pdf.

10. Mansky, J. (November 22, 2010). Abrams explains the neglected "fourth dimension" of a poem: "Oral activity" in its reading. Cornell Chronicle. https://news.cornell.edu/stories/2010/11/abrams-explains-four-dimensions-poem.

11. Abrams, M. H. On reading poems aloud. Cornell University. https://www.youtube.com/watch?v=d1Ofwljw4Y0.

12. Hasson, U. (2016). This is your brain on communication. Ted Talk. https://www.ted.com/talks/uri_hasson_this_is_your_brain_on_communication?language=en.

13. Visual patterning. Purdue OWL, Purdue University. https://owl.purdue.edu/owl/subject_specific_writing/creative_writing/pattern_and_variation_visual/index.html.

14. The benefits of reading aloud to your students. Walden University. https://www.waldenu.edu/online-bachelors-programs/bs-in-elementary-education/resource/the-benefits-of-reading-aloud-to-your-students.

15. Lawrence, D. H. https://www.poetryfoundation.org/poems/148471/snake-5bec57d7bfa17).

16. Jamboard. https://jamboard.google.com.

17. Christie, C. P. The sky is busy. https://www.sfu.ca/lovemotherearth/02poetry/tea_and_bannock.pdf.

18. Kiger Lee, B., Enciso, P., & Austin Theatre Alliance. (2017). The big glamorous monster (or Lady Gaga's adventures at sea): Improving student writing through dramatic approaches in schools. *Journal of Literacy Research, 49*, 157–180.

19. Blecher, H. The Lewis Carroll Project.

6

PROMPTS FOR WRITING PROSE

PROFESSIONAL CONVERSATION STARTERS

1. Which writing prompts work best for you?
2. Why do you think the outdoors can be an inspiring prompt for student writing?
3. Why is it necessary to consider prompts as a phase of writing?

What kinds of writing prompts stimulate one's imagination? A single word, a phrase, a sentence, a piece of instrumental or lyrical music, an experience, an artifact, messages on social media, or a teacher wearing a costume have the potential to elicit a range of genres for student fiction or nonfiction writing. The following writing prompts,[1] for instance, could inspire engaged work, provided that time is allocated to research, edit, and polish the work:

- silk
- red eyes
- He woke to birdsong.
- The garden was overgrown now.
- Stars blazed in the night sky.
- the smell of freshly cut grass

- This time her boss had gone too far.
- It was the first snowfall of the year.
- She studied her face in the mirror.
- They came back every year to lay flowers at the spot.
- "Shh! Hear that?" "I didn't hear anything."
- He'd always hated speaking in public.
- He'd never noticed a door there before.
- "I told him not to come back, too!"
- His feet were already numb. He should have listened.
- He hadn't seen her since the day they left high school.
- The streets were deserted. Where was everyone? Where had they all gone?

Although the web is chock-full of prompts, when released into the classroom, they are simply not enough to engage *all* learners. Some students will write away and complete the task with unwavering focus; others will go through the motions of spilling out words to fill a paragraph; and finally, others will choose avoidance strategies that take the teacher away from conferencing into the disruptive world of classroom management.

Writing Outdoors

Writing on the sidewalk with chalk, writing in the sand, using a stick to draw in mud or a puddle. What do these have in common? This is writing. This is the act of using an implement to make a symbol. This action takes place outside of physical walls. It is outdoors.

During the COVID pandemic, getting outside became a common theme for wellness. Take a break, take a walk, hug a tree, jump in a puddle, feel that breeze, smell the flowers, and more were noted in advertisements, infomercials, articles, and media posts. Homeschooling and camping showed a marked increase during the pandemic.

What does Mother Nature have to do with writing? How can educators connect the outdoors with students' writing development? It is of note that this question starts with how and not with can. As Charlotte Mason suggests: "We are all meant to be naturalists, each in his own degree, and it is inexcusable to live in a world so full of the marvels of plant and animal life, and to care for none of these things."[2]

A large and growing body of evidence-based research demonstrates the benefits of outdoor learning for mental health and well-being, stress reduction, physical health, student engagement, and academic success.[3] This is part of the impetus for the North American Association for Environmental Education (NAAEE) Outside for 5 campaign.[4] Teachers, educators, parents, and students are being asked to get outside for five minutes a day.

Patients are getting prescriptions from their doctors for a dose of the outdoors. As reported in Park RX America, evidence shows the impact of being within nature on lowering obesity, anxiety, stress, and depression, and increasing focus and attention levels.[5]

Outdoor education has existed in other countries and is getting more attention in the United States. Organizations such as the Forest School Teacher Institute (FSTI)[6] provide training opportunities for people interested in outdoor education. Leaders Jean Lomino and Joe Pounds primarily work with adults in preschool and elementary-age programs, but participants represent a cross section of ages and stages of educational backgrounds. They saw an increase in interest and enrollment in their programs throughout the pandemic.

Whether it is five minutes a day, or 300 seconds, the traditional schedule includes time to go outside. Why do students need to go outside? Why should they engage with nature in urban, suburban, or rural areas? Being in the outdoors has an impact on learning. Connecting with natural elements not only has academic benefits, but such experiences can enhance a student's sense of community.

Among the positives of incorporating place- and play-based nature education into schooling are an awakening or reawakening of one's senses. Students can experience distinctions, beyond sight and sound, that include smell and taste. Comparing what is sweet, tangy, tart, spicy, colorful, and tangible requires students to build a bank of sensory experiences.

A teacher can bring nature into the classroom by examining plant life; taking virtual tours; viewing illustrations in books, magazines, and websites. Teachers can also invite farmers, gardeners, and cultivators to be guests. Bringing experts to the classroom can involve students learning to craft invitations and thank-you notes.

During the COVID pandemic, many doctors prescribed being outdoors to patients. Every community is full of sound educational options. For instance, in the Catskill Mountains of New York, Blecher often stopped by taking visitors to say hello to a few potbellied pigs at Arthur's Acres Animal

Sanctuary.[7] The experience felt like *Charlotte's Web*[8] came to life before their eyes. Blecher began volunteering as a poopy scooper and later as a literacy volunteer at the sanctuary. Fields of friendships, photos, and fodder for newspaper articles soon followed.

Arrowhead Ranch and Rescue[9] also offers powerful learning experiences in the Sullivan County, New York, area. Much education can happen at a local animal shelter, a community garden, or at one's own flowerpot or windowsill. Being in the outdoors can support all kinds of learners. Such exposure can enhance the learning experiences of English as a new language (ENL), gifted and talented (G&T), and students with individual educational plans (IEP). Such students may have different life experiences than other students, but they, too, can be enriched by nature.

Gardner and Kuzich studied writing samples from 97 9- and 10-year-old students in Western Australia and found that "students' poetic writing is enhanced through direct contact with nature." The implications of such a finding?

> Teachers in both England and Australia, countries where "high stakes" testing dominates the literacy curriculum, may find that standards of writing improve when students are given direct contact with natural spaces and are scaffolded to elicit their poetic voice.[10]

The use of our senses and becoming part of a natural context through a variety of lenses will impact their illustrations. As well, being in nature can inspire the cultivation of an array of rich sensory language for prose and poetry.

From the "Colors of the Wind" in *Pocahontas*[11] to the prose of Byrd Baylor,[12] from *It Looked Like Spilt Milk* by C. Shaw[13] to *Walden* by Thoreau,[14] books, lyrics, poetry, and prose are available to teachers and students. These examples can serve as mentor texts, springboards for observations, reflections, conversations, and writing. From ROYGBIV (the sequence of colors in the rainbow) to onomatopoeia, seasons to constellations, the natural world has a richness available to the teacher and student who step outside.

Developing one's senses and writing while in a natural environment or about nature can occur with a variety of implements, thus increasing the accessibility of these experiences. What for one student is a tar beach or a tree growing in Brooklyn[15] is a fish named Dory or a commotion in the ocean to another student.[16]

Focus upon a tree. In literature teachers and parents can share *The Giving Tree*,[17] *The Survivor Tree*,[18] and *The Lorax*.[19] Students can be engaged through read-alouds, improv, and social justice. These texts become prompts for interdisciplinary and cross grade-level assignments that teachers can design with intentional depth and breadth while also differentiating for individual students and families of learners.

Some charismatic teachers may keep more students on task, but without planning with purpose and sustained time to develop writing, it is doubtful that a prompt will increase the critical mass of writers in any classroom. The deliberate focus on the writing task requires that student writing be propelled both by an audience and the relentless writers' will to fiercely convey their own voice.

NOTES

1. Kewin, S. Writing Prompts 101. Daily writing tips. http://www.dailywritingtips.com/writing-prompts-101.
2. Mason, C. Simply Charlotte Mason. https://simplycharlottemason.com/blog/nature-study-in-a-nutshell/.
3. CBS Chicago. (April 21, 2017). Doctors are prescribing a daily dose of the outdoors. https://www.cbsnews.com/chicago/news/doctors-prescription-outdoors-health/.
4. James, T. (August 8, 2019). Doctors in Oregon are writing prescriptions to get outside. That Oregon Life. https://thatoregonlife.com/2019/08/doctors-in-oregon-are-writing-prescriptions-to-get-outside/.
5. PRA. Nature Prescribed. parkrxamerica.org.
6. Forest School Teacher Institute (FSTI). forestteacher.org.
7. Arthur's Acres Animal Sanctuary. https://www.arthursacresanimalsanctuary.org.
8. White, E. B. (1952). *Charlotte's web*. New York: HarperTrophy
9. Arrowhead Ranch and Rescue. https://arrowheadranch.org.
10. Gardner, P., & Kuzich, S. (2017). Green writing: The influence of natural spaces on primary students' poetic writing in the UK and Australia. *Cambridge Journal of Education, 48*, 427–443. https://www.tandfonline.com/doi/abs/10.1080/0305764X.2017.
11. Disney, W. "Colors of the wind." *Pocahontas*. https://youtu.be/O9MvdMqKvpUt.
12. Baylor, B. *Everybody needs a rock*. https://blogs.scientificamerican.com/rosetta-stones/a-perfect-book-for-hooking-kids-on-rocks/.
13. Shaw, C. G. (1947). *It looked like spilt milk*. Malaysia: HarperCollins.
14. Thoreau, H. D. (2012). *Walden*. Princeton, NJ: Princeton University Press.
15. Ringgold, F. https://www.faithringgold.com; Smith, B. https://en.wikipedia.org/wiki/Betty_Smith.
16. *Finding Nemo*. Pixar. https://en.wikipedia.org/wiki/Finding_Nemo.
17. Silverstein, S. (1964). *The giving tree*. New York: Harper & Row.
18. *The survivor tree*. https://en.wikipedia.org/wiki/Survivor_Tree.
19. Dr. Seuss. (1971). *The Lorax*. https://en.wikipedia.org/wiki/The_Lorax.

7

PLANNING TO WRITE PROSE

PROFESSIONAL CONVERSATION STARTERS

1. Which criteria would you include to assess a quality outline?
2. Look at a piece of writing and backward design it to an image with labels.

Plans for writing can be enhanced using various tools. Graphic organizers are very popular in many classrooms. Illustrating ideas can be viewed as an optional prewriting activity, but when employed as a starter for writing, it can lead to creation of impressive written work.

A visual outline of ideas can help prepare a roadmap for writing. Visual representations of ideas provide some of the best opportunities for widespread student buy-in. Many writers respond well to creating a detailed image for labeling rather than a conventional listing of ideas. The bigger the page, the better. In a performing arts school in the District of Columbia, one boy in grade 4 enjoyed drawing but was hesitant to write. By using an image at the front end of the writing experience, this student added as many labels as he could. After drawing and labeling, it was much easier for him to write many sentences around the words for a first draft. In this case, the question "I don't know what to write" was virtually eliminated.

Grade 4 Paired Outline of an Ideal School

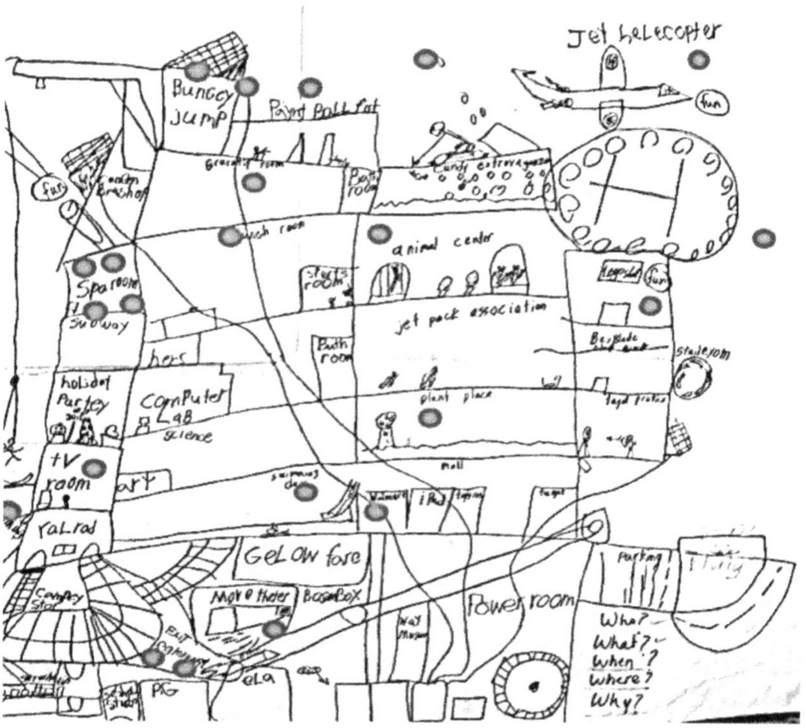

Figure 7.1. Illustrated Outline of an Ideal School (Grade 4 Student Pair)

Figure 7.1 illustrates the collaboration between this boy and his partner: their image outline for what would become three paragraphs reflecting their thoughts about the "ideal school."

Students first generated their ideas on large poster paper, which they labeled and edited. Students can use webbing, graphic organizers, or lists to prepare a detailed outline of a writing plan. The creation of Bitmoji[1] images can also be used to plan for writing. Having choices at the early stages for which tools students use can be motivating; some may need to be guided to try certain tools if the selection does not lead to gathering rich ideas. Exploring multiple tools can help students determine which tools help them improve their writing the most.

A great outline should leave room for plenty of ideas. Giving students large sheets of paper opens space for more words to populate the outline. The initial outline should not take more than 45 minutes to organize; however, students should be afforded additional time to edit their plans throughout the writing process. The image should not be judged according to its artistic prowess; rather, it should be considered an initial sketch created to build a bank of words and phrases as starter points for future sentences.

It is important to make time for students to conference with a peer or teacher about their plans. The visual image acts as a stimulus for getting started and planning an overview. It gives others a chance to provide input at the early stages of the work. An effective outline for an "ideal school" project should include the following:

- at least 10 detailed images about an ideal school
- at least 20 words to label the images
- at least three original ideas distinct from other plans
- feedback from classmates about the strength of the ideas presented in the plan
- conferencing with the teacher to discuss the quality of the plan

It is not commonplace for teachers to meet with students as part of the planning process, but giving students a chance to talk about their plans can lead to improving them, at the same time gaining suggestions about the organization of ideas and whether students need to invest more time in the planning stage.

Rather than head right to writing the first draft, the image should be edited so that additional details can be added to the overall plan. The initial outline should not be rushed; time spent on planning is usually well worth it. In a quality writing classroom, students are accustomed to returning to their images and outlines to make ongoing adjustments.

Students should not be permitted to move on until they have organized their ideas in their outlines first. Without deliberate modeling of how to draft and redraft plans, students can miss out on emulating such organizing practices of professional writers.

Ideally, students should have opportunities to work in pairs, so they can read each other's first thoughts and provide suggestions to enhance the outline. Once the sketches have enough details, the teacher can give students the go-ahead to write their first drafts. Students who do not meet the expectations can be supported to improve their sketches and labels until they are ready to serve as a support for the drafting stage of writing.

These outline labeled sketches should be handed in with each draft and the final copy. Teachers need ample evidence that student writing has transformed throughout the process. It is important to build into the writing process emulating the work and constant revising by real writers.

Novels, short stories, and poems were rarely built in a day. In fact, quality works can take months and years to craft, yet in English classrooms the time to craft an authentic piece of work is often shortchanged.

When teachers review the work in each phase, more value is placed on each step; as well, plagiarism concerns are minimized, eliminating the temptation for students to cut and paste work that others have written. When each stage of writing is examined, it should be easy to see that students have moved their written work from point form to revised drafts to final copy in a logical manner.

Teachers can trace development of the writing to help students be aware of the intricacies of the process, providing feedback along the way, much like an expert supports an apprentice or a novice master the writing craft. A solid detailed plan can be developed in many forms. The idea of beginning with images on a blank canvas is one way to help students generate words in preparation for getting their thoughts on paper and drafting sentences—the next phase of writing.

NOTE

1. https://www.bitmoji.com.

8

PRODUCING A FIRST (PROSE) DRAFT

PROFESSIONAL CONVERSATION STARTERS

1. Which criteria would you use to guide a student's first draft?
2. How can students use specific criteria to provide peer feedback in the early stages of writing?

The first draft of a piece of writing can be initiated as a skeleton consisting of first rough draft sentences. The directions for writing ideally should include a detailed account of how the writing will be assessed, viewed, and lead to action by the reader. The directions should outline the expected genre or writing style that will best convey the message for ease of understanding by the reader.

To illustrate the transformation of a high school piece of writing from the draft stage through the polished and presenting stages, the following draft about an experience volunteering at a homeless shelter will be used as an example. Students were expected to reflect on their experiences, using an outline to begin a first draft of their response. The teacher listed these criteria for the response:

- follows directions for writing a response
- includes a starter title

- includes a social justice claim
- has at least three distinct points
- backs up points with evidence or examples
- describes a detailed setting
- is double-spaced

After listing ideas in an outline, the writer crafted the first draft of Hope for the Homeless.

Hope for the Homeless

The Studio gives the opportunity for homeless to earn money through the creation of their stories. The studio is especially good because it allows for homeless to make money, and the expressive writing they take part in acts as a therapy as well. There need to be more opportunities like The Studio in the downtown east side, so that it can prevent homeless to resorting to illegal activities for survival.

For the most part, this draft accomplished what was asked. The author shared three benefits of The Studio program and, therefore, met most of the requirements of this first draft. It is important to note that the first draft is not a written piece where grammar, punctuation, unity, or clarity must spill out automatically.

The first raw response in sentence form followed the directions of the task, which is precisely why this phase is called the rough draft. In the first draft of Hope for the Homeless, the writer needed to convey more than just listing the benefits of a writing program for the homeless. A peer reviewer recommended that the writer use more words that create visual images of the setting as well as provide concrete examples demonstrating evidence to support each claim. Finally, the writer was prompted to ask a question or share a theory about why many cities have homeless citizens.

The teacher and student would use the criteria to discuss the written response during the writing conference. During this feedback stage when the teacher and student view the draft together, they can discuss the criteria in terms of what's there and what's missing. Students need to know that a first draft is never a final copy but just a skeleton of the final work. Writing the first draft of prose can involve researching settings and gathering information to ensure that the writing piece has enough meat to polish in the editing phase to follow.

9

POLISHING WRITTEN WORK

PROFESSIONAL CONVERSATION STARTERS

1. What are creative ways to teach mini lessons about common writing mistakes?
2. What engaging resources for students are you aware of that can support learning about quality writing practices?

Polishing a piece of writing can be enhanced when writers pay particular attention to word choice and deliberate revision and heed the advice of reviewers. The polishing stage of writing requires time, consultation, and hard work. This is when the writers need to roll up their sleeves and emulate how real writers behave.

It is important to have a way for students to *see* the changes made to each draft. Technology can make it easy for students to write and revise their work; however, it can be challenging to keep track of the writing transformation as students write a draft one day, save it in a folder, then return to it the next day—making changes that are not tracked. In this way, it is difficult for students and teachers to see the value and evidence of editing without marking hard copies of their work.

It can be helpful for young writers to print drafts and use a pen or pencil to make their changes. Modifications may also require shifting sentence order or including additional sentences, so it makes sense to double-space drafts to make room for such adjustments. The use of track changes (recommended for middle or high school students) when saved as separate files on a computer can also provide a visual record. It is important for young writers to provide evidence of their edits, which can be easier, at first, with paper and pen/pencil.

Teachers also need to see the effort students put into the process to gauge conferencing support that can meet students where they are and move them forward. Without a reference to the original work and various changes in drafts, it is almost impossible to compare and determine the extent of editing.

Enhancing Word Use

The use of an enhancing word chart can allow both the writer and the reviewer to take stock of the word inventory to gauge the depth of language use in a passage. For instance, in the first draft of Hope for the Homeless, the following words and phrases added to the reservoir of strong word choices: therapy, expressive, opportunities, dismal, survival, hopeless, committed, especially, designed, and impressed.

Grammar can help the reader identify and use parts of speech as a tool to improve word and phrase choices. Writers can remove simple words and slang (e.g., "got") and use a thesaurus to edit in rich vocabulary. Mini lessons about grammar, slang (e.g., removing "anyways"), and clichés (e.g., "at the speed of light") can also help writers with word revision.

The challenge for teachers is how to help young writers view their own writing through many different lenses. The mini lessons and conferencing can help, but clarity of the rubrics is also necessary. Ideally, schools have set up writing buddies, so older students emulating teachers can view other writing pieces and talk and teach their younger buddies why certain words and sentences need more work. According to experts at the Dartmouth Institute, collaborative writing is a powerful skill:

> Collaboration helps students understand writing as a public, communal act, rather than a private, isolated one. Many students write papers that make sense to them but aren't clear or persuasive for others. Peer reviewers help students to understand that they aren't writing for themselves, but for readers.[1]

Building in an advise and revise stage within the polishing stage is a way for partners to learn and use the rubrics and their own listening skills to support each other's writing. At the advise and revise stage of writing, the focus shifts from content to word use and sentence construction. To fine-tune writing so that the style enhances the message, the writer can work with others to make changes to most sentences in the first draft. Use a read-aloud in concert with dialogue about the criteria in the rubric and focused short mini lessons with only a few students at a time.

Ideally, the draft is read aloud at least twice—once by the writer and once by the reviewer. Hearing the written words can help the writer begin to make revisions. Students need to ask their writing partner (a student sitting next to them) to read aloud their drafts. The writer may ask the reader to stop at any time to make revisions, but the partner must read the full draft out loud.

At certain stages, writing can be a social process. Outside advice should be sought to help reduce the critical mass of mechanical and word choice errors that can be pervasive in weaker writing. Students need to understand that it is easy to leave out words when your mind is racing; when they hear their words aloud, it can be easier to detect what might be missing. Students often find mistakes in their peers' work, helping them gain further capacity to clean up their own writing. Reading aloud and listening to someone read aloud a piece of written work is a powerful approach for stimulating revisions.

Self-Assessment and Conferencing Feedback

Expecting fewer careless writing errors is augmented by clarifying what the teacher looks for when providing feedback for a piece of work. By making mistakes explicit, assessment tools can serve as teaching tools. After students have experience using interactive rubrics, they can generate their own assessment criteria, individually or collaboratively with others. According to Peha: "It's much more effective to give students a hand in creating their own criteria based on authentic models."[2] The writer and reviewers can make their goal to streamline sentences. Can words be removed to make the message smoother? Can sentence order be changed for added impact?

After reading and listening to the text, focusing on word use and grammar, the writer can assess the draft to make final changes. At this stage, student writers can self-assess their draft according to criteria listed on an interactive rubric. Writers should read their work many times to make changes that address the features of quality writing. They should ask themselves which criteria are present in their writing and which criteria might be missing.

Following peer review and self-reflection, students can make changes to their draft and complete the self-assessment portion of the rubric (see table 9.1), giving it and the draft to the teacher for more formal feedback. Based on this initial self-assessment, and the changes recommended during the reading aloud and the analysis of word use, the following revisions (in bold) were made to the first draft of the grade 11 student reflection:

Hope for the Homeless

For some, the sidewalks of Vancouver's **east side** can be a **damp and** dismal place. Thanks to The Studio, there are fewer homeless people **spending time lying on the vents of high rises**. The Studio is a program designed to help the homeless gain some career entry skills. **This practical program provides an opportunity for the homeless** to earn money **by writing and sharing** their **own** stories. The studio is especially good because it allows for **the** homeless **to use** expressive writing as therapy as well. When I observed the program, I was impressed with how Neal, **a tall, thin, unshaven forty-ish man**, wrote about how he cared for his dog: "Molly keeps me warm and doesn't let anyone take my stuff," he shouts. Even though he **rarely smiled**, I could see that his **companion** brought him joy. I could also see that the coordinators of the program were committed to helping each homeless writer. Neal was asked to add more details and explain why he felt helpless and what he could do about it. Through writing the homeless could learn to solve their own problems. **Drugs are a serious issue for** many homeless people, and the time Neal spends writing takes his mind off when and where he is going to **find** his next fix. By writing about his problems, he is beginning to see that drugs will not solve them, and stealing to find the money to pay for **his habit** will only lead him back to jail.

The Studio place is much more than a government handout. If the homeless could learn to take care of themselves, they could get out of their situation. Neal and the others taught me that the homeless are not homeless by choice **but by tragedies beyond my imagination**. No one wants to steal **or beg for food** for a living. There needs to be more opportunities like The Studio in the downtown east side, so that **such programs** can prevent **many** homeless **people from** resorting to illegal activities for survival. We need to understand the homeless and **realize** that they can break free from a hopeless cycle of living **in dark corners of our cities**.

This piece has not improved simply because it is a thicker description; it is richer because it embellishes more qualities of strong writers, most notably the use of evidence, setting, abstract themes, and quotes. The work now meets the expectations as outlined in the criteria.

Students can then self-score, and teachers and peer reviewers then assess this work using the interactive rubric in table 9.1.

Hope for the Homeless is becoming a powerful piece of writing. Please consider sending this to your internship coordinator, as he would enjoy reading

Table 9.1. Interactive Rubric for Hope for the Homeless

	Interactive Rubric for Writing Reflection Assignment	
Student Self-Score	*Quality of Writing: (2) strong skill, (1) developing skill (still learning), (?) missing*	*Teacher Score*
Substance: This piece of writing . . .		
2	has at least three great details about the Studio Program	2
2	has at least three distinct details about setting	2
2	has at least three distinct details about evidence	2
2	develops an abstract idea/theory that addresses a social justice issue	1
Organization: This piece of writing . . .		
2	uses words properly (does not use slang: "ain't," "guys," "thing")	2
1	does not use run-on sentences, contractions, or hyphens	2
1	does not use repeated words	1
1	demonstrates sequential flow of sentences	2
2	uses a variety of sentence types	2
1	has a clear and captivating introductory sentence	2
1	has a clear and captivating concluding sentence	2
2	includes compelling words and phrases	2
2	read writing aloud to partner and made changes to draft	2
2	made changes when writing was read aloud	2
2	is double-spaced and shows changes made to most sentences	2
25/30		28/30
Comments:		

what you have read. When we meet to conference, let's discuss how poverty is a social justice issue and how that abstract idea might be emphasized more in your writing piece. We can also discuss where you thought you made any organization errors, but from my view this is incredible work.

How a teacher uses the scores can vary. At first, the student may need support with scoring their own work. After comparing assessments over time with the teacher's scores, students can improve their self-awareness and often mirror the same assessment as the teacher. Teachers may add both scores together or only use their score.

The rubric is more than a checklist: it focuses attention on whether criteria have been addressed as "some" or "more" or "?," meaning that an expectation seems to be missing. Rather than traditional grading schemes where the "some" is broken down in multiple deviations of "not meeting" expectations, this reduction in layers of assessment makes the tool less cumbersome and, it could be argued, more objective. What's important is that the interactive rubric support draft revisions.

The teacher can use an interactive rubric as a guide for mini lessons prior to editing and again throughout the editing process when conferencing about the student's writing. Teachers can discuss what they think is missing and invite students to show them where a criterion is present in the work. The teacher may adjust the assessment or ask the student to make the evidence more explicit, just as writers and editors interact in the real world.

Students should have every opportunity to improve their scores. Thus, the rubric serves as a formative tool until the student has completed upgrades, noting that the goal is to ensure student mastery of writing, not a range of writing scores in the classroom.

Should the draft scores count toward a grade? Should the upgraded work, after input, be part of the overall writing score? It is often assumed that formative assessment does not count. But if editing is a valued skill, it should count even after students have received support along the way. In this way, they can cultivate genuine polishing habits and heed peer and teacher review recommendations.

To prevent writers from moving to a final copy that requires more work, a teacher could determine a minimum mastery score that students must achieve. For instance, if a student scores less than 80% on the teacher-score side of the rubric (i.e., 24/30), the student can be asked to go back and make improvements to the draft before getting the go-ahead to complete a final copy.

The final stage of polishing should address spelling, punctuation, formatting, and an overall impression about the readiness of the piece for others to read formally. Such assessments should occur at the final polishing stage when the writing shifts from the double-spaced draft to the form and shape of the genre of writing required.

Leaving the review of spelling and punctuation until the assessment of the final copy is deliberate. Too often students rush an edit by scanning for spelling errors; instead, this should be one of the final tasks after the writing has been modified.

~ *Spelling Mini Lesson*

It's important to keep several points in mind at this stage of the editing process. Writers who tend to rush only edit for spelling. Students who have difficulty with spelling tend to mix up homonyms (e.g., "there, they're, their"; "to, too, two"; "our, are"; "your, you're"). Wise advice to writers: pause each time you see a homonym to make sure you chose the correct word.

A reader can interpret spelling mistakes as sloppy, noting that care was not taken to proofread thoroughly. Weak spellers need to check their work for accuracy. They should never assume the spelling is correct. It takes time to check, but it is worth removing this distraction. Weaker spellers often rely on spell check, a practice that is not recommended; many words can be replaced with words that have correct spellings but have nothing to do with the sentence.

It is also easy to be careless about word endings, particularly when students make frequent changes to their drafts. Final checks of writing pieces should include a second look at word endings (e.g., "ed," "ing," "s"). Racing minds can lead to careless errors. An extra read-aloud usually catches these typos.

Writers can miss adding apostrophes or add them where they do not belong. For instance, formal writing should not use contractions (or hyphens). It is also easy to make mistakes among Canadian, American, and British versions of spelling.

Mini lessons about common mistakes can be shared during conferencing at any stage of the drafting process. Help the student look through more lenses to improve the draft. Deliberately teach students and student reviewers in mini lessons throughout the writing process to be aware of common mistakes in writing.

~ Common Mistake Mini Lesson

- commas used instead of periods (no commas between complete sentences)
- run-on sentences (Count the number of verbs in a sentence. If more than three are present, the sentence may be tempting the hideous run-on sentence.)

The following list of other common mistakes can be reviewed during teacher or peer conferencing:

- repeating words
- using fragments
- using improper past-tense words
- using too many simple words
- missing a subject before a verb
- using excess or extraneous words
- using or misusing contractions and apostrophes
- not aligning for first- or third-person agreement
- using absolutes (i.e., "best," "always," "every," "never," "only," "safe")
- careless about word endings (i.e., "ed," "ing," "s")
- lack of accurate use of "this" or "that" (i.e., when "that" is used as a subject)

Simply listing common mistakes and telling students not to make them will not be as effective as using deliberate strategies in the context of student writing.

~Title Making Mini Lesson

After the writing is polished, it is time to pay special attention to a title for the text. Some texts do not require titles (letters, journal entries, texts with predetermined titles), but for those that require a title, it is best to think carefully about this first impression. The title should give a strong hint about the main idea, but it should also draw in the reader with a creative, ideally, one-of-a-kind headline. Title mishaps, which can distract the reader, need to be reviewed prior to printing the final polished copy.

Common Title Mishaps

- use of period at the end
- improper or no use of capitals
- lack of creative title (or no title at all)
- title does not seem to connect to the main idea

Which expectations to include in an interactive rubric vary depending on the age level and type of text written. In the case of Hope for the Homeless, the formatting needs to fit a persuasive writing style, which would be assessed as substance in earlier assessed versions of the writing draft. Table 9.2 provides an example of an assessment tool for a final copy.

The final written copy requires a review of the text and the title. People are not born great writers; they have been helped along the way, especially if they have not picked up the art of writing via osmosis from reading. Preparing writing worth reading does not happen overnight. The presentation of writing can make the process complete and meaningful for many writers. The next chapter features several engaging ways to present writing to be read by others.

Table 9.2. Teacher Scoring of the Final Copy

The final copy: This piece of writing has . . .	*Teacher Score* *(2) meets expectations* *(1) almost meets expectations* *(?) has not yet met expectations*
Accurate spelling	
Accurate punctuation	
Accurate grammar	
Accurate capitalization	
A creative and compelling title	
Total Score	/10 points
Comments:	

NOTES

1. Dartmouth Writing Institute. http://dartmouth.edu/writing-speech/teaching/first-year-writing-pedagogies-methods-design/collaborative-learninglearning-peers.

2. Peha, S. (1995–2003). Assessing writers assessing writing. https://www.ttms.org/PDFs/09%20Writing%20Assessment%20v001%20(Full).pdf.

10

PRESENTING WRITTEN WORK

PROFESSIONAL CONVERSATION STARTERS

1. How do students like to present their writing?
2. Why is it an advantage to combine written and spoken assignments?
3. How can technology provide an engaging medium for presenting written work?

Typically, assessment of writing focuses on the product rather than the process. If something is worth reading, it is important to read and assess the work at all stages of the process. It is prudent, therefore, to develop rubrics to support the growth of writing in action; interactive rubrics can be designed to shape the ways writers share their work with others. Written work can be shared in published, verbal, and mixed-media formats. Different from contests, classroom or school anthologies include all students interested in having their written work published.

Writing can be published within anthologies, or as short stories or individual novels. Taking extra steps to have copies in classrooms, libraries, and other public spaces can further honor the work of students. Written works that are reports of research can be cataloged in school libraries, and students can be required to reference such research in future inquiries as another way to build writing legacies.

When students emulate the process of the doctoral defense, they link a mastery of the text they have written by articulating clearly the message of the text. Whether speaking to slides or in the formality of a Ted Talk[1] presentation, students have much to gain by talking about their writing. Finding opportunities for students to have audiences for their writing beyond their teacher only adds to the authenticity of the assignment.

The expression of writing can happen within the context of many different art forms. When poetry is fused as lyrics with music, writing can be experienced as song, and the message takes on a richer texture. Similarly, just as illustrated manuscripts embedded within texts in the Middle Ages added value, visual arts and graphic forms add further ways to interpret the message.

Writing scripts so they can be implemented as plays and dramatic renditions allows messages to be presented in the form of a story. Unfortunately, student writers rarely have an opportunity to write scripts for theater, film, or television productions.

The arts can be an incredible framework for presenting ideas. Expressing written messages by combining movement with a narrative can be a creative way for presenting text through dance; at one time a thesis could be presented as a choreographed message through movement. Similarly, at a highly recognized institution of higher education, a 20-foot-high and 10-foot-wide tapestry hung at the entrance for decades, accenting the acceptance of a nonlinear, less fixed form of a creative dissertation.

Images combined with text provide an opportunity to enhance the potential emotional connections with the message. The illustrations in a Shel Silverstein poem can add much to the humorous theme. Spiegelman's graphic novel *Maus* features deep social justice themes as the story portrays in print and image his father's Holocaust survivor story as a Polish Jew during World War II. It is the first and only Pulitzer Prize winner for a graphic novel.[2]

Magazines, websites, and other media include images as powerful tools for enhancing messaging. The hundreds of font choices and emojis have transformed the way text can be presented to the reader. Audiobooks, podcasts, webinars, and videos also incorporate sound to augment the message of the text. Students should have opportunities to express their work in written forms that reach beyond the printed text.

The presentation of student work is often overlooked. When young writers *write to be read*, they take more responsibility for improving their own writing and the way others can experience it. Chapters 12 through 16 provide examples of distinct modes of presentation that support student writing from kindergarten through high school.

NOTES

1. TedTalk. https://www.ted.com/talks.
2. *Maus*. https://en.wikipedia.org/wiki/Maus.

11

PURPOSE-BASED (PB) WRITING MODEL

PROFESSIONAL CONVERSATION STARTERS

1. Do teachers use a common approach to teach writing at your school?
2. Should every piece of writing instruction address prompts, plans, drafts, edits, and a presentation?

Purpose-based (PB) writing is about creating written work to be read by the writer and other readers. PB is a comprehensive approach to writing that emerged from work with students in public, charter, independent, and international elementary and high schools, as well as work with student teachers in colleges of education.

After the teacher presents an engaging, purposeful prompt, the writer is ready to organize and research ideas in an outline or plan. Reading one's own writing as the plan outline emerges, as well as reading ideas gathered from research, draws attention to the interdependence of reading and writing within writing tasks. A key purpose of reading is to share responses, feedback, and ideas to further develop writing. All writing at any stage can be improved.

This PB option emerged from an extensive literature review as well as more than 80 years of teaching and learning experiences with students garnered in the context of their use. Five "P" words represent simple steps in the PB writing model:

- P = Prompt
- P = Plan
- P = Produce
- P = Polish
- P = Present

Focusing on distinct phases of writing, from the initial stages of word-to-sentence formation and from poetry to prose, gives students time to improve their capacity to write. Rather than indicating that it is "the" best way to teach writing, it is most humbly, an informed sample that English language arts and other teachers committed to cross-curriculum writing can use to create common approaches to teaching writing.

What makes the PB writing process the same and different from current practices in teaching and learning writing? Whereas the words "draft," "edit," and "revise" are commonplace in many writing models, the notion of illustrating outlines, as well as reading and listening to written work, are not.

Even though significant research suggests that illustrating diagrams and images can be appealing prewriting options, they are not considered key components in popular writing models. Having students read their work and listen to others read their work may be an activity of interest, but rarely are such actions integrated directly into the writing process itself.

Conferencing with a teacher or peers is often an option near the final stages of writing, but rarely is such talk about writing throughout the process required as regular practice. Presenting a piece of work may be part of an integrated project but not necessarily a requirement for all written work.

To make writing lessons more engaging and effective, it could be advantageous to consider a PB approach. The idea of writing to be read can be integrated into a school curriculum and can transform it. If students work using this approach over several years in an elementary setting, it could reduce the need to have writing taught explicitly at the secondary or college level.

Students in high school, college, and the workforce who lack writing basics can improve their writing by using a common language and systematic process. The PB approach can help unpack and improve the quality of anyone's writing at any age, and it has been used with students in first grade through college.

The next five chapters feature primary, grades 3 through 5, grades 6 through 8, grades 9 and 10, and upper high school writing as samples of applications of a PB approach to written work.

Part III

WRITING FOR A PURPOSE, ONE GRADE AT A TIME

We've all heard the advice to have students write for authentic audiences. But the truth is that too many times, even when we try to follow that advice, we accidentally end up just having students pretend to write for someone other than us. So, our students write letters to the school board about lunch or the parking lot, but do we really deliver the letters? Is there a conversation with members of the board afterward?

—Anne Elrod Whitney

12

PRIMARY WRITING CLASSROOM

PROFESSIONAL CONVERSATION STARTERS

1. What kinds of activities are engaging for students in primary grades (PK through grade 2)?
2. How can pre-kindergarten through grade 2 writing experiences prepare students for writing in grades 3 through 5?

This section reveals ideas for addressing how learning can progress from letters to words, to sentences and short paragraphs. Ideally, students in the prewriting stages would focus on letter recognition to form words by kindergarten, and through word combinations master the formation of sentences in grade 1. By grade 2, most students should be ready to write short paragraphs and, therefore, apply the complete writing process. Table 12.1 illustrates sample prewriting activities for PK through grade 2.

To show progression of expectations with the same writing assignment theme (i.e., Invisible Things), the following distinctions could be made between PK and grade 2:

- PK Writing—Dictate three words about an invisible thing.
- SK Writing—Dictate a sentence about an invisible thing.
- Grade 1—Print a sentence about an invisible thing.
- Grade 2—Print three sentences about an invisible thing.

Table 12.1. Prewriting Activity in PK to Grade 2

PK (pre-kindergarten)	*SK (senior kindergarten)*	*1*	*2*
• uppercase letters • two-letter words (first consonant) • first name • numbers 1–9	• uppercase and lowercase letters • three-letter words (first and ending consonant) • first and last name • copy words to label pictures • numbers 11–20	• three- to four-letter words with basic vowel combinations • verbs • statement sentences • label pictures with support • numbers 21–100	• words with complex vowels and blended letter combinations • proper and common nouns • statement and question sentences • label pictures without support • combining words and numbers (dates, addresses)

Prompt

- Blindfold one partner while the other partner gives them verbal directions to complete a simple task.

  Teacher can ask a series of reflective questions such as:
  - What did you hear on your blind adventure?
  - Did you smell anything on your blind adventure?
  - What did you feel on your blind adventure?
- Class can talk about feelings as invisible things.
- Teacher can list other invisible images (e.g., air, hot, cold, hunger, sound, germs, gas, feelings [happy, love, sad, proud, disappointed], qualities [courage, selfishness])

Planning

- Students can draw one invisible thing they did not see on their adventure.
- They can label it by asking the teacher to place the image on the word wall.
- Students can be asked to add details and labels to their adventure picture.
- Students can label these parts of their pictures with more words that can be added to the word wall.

Produce (PK sample)

- They can dictate words to label the images in the pictures story. (Teacher prints out first draft under images.)
- PK students can practice printing one- and two-letter words from the story using uppercase letters.

Produce (SK sample)

- Discuss how stories have a beginning, middle, and end.
- Students add more images or details to story.
- Students dictate a sentence using the images in the picture story.
- SK students review and practice sounds of three-letter words in story.
- SK students practice printing two- and three-letter words from the story with lowercase letters.

Produce (Grade 1)

- Talk about invisible things that are not real (ghosts, dragons) and things that are real (feelings, truth).
- Students can add more images of real and unreal invisible things to their picture story.
- Discuss how stories have a beginning, middle, and end.
- Students print a sentence about the image for an adventure story using phonetical sounds of each word.
- Students label two-, three-, and four-letter words with simple vowel combinations under images in the plan.

Producing the Sentences (Grade 2)

- Students can talk about invisible things that are not real (ghosts, dragons) and things that are real (feelings, truth).
- Students can add more images of real and unreal invisible things to their picture story.
- Discuss how stories have a beginning, middle, and end.
- Talk about which images could represent the beginning, middle, and end of a story about invisible things.
- Students print three sentences about invisible things using phonetical sounds of each word.
- Students label simple, compound, and blended letter words on plan using simple and complex vowel combinations.

Figure 12.1 illustrates PK to grade 2 writing samples.

<table>
<tr><th>Image</th><th>Script/Writing</th></tr>
<tr><td>PK Writing
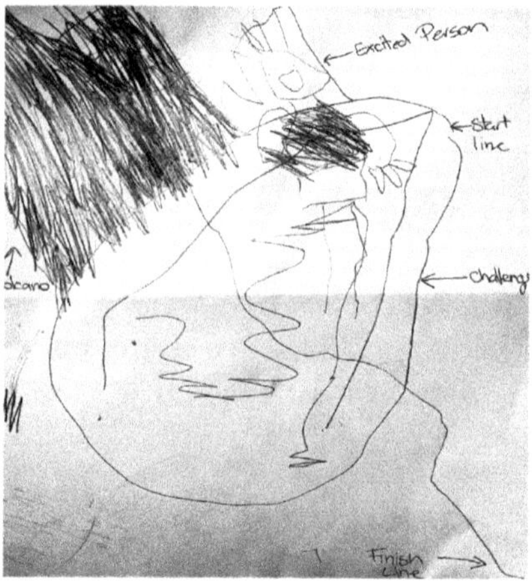
</td><td>I am excited doing a race from the volcano.</td></tr>
<tr><td>K Writing

</td><td>A unicorn that's yellow and flying over purple sea and orange sky.</td></tr>
</table>

Figure 12.1. PK to Grade 2 Writing Samples

<table>
<tr><th>Image</th><th>Script/Writing</th></tr>
<tr><td>Grade 1 Writing

</td><td>My octopoos is brushing his hair and the octopoos is not real becues he is ranbow.</td></tr>
<tr><td>Grade 2 Writing

</td><td>A old dragon with smaoth wings. Was walking by when he heard a big exsploshin. He said to himself I have to help.</td></tr>
</table>

Presenting the Sentences

Students can talk about their plans and sentences with the rest of class and then place them in their portfolios after being displayed, for example, on a dedicated bulletin board. Each plan can also be photographed and gathered into a digital collection to share in a classroom newsletter or magazine.

It is a practice in some schools to display only perfect products. Some students, therefore, never have their work featured, or they must spend countless minutes perfecting their work. Celebrating perfection should not be the goal. Hallways and classrooms are ideal spaces to document and pay tribute to the full transforming process from word to sentence (and their edits) to print. The joy of writing needs to be cultivated through the process *and* the product.

Expecting multi-paragraphs from all students in primary grades may produce a subculture of reluctant writers. If a staff can determine the ceiling in each grade, then all students can have extensive opportunities to achieve mastery. A vertically aligned curriculum similar to the example in table 2.3, with clear expectations, can help.

There is no need to rush primary writers to be paragraph writers. Those who can compose solid sentences by grade 2 are ready for an enriched experience, but this should not be a target for primary writers. In the next chapters, samples based on the purpose-based (PB) writing approach are featured to examine student written expression in grades 3, 4, and 5.

13

GRADES 3 THROUGH 5 WRITING

PROFESSIONAL CONVERSATION STARTERS

1. When is teaching a friendly and business letter formalized in curriculum in your school or district? Why is this an important medium for writing?
2. Why is it helpful for a student to focus on one year and genre at a time?
3. How can it be helpful for students to only focus on a few literary terms in one school year?
4. How would an English curriculum at the school or district level be affected by a grade concentration of a single genre per year, as well as the mastery of grammatical, punctuation, and literary devices?

The grades 3 through 5 writing experience should prepare students for success as a middle school writer. This chapter features examples of three writing activities: write a friendly letter to a new e-pal; write a three-paragraph book review about a humorous novel; and write a five-paragraph creative myth.

E-PAL WRITING (GRADE 3)

Prompt

- Research about e-pals; set up a plan to write to an e-pal at least once each term.
- Brainstorm what you might share with someone about your home, school, community, and country.

Plan

- Draw and label things you might want to share in your three or more letters to an e-pal.
- Be sure to include funny things.
- Self-assess your plan, and then gather feedback about it from your teacher using the interactive rubric in table 13.1.

Table 13.1. Writing Plan for E-Pal Letters

Writing Plan for E-Pal Letters *This Plan* *(2) You did it!* *(1) You still need some work.* *(?) Missing part.*	*Self-Review (Student Score)*	*Teacher Feedback (Teacher Score)*
created at least 15 detailed images		
labeled each image		
included funny things to share		
images and labels included descriptions of interesting settings		
used color-coded stickers to show which points would be included in the first e-pal letter		
Total	Score: /10	Score: /10
Comments:		

Producing the First Draft

- Students write the first draft of the e-pal letter by forming sentences around selected words on the plan and adding questions to start the conversation.
- Then students self-assess and conference with the teacher to determine whether expectations for the first draft have been met.

Chris wrote the following first message to her e-pal:[1]

March 16, 2023

Dear Global e-pal,

I am looking forward to emailing you this year. I'd love to know more about you and your school and your country. How do you start your day? What do you eat for breakfast? If you eat eggs, what kind are your favorite.

Here's a funny story about this morning when dad was in a hurry to go to work. It didn't take long for the smell of burnt toast to move upstairs, under my door and wake me. The words NOT AGAIN sprang in my head. I'd like to hear more about your mornings and other parts of the day.

Your e-pal,

Chris

Table 13.2. Sample Feedback Tool for the Initial Drafting Stage

Feedback Tool of the Initial Drafting Stage		
Student Self-Score	*Quality of Writing* *(A) ample evidence, (S) some evidence, (NY) no evidence yet*	*Teacher Score*
	creates images of setting (i.e., home, school, or country)	
	introduces a humorous event	
	letter is one paragraph in length	
	asks questions to help get a conversation started	
	has been written on every other line (to make room for future edits)	
Comments:		

Polishing the Drafts

- Students can print the first draft and begin editing.
- In the first round of edits, students should use a thesaurus to find synonyms to revise and add richer words, particularly, adjectives, nouns, and verbs.
- In the next edit round, students can add similes using "like" or "as."

~ *Enriched Language Mini Lesson*

Students can complete the Enriched-Language Chart (table 13.3) to track the use of powerful verbs, nouns, adjectives, and similes. The teacher may assign scores if students are aware that the identification of parts of speech and similes would be assessed either formatively or summatively.

Table 13.3. Sample Grade 3 Enriched-Language Chart for E-Pal Letter

three powerful verbs	*three powerful nouns*
creeping	offerings
dream	awakening
ignored	
three powerful adjectives	*one simile*
chocolate-chip dotted	syrup tastes like honey
humorous	
rude	
Score:	9/10
Comments:	

~ *Adjectives, Synonyms, and Thesaurus Use Mini Lesson*

Descriptive writing can be supported by access to stronger adjectives. The thesaurus can not only reduce repetition of words, but it can be a source of powerful descriptive words. Whether the thesaurus is digital or on paper, it is a critical tool in the writer's toolbox. Lessons on synonyms can also reveal alternative nouns and verbs to enhance the writing.

Prior to grade 3, the writing emphasis is on sentence formation, which requires nouns and verbs. When writing advances to the paragraph stage, it is time to introduce adjectives as descriptive words that modify nouns. Many digital resources can help students identify adjectives; popular choices include Flocabulary[2] and My Vocabulary.[3]

- https://www.flocabulary.com/unit/adjectives/
- www.myvocabulary.com

A mini lesson in the context of student writing can make learning grammar more relevant and authentic. Other grammar sources include:

- https://www.turtlediary.com/games/adjectives.html[4]
- https://grammar.yourdictionary.com/parts-of-speech/adjectives/adjective-games.html[5]
- https://www.englishclub.com/esl-games/grammar/adjectives.htm[6]

Some resources may list grades for various learning activities, but such distinctions may not align with the curriculum plan of the school. For instance, in this case, the recommended emphasis for mastering adjectives is grade 3, but IXL, for instance, refers to them being taught in every grade:

- https://ca.ixl.com/ela/adjectives-and-adverbs[7]

As part of the revision process, students should complete two audio reads: first, when the reader reads her own work aloud; and the second, when someone else reads the work aloud. When it sounds funny and doesn't make sense, this can be a clue for where to make changes. Based on feedback gathered from the teacher conference, the assessment of the Enriched-Language Chart, and the audio reads, the revision to the first draft emerged as follows with new words added bolded and underlined.

March 16, 2023

Dear Global e-pal,

I am looking forward to emailing you this **school** year. I~~'d~~ **would** ~~love~~ like to know more about you, ~~and~~ your school and **all about** your country. How **kinds of things** do you do **at home** to start your day? What **is your favorite meal at** ~~do you eat for~~ breakfast? If you eat eggs, what kind **do you prefer?** ~~are your favorite.~~ **I often dream of pancakes because maple syrup is delicious! It takes like honey, especially if you are a fan of sugar, like me.**

Here~~'s~~**is** a ~~funny~~ **humorous** story about the smell of burnt toast ~~to~~ **creeping** up **the** stairs **and** under my door. What a rude awakening! ~~and wake me~~. The words **"**NOT AGAIN**"** **sprang in my head, but it wasn't the first time my dad ignored the toast, too long in the toaster. I hope you do not have to eat burnt offerings!** I'd like to hear more about your mornings, ~~and~~ other parts of **your** day **and what it's like to live in your country.**

Your e-pal,
Chris

The teacher then scored the polished draft using the following interactive rubric (table 13.4).

If the score did not add up to at least 24/30, the student was asked to make more changes to improve the paragraph. The teacher would then work with the student to help edit the next draft. During the teacher conference, the teacher noted that the letter had a fun, friendly message, with excellent questions to start the conversation. The teacher also used the conferencing opportunity to remind the writer that future correspondence should include details about the school, community, and country.

Although this introductory letter needed one more simile, the overall message was ready to email. The final copy is written when the student polishes the work for accurate spelling, punctuation, and formatting.

Table 13.4. Sample Interactive Rubric for Assessing Revision of the E-Pal Letter

Interactive Rubric for Assessing Revision of the E-Pal Letter		
Student Self-Score	*(2) strong skill, (1) developing skill (still learning), (?) missing part*	*Teacher Score*
Substance: This piece of writing . . .		
1	has at least three descriptive details to share with the E-Pal	1
2	asked at least two questions	2
2	shared something funny in the letter	2
1	included two similes in the letter	1
2	included at least three powerful adjectives	2
Organization: This piece of writing . . .		
2	uses words properly (does not use slang: "ain't," "guys," "thing")	2
2	does not use run-on sentences or contractions	2
2	demonstrates sequential flow of sentences	2
2	uses a variety of sentence types	2
2	has a clear and captivating introductory sentence	2
2	has a clear and captivating concluding sentence	2
1	includes compelling and enriched nouns and verbs	2
2	read writing aloud to partner and made changes to draft	2
2	made changes when writing was read aloud	2
2	is double-spaced and shows changes made to most sentences	2
27/30		28/30
Comments:		

~ *Friendly Letter Formatting Mini Lesson*

Friendly letters usually have the date written in the upper right corner, called the Heading. This is followed by the Greeting, "Dear___." The featured paragraph is called the Body; The Closing can be a number of phrases or words, such as "Your friend," or in this case, "Your e-pal," which is followed by the student's signature (first name only). Teachers (or students) can make anchor charts as reminders about the formatting.

The final copy of the letter that follows features the revisions that were cleaned up and prepared on every line for distribution via email.

March 16, 2023

Dear Global e-pal,

I am looking forward to emailing you this school year. I would like to know more about you, your school and all about your country. What kinds of things do you do at home to start your day? What is your favorite meal at breakfast? If you eat eggs, what kind do you prefer? I often dream of chocolate-chipped dotted pancakes because maple syrup is delicious! It takes like honey, especially if you are a fan of sugar, like me. Here is a humorous story about the smell of burnt toast creeping up the stairs and under my door. What a rude awakening! The words "NOT AGAIN" sprang in my head, as it was not the first time my dad ignored the toast, too long in the toaster. I hope you do not have to eat burnt offerings! Seriously, though, I would like to hear more about your mornings, and other parts of your day and what it's like to live in your country.

Your e-pal,
Chris

Table 13.5 is a sample assessment tool for a final copy.

Table 13.5. Assessment Tool for Final Written Copy

Final copy: This piece of writing has . . . *(2) strong skill* *(1) developing skill (still learning)* *(?) missing*	*Teacher Score*
accurate spelling and proper use of homonyms	
accurate punctuation	
accurate grammar	
accurate capitalization	
effective formatting of friendly letter	
Total	/10 points
Comments:	

Learning to write is not easy. Having students learn how to craft a paragraph and revise it can be much more beneficial than hoping that completing lots of paragraphs will magically transform their writing.

FIVE-STAR BOOK REVIEW WRITING (GRADE 4)

Prompt

- Students can discuss qualities of the mystery of Vinland map by viewing parts of two videos:
  - https://www.youtube.com/watch?v=XUCMiJj4VAU
  - https://www.youtube.com/watch?v=xXn0TukpBtE
- Students can then discuss the mystery of whether Columbus or the Vikings were the first Europeans to cross the Atlantic Ocean.
- View on https://www.youtube.com/watch?v=nIbUtLTvUOk&t=14s.
- Although the Vinland artifact has now been discredited as a forgery, this does not mean that science has not provided evidence that the Vikings did arrive in Newfoundland, Canada.
- Students discuss how science can play a role in solving mysteries.

~ Mystery Genre Mini Lesson

Students can discuss the mystery genre that uses clues to solve or make sense of the possible cause of crimes. The mystery genre, as defined by https://literarydevices.net/mystery/, claims that "mystery literally means something that is a dilemma for the public. It is difficult for people to understand the mysteries of the universe. . . . It was a derivative of the old French term, *mistere*, which means a secret."[8]

- Students can then read this review of the book *Book Scavenger*[9] by Jennifer Chambliss Bertman.

Adventure + Books + Kids + San Francisco = Totally Enjoyable Family Read-Aloud *5.0 out of 5 stars.*

We all loved BOOK SCAVENGER. A lot. Even my hubby and clue-sniffing hound, Betsy got in on the action trying to solve the mystery of the missing/hidden books peppered throughout San Francisco. The storytelling is dynamic, the characters highly engaging, and the historical-literary element a fun surprise.

THE BOOK SCAVENGER revolves around middle school students Emily (the protagonist) and her friend, James as they solve ciphers and more in Edgar Allen Poe's 1843 little-known short story, THE GOLD-BUG. But there's so much more: middle school angst, big brother issues, a family's quest to live in all 50 states, bad guys, and of course, the city of San Francisco. When I got to the end of a chapter, signaling an end to our reading session, the kids would let out a chorus of "Nooos." They liked it that much.

The story reminded me a bit of . . . Nancy Drew meets A WRINKLE IN TIME, meets WILLY WONKA AND THE CHOCOLATE FACTORY . . . but those might not be the best comparisons. Truly a fun family read-aloud, but great for motivated 9+ year old kids (boys and girls) to read on their own. While THE BOOK SCAVENGER is technically part of a series, this is the first one, and can most definitely stand-alone.

- Students can discuss why Emily might be the protagonist.
- Students can then make a mystery list of places the book could be hidden in their own communities.

Students should realize that book reviews are not always positive. For instance, the following review of the same book did not share the same perspective as the first review.

Way overrated—3/5 Stars. Reviewed in the United Kingdom on January 15, 2018.

Why is this book so highly rated? Yes the idea of a book scavenger hunt is a clever one. But after a few chapters. . . . Its still hard to connect with the main character. Much of the text is spent describing the technical way geocaching works but with more ciphers. The story itself is humorless. It is not understood just WHY the parents chose the locations they chose to live in except that they are self absorbed. The target book of interest is really uninteresting. Don't expect this to be another Basil E Frankweilker quality story. Unentertaining. Give it a pass.

- Students can research more book reviews about other adventure or mystery books from various online sources: Amazon, Goodreads, Barnes & Noble, Chapters-Indigo.
- Students can choose their favorite reviews and read them aloud to the class or in small groups.

Planning

- Students can draw and label images on the plotline of a novel they plan to review.

~ Plotline Mini Lesson

Students will learn about mapping a plot in a story (problem, rising action, climax, falling action, and resolution) to identify key events to prepare a plan for writing a review.

- Students should then self-assess their plan and gather feedback from their teacher.
- Students should be encouraged to revise the images and the labels on the plan throughout the writing experience.
- The teacher should conference with every student about their plans to give them the go-ahead, when ready, to produce their first draft.

Producing the First Draft

- Students form sentences around selected words on the plan for the first draft of the review.
- Then students self-assess and conference with the teacher to determine whether expectations for the first draft have been met.

Polishing the Drafts

- Students can print the first draft of their review to begin making revisions.
- Students need to use a thesaurus to find synonyms to revise and add richer words, particularly adjectives, nouns, and verbs.
- In the second round of edits, students can add at least one hyperbole to exaggerate a point in the review.

Prior to grade 4, the writing emphasis is on forming a single paragraph using more powerful nouns, verbs, and adjectives. When the writing advances to the multiparagraph stage, then adverbs and literary devices such as hyperboles can be introduced to add further depth to the writing.

~ *Adverb Mini Lesson*

Descriptive writing can be supported by using adverbs in sentences, especially to provide variety as a sentence starter (e.g., "Strangely" or "Fortunately"). The easiest adverbs to identify end in "ly," but other words such as "again" and "yesterday" also modify or adjust the meaning—when something happens, or how "well" something is done. Adverbs usually modify verbs, but they can also modify other adverbs and adjectives.

Students can review and rank four websites that teach about adverbs:

- https://www.flocabulary.com/unit/adverbs/[10]
- https://www.youtube.com/watch?v=kKw1j7sZni0[11]
- https://www.youtube.com/watch?v=Io0dCPwFPTo[12]
- https://www.youtube.com/watch?v=cfenLGAYDeg[13]

~ *Hyperbole Mini Lesson*

Q: What is a hyperbole? A: "Hyperbole is a figure of speech and literary device that creates heightened effect through deliberate exaggeration. A hyperbole is often a boldly overstated or exaggerated claim or statement that adds emphasis without the intention of being literally true. In rhetoric and literature, hyperbole is often used for serious, comic, or ironic effects."[14]

A fun way to introduce or reinforce hyperboles is through Flocabulary:

- https://www.youtube.com/watch?v=kuzWLDWm6Zs[15]

In addition to adding adverbs to the review, students need to use the thesaurus to eliminate word repetition and add more powerful nouns, verbs, and adjectives. Students can complete an Enriched-Language Chart to track the use of powerful verbs, nouns, adjectives, adverbs. and at least one hyperbole.

Just as various parts of speech and literary devices can be the focus of different grades, punctuation and other grammatical lessons can be emphasized in small chunks in an English language arts curriculum each year. For instance, grade 4 could be an ideal time to introduce a mini lesson on hyphens and dashes.

~ *Hyphens and Dashes Mini Lesson*

Students may use hyphens to divide words; however, hyphens (-) should not be used for formal writing. Similarly, dashes (—) that are used to separate ideas in a sentence should not be used for writing assignments. When students are journaling, which is an informal writing activity, they are not subject to grammar or punctuation rules.

Email or social media writing can fall into the informal or casual writing area, but it often depends on the purpose of the message and who is the recipient. When you email a friend, the quality of the writing is different from what you write to your boss.

- The writer reads his work aloud to determine whether more revisions are required.
- Then someone else reads the work aloud to make sure word endings are accurate and that no words have been left out.
- Students can use the sample rubric (table 13.6) with the teacher during a writing conference.

The final copy emerges when the writer polishes the work for accurate spelling and punctuation and constructs a creative title. The teacher examines the final copy to determine whether it is ready to be published as a review online.

Table 13.6. Sample Rubric for Assessing a Draft of a Novel Review

Rubric for Assessing Draft of a Novel Review		
Student Self-Score	*Quality of Writing* (2) *strong skill,* (1) *developing skill (still learning),* (?) *missing part*	*Teacher Score*
Substance: This piece of writing includes . . .		
	key details about the conflict	
	key details about the characters	
	key details about the setting	
	two hyperboles	
	at least two powerful adverbs	
Organization: This piece of writing . . .		
	uses words properly (does not use slang: "ain't," "guys," "thing")	
	does not use run-on sentences	
	demonstrates sequential flow of sentences	
	uses a variety of sentence types	
	has clear and captivating introductory sentences for each paragraph	
	has clear and captivating concluding sentences for each paragraph	
	includes compelling and enriched nouns, verbs, and adjectives	
	was read aloud by writer to a partner, which led to changes made to draft	
	was revised when writing was read aloud by a partner	
	is double-spaced and shows changes made to most sentences	
/30		/30
Comments:		

Presenting

Once the final copy of the text is ready, students need to work with their teacher to cut and paste their work onto a safe website. Links to Goodreads and details on how to submit a review on Amazon.com are featured below:

- https://help.goodreads.com/s/article/How-do-I-write-a-book-review-on-Goodreads-1553870933519[16]
- https://www.wikihow.com/Leave-a-Review-on-Amazon[17]

Bookstores usually feature a space on their website for publishing reviews. Barnes & Noble in the United States and Chapters/Indigo in Canada also provide safe places for sharing reviews.

CREATIVE NARRATIVE FOR SUPERPOWER SLIDE SHOW (GRADE 5)

Prompt

- Students can begin by listening and viewing the myth about Curupira:[18] https://www.youtube.com/watch?v=ahSm_Bk2HQE
- They can then discuss questions about a Brazilian myth:
    - Myths are told like they were factual, offering reasonable explanations. Long ago people believed these stories to be true. (Which parts of the Curupira myth seemed real?)
    - Myths can include characters with superpowers such as gods and/or goddesses. (What superpowers did Curupira have?)
    - Myths explained such things as lightning in a time before science. (What explanation was given for why Curupira had feet that faced backward?)
    - Myths usually teach life lessons. (What is the moral of Curupira's story?)

Mythical stories are common in many societies around the world.

- Students can read about bee myths from different continents. Bees exist on every continent except Antarctica.
- Students can take notes from these two sites to discuss how some are the same and different from each other:
    - https://www.hobbyfarms.com/5-honeybee-myths-legends-folklore/[19]
    - https://www.raymondhuber.co.nz/honey-bees-ebook-life-cycle-honey-stings-crisis-myths/bee-mythology/[20]
- After the discussion, students can determine what kind of myth they will create to feature in the class Superpower Slide Show.

Planning

- Students can draw and label images to illustrate their setting, characters, and challenge in their own myth, keeping in mind the key features of myths.
- Students can self-assess their plan using the interactive rubric in table 13.7 and then gather feedback about the plan from the teacher.

Table 13.7. Interactive Rubric for Creative Myth Plan

Plan for Writing a Creative Myth	*Self-Review (Student Score)*	*Teacher Feedback (Teacher Score)*
This plan included: *(2) You did it!* *(1) You still need some work.* *(?) Missing part.*		
detailed images with labels of character(s)		
detailed images with labels of setting		
detailed images with labels of conflict(s)		
evidence of character(s) with superpowers		
images and labels are easy for reader to follow		
Total	/10	/10
Comments:		

- Students can revise the images and labels on the plan at all stages of the writing process.
- Following the teacher conference about the plan, if expectations of the plan have been met, students can begin to produce their first draft.

Producing the First Draft

- Students build sentences from the words in the plan.
- Student then organize the sentences into five paragraphs.
- They can then self-assess their first draft and discuss ideas during the conference with the teacher.

Polishing the Draft

- Polishing the writing can begin on a printed copy of the first draft.
- Revisions should include using phrasing within sentences as well as including literary devices (e.g., onomatopoeia, assonance).

~ *Prepositions and Phrasing Mini Lesson*

Prepositions begin phrases, and phrases end with nouns or pronouns. Most phrases are adverbial phrases because they answer where and how; adjectival phrases describe a noun.

Students can review these videos to discover more examples of phrases and prepositions:

- https://www.youtube.com/watch?v=brxQFHE3b6Q[21]
- https://www.flocabulary.com/unit/prepositions/[22]
- https://www.khanacademy.org/humanities/grammar/parts-of-speech-the-preposition-and-the-conjunction/types-of-prepositions-and-phrases/v/prepositional-phrases[23]

Students can review the poems to identify phrases. In the following poem, "Who am I?," the phrases are underlined. Students can discuss which are adverbial phrases and which are adjectival phrases. They all begin with prepositions.

Who am I?

I am the color <u>of the worn-out leather seats</u>.
I am the color <u>of the pale dreaming face</u>.
I am the purse slung tightly <u>around a woman's waist</u>.
I am cover-up <u>for stray spots on a young face</u>.
I feel light and bold.
I feel weightless <u>in a night's sky</u>.
I sometimes feel the joy and pain
<u>Of a world</u> mixed <u>with shades of gray</u>,
I feel the urges <u>of glory and passion</u>
but my color remains the same.
I am not red or black or white
but feel them all the same.
If looks could tell, I'm undecided.
I simply am beige.

—Anonymous

~ Onomatopoeia Mini Lesson

Onomatopoeia is a literary device that uses words that imitate sounds. Some examples include "smash," "crash," and "boom." Students can list at least five more after listening to these videos:

- https://www.youtube.com/watch?v=f1b5kCvVBo8[24]
- https://wordwall.net/resource/44391/english/onomatopoeia-match-up[25]
- https://www.flocabulary.com/unit/onomatopoeia/[26]

Students can also view comics to find examples of onomatopoeia.

~ Assonance Mini Lesson

Assonance is when words repeat the same vowel sound. Students can listen to a lesson about assonance on this YouTube channel:

- https://www.youtube.com/watch?v=5dLGAjMGhZs[27]

Sometimes students mix up assonance with alliteration. Students can view the following videos that clarify the distinctions:

- https://www.flocabulary.com/unit/alliteration-assonance/[28]
- https://www.studiobinder.com/blog/what-is-assonance-definition/ (review of alliteration)[29]

Students should use a thesaurus to integrate more synonyms into writing. Students can complete the Enriched-Language Chart (table 13.8) to provide evidence of powerful verbs, nouns, adjectives, adverbs, phrasing, onomatopoeia, and assonance.

Table 13.8. Sample Enriched-Language Chart for Creative Myth

Enriched-Language Chart for Creative Myth	
three powerful verbs	three powerful nouns
three powerful adjectives	three powerful adverbs
three examples of phrases	three examples of onomatopoeia
Total: /20 points	two examples of assonance
Comments:	

~ *Possessive Apostrophes, Not Contractions Mini Lesson*

Students need to be taught the deliberate rules of using apostrophes that align with who possesses something. Where the apostrophe is placed depends on whether the owner is more than one person. The general rule for a singular noun is to add an "s" after the apostrophe as in the examples below:

- The coach's fee
- The child's book
- The boy's grandparents

When the noun is plural and does not end in an "s," the same rule applies.

- The children's books

However, when the plural ends in a "s," the apostrophe is placed after the "s."

- The twins' grandparents
- The girls' hockey team
- The coaches' fees

Examples of more apostrophe lessons can be found in the following websites:

- https://www.thepunctuationguide.com/apostrophe.html[30]
- https://www.grammarbook.com/punctuation/apostro.asp[31]
- https://www.youtube.com/watch?v=My6oGvkHnfY[32]
- https://www.youtube.com/watch?v=KFdTz6GlUeg[33]

It is important to know that the use of apostrophes for contractions is not preferred in formal writing. Examples of contractions include: "it's" shortened from "it is," and "they're," shortened from "they are." Students should revise writing to eliminate or limit contractions in assignments. Understanding how to combine words to make contractions is useful for informal writing, but removing the contraction to expand to two words can help ensure that the word usage fits with more formal applications.

Following the series of mini lessons, the writers can read aloud their myths, then listen to a partner read the text read aloud to determine whether more revisions are required. Then students can self-assess their polished work and use an interactive rubric (table 13.9) with the teacher to gather further feedback about the revised draft.

Table 13.9. Sample Rubric for Assessing Revisions to Creative Myth

Rubric for Assessing Revisions to Creative Myth		
Student Self-Score	*Quality of Writing* *(2) strong skill, (1) developing skill (still learning), (?) missing part*	*Teacher Score*
Substance: This piece of writing includes . . .		
	key details about the conflict or challenge	
	key details about the characters	
	key details about the setting	
	compelling use of superpowers	
	three examples of onomatopoeia	
	three examples of assonance	
	at least three examples of phrasing	
Organization: This piece of writing . . .		
	does not use run-on sentences, contractions, hyphens, dashes, or slang	
	demonstrates sequential flow of sentences	
	has clear and captivating introductory sentences for each paragraph	
	has clear and captivating concluding sentences for each paragraph	
	includes compelling and enriched nouns, verbs, and adjectives	
	was read aloud by the writer to a partner, which led to changes made to draft	
	was revised when writing was read aloud by a partner	
	is double-spaced and shows changes made to most sentences	
/30		/30
Comments:		

After reaching a proficient polishing level, the student can record the final copy after ensuring that spelling and punctuation are correct, and a creative title has been established. Table 13.10 provides an example of an assessment tool for a final copy.

Table 13.10. Assessment Tool for Final Copy of Creative Myth

Final copy: This myth has . . . *(2) strong skill* *(1) developing skill (still learning)* *(?) missing part*	*Teacher Score*
accurate spelling and proper use of homonyms	
accurate punctuation	
accurate grammar	
accurate capitalization	
a creative title	
Total	/10
Comments:	

Presenting

A Superpower Slide Show can be created so that all students can read their myths live or in a recorded fashion. Teachers can then acquire evidence of students' speaking skills.

- Students can choose one image for each paragraph from their plan. A photo of the images can be scanned and incorporated into a class slide show.
- Students can celebrate their collated work in a Superpower Slide Show presentation.

Presentations of this kind contribute much to making fond memories of writing.

NOTES

1. Global E-pals. https://www.epals.comc.
2. Flocabulary. https://www.flocabulary.com/unit/adjectives/.
3. My Vocabulary. www.myvocabulary.com.
4. Turtle Diary. https://www.turtlediary.com/games/adjectives.html.

5. Kittelstad, K. 7 Awesome adjective games. https://grammar.yourdictionary.com/parts-of-speech/adjectives/adjective-games.html.

6. English Club. https://www.englishclub.com/esl-games/grammar/adjectives.htm.

7. IXL. https://ca.ixl.com/ela/adjectives-and-adverbs.

8. Literary Devices. https://literarydevices.net/mystery/.

9. Chambliss Bertman, J. (2016). *Book scavenger*. New York: Henry Holt.

10. Flocabulary.com. https://www.flocabulary.com/unit/adverbs/.

11. Grammaropolis. Adverb song. https://www.youtube.com/watch?v=kKw1j7sZni0.

12. Learn English. How to start a sentence in English with an adverb. https://www.youtube.com/watch?v=Io0dCPwFPTo.

13. MC Grammar. The adverb song. https://www.youtube.com/watch?v=cfenLGAYDeg.

14. Literary Devices. https://literarydevices.net/hyperbole/.

15. Flocabulary. https://www.youtube.com/watch?v=kuzWLDWm6Zs.

16. Goodreads. https://help.goodreads.com/s/article/How-do-I-write-a-book-review-on-Goodreads-1553870933519.

17. Amazon. https://www.wikihow.com/Leave-a-Review-on-Amazon.

18. Brazilian Myth. Curupira. https://www.youtube.com/watch?v=ahSm_Bk2HQE.

19. Urquhart, K. M. (May 2, 2017). 5 Honeybee myths, legends & folklore. https://www.hobbyfarms.com/5-honeybee-myths-legends-folklore/.

20. Huber, R. Bee myths & folktales. https://www.raymondhuber.co.nz/honey-bees-ebook-life-cycle-honey-stings-crisis-myths/bee-mythology/.

21. Stowell, D. Prepositions and prepositional phrases. https://www.youtube.com/watch?v=brxQFHE3b6Q.

22. Flocabulary. https://www.flocabulary.com/unit/prepositions/.

23. Khan, S. https://www.khanacademy.org/humanities/grammar/parts-of-speech-the-preposition-and-the-conjunction/types-of-prepositions-and-phrases/v/prepositional-phrases.

24. Bauer, M. Onomatopoeia. https://www.youtube.com/watch?v=f1b5kCvVBo8.

25. Word Wall. https://wordwall.net/resource/44391/english/onomatopoeia-match-up.

26. Flocabulary. https://www.flocabulary.com/unit/onomatopoeia/.

27. The Touring Teacher. Assonance examples for kids. https://www.youtube.com/watch?v=5dLGAjMGhZs.

28. Flocabulary. https://www.flocabulary.com/unit/alliteration-assonance/.

29. Studio Binder. https://www.studiobinder.com/blog/what-is-assonance-definition/ (review of alliteration).

30. The Punctuation Guide. https://www.thepunctuationguide.com/apostrophe.html.

31. Grammar BOOK. https://www.grammarbook.com/punctuation/apostro.asp.

32. McClure, L. When to use apostrophes. https://www.youtube.com/watch?v=My6oGvkHnfY.

33. A7 Learning. Plural S and possessive S. https://www.youtube.com/watch?v=KFdTz6GlUeg.

14

MIDDLE SCHOOL WRITING IN AN UPPER ELEMENTARY SCHOOL SETTING

PROFESSIONAL CONVERSATION STARTERS

1. Which writing strategies engage middle school students?
2. What do you think students need to master before writing essays or extended compositions?
3. It is recommended that detail paragraphs be drafted in advance of introductory and concluding paragraphs. How can such a strategy help organize a writer's ideas?
4. It can be confusing for students to learn the parts of speech and the parts of a sentence at the same time. Do you think it makes sense for students to master the basic parts of speech (nouns, pronouns, verbs, adjectives, adverbs, prepositions, and phrases) first before being expected to have a solid understanding of subjects, predicates, and clauses?
5. Do you think middle school students would be able to design assessment tools to guide their writing?

There is no simple way to describe a grade 6, 7, or 8 middle school writer. Students who have struggled with writing prior to middle school may bring unpleasant memories with them and as such, they may find written assignments painful. Although in some cases the computer can help, it can also tempt students to cut and paste work from other writers. If students are not invested in the writing, then plagiarism can be a more convenient way to manage work, especially if the volume of assignments is too great.

Individuals who love to read tend to be more prolific writers. Although it is important to encourage reading, relying on a reading prompt is not the only way to improve student writing. Including targeted mini lessons, customized within project work, can be powerful and engaging.

Plenty of writing skills and authentic experiences help students be successful writers in middle school. Students can continue working through the purpose-based (PB) approach using a prompt to design a plan, write a first draft, polish the drafts, and present texts in a variety of authentic ways. This chapter will feature three engaging writing projects in three different middle school grades:

- Grade 6—Current Event or Article
- Grade 7—Future World
- Grade 8—Social Justice

This chapter also features a description of a novel-writing activity that can be organized over three years as a sample of a sustained writing project. It is rare for curriculum planning to reach beyond traditional school year time limits, but novelists and nonfiction writers do require significant time to develop their texts. Schools that give students opportunities to emulate conditions of professional writers can enhance their writing lives.

CURRENT EVENT NEWS ARTICLE WRITING (GRADE 6)

Prompt

If the school does not have a student-run newspaper or magazine, then students can research how to set up one. Here are sample suggestions:

- https://schools.firstnews.co.uk/blog/journalistic-writing/how-to-start-a-school-newspaper/[1]
- https://makemynewspaper.com/how-to-start-a-school-newspaper/[2]
- https://www.wikihow.com/Start-a-School-Newspaper[3]

Planning

- Students can work alone or in pairs to create an outline for a multi-paragraph article (five or more small paragraphs) about a current event.
- Outlines can be a point form list or graphic representations with labeled images.

~ *Investigative Reporting Mini Lesson*

What does an investigative reporter do? Students can view the following link and then discuss what investigative reporters do:

- https://life.lfny.org/2018/01/31/behind-the-scenes-in-the-broadcast-room-2/[4]

Students can review the following example of an investigative inquiry into local/family heroes in a community.

First paragraph (3–5 sentences)

- introduction; famous heroes
- heroes in different cultures
- introduce three local/family heroes

Second paragraph (at least 4–5 sentences)

- background of first hero
- challenge hero faced
- describe hero's actions

Third paragraph (at least five sentences)

- background of second hero
- challenge hero faced
- describe hero's actions

Fourth paragraph (at least five sentences)

- background of third hero
- challenge hero faced
- describe hero's actions

Concluding paragraph (2–3 sentences)

- link heroes to protagonist in books
- link heroes with awards (e.g., *CNN Heroes*)
- imagine future for heroes
- discuss why heroes matter in the local community

Students can research details about their heroes, their specific challenges, and their actions that made them stand out. Students can conference with their teacher about the quality of the outline.

Plan

Without more details and evidence of suggestions for solutions, the outline list would not meet the requirement to move to writing the first draft. Article writing requires the work of an investigative reporter. Table 14.1 features a sample plan for writing a current events-focused piece of writing.

Table 14.1. Plan for Writing a Current Event Article

Plan for Writing a Current Event Article	*Self-Review (Student Score)*	*Teacher Feedback (Teacher Score)*
This plan included . . . *(2) You did it!* *(1) You still need some work.* *(?) Missing part.*		
detailed points about three heroes	1	?
detailed points about setting/context	1	1
detailed points about problem or challenge heroes faced	2	2
evidence of hero actions	?	?
breakdown of ideas and organization for each paragraph easy for reader to follow	2	2
Total	Score: 6/10	Score: 5/10
Comments: You've identified many challenges each hero faced. It would be a good idea to research more about the individuals and the setting for the story. When you have this information, it should be easier to figure out what actions the heroes took to help in the community. Keep working away at this as it is not yet ready to move to a first draft. Let's meet again to go over your expanded outline.		

- Students should revise the original plan based on the findings gathered from further research.
- Following another teacher conference about the plan, if expectations of the plan have been met, students can begin their first draft.

Producing the First Draft

- Students begin their first draft by building sentences from the words in the outline.
- Student then organize the sentences into at least five paragraphs.
- Students should write the draft of each of the three detailed paragraphs first.
- Students then write the more general introductory and concluding paragraphs.
- Students reorganize the paragraphs in order (introductory, followed by the first, second, and third detailed paragraphs, followed by the concluding paragraph).
- After the first draft has been written, students self-assess their initial work and discuss further ideas during the conference with the teacher.

Polishing the Drafts

- Begin to polish each news article draft by using track changes on the toolbar of the Word document.
- It's important for students to save the different versions of each draft in a writing folder, so they have evidence that the writing was revised throughout the process.
- By middle school, revisions should include using literary devices such as symbolism, metaphors, and more elaborate sentences with adverbial clauses.

~ *Symbolism Mini Lesson*

Symbols are used in writing to represent something beyond the literal meaning of a word. The green light can be a symbol for moving forward; a four-leaf clover can mean good luck; and in today's digital world, a shopping cart can represent an online purchase. Emojis are symbols commonly used in casual media communication; however, they are not featured in newspapers.

Students can discuss more ideas about symbolism after viewing the following websites:

- https://www.youtube.com/watch?v=Xc7Qt5sGPeg[5]
- https://www.youtube.com/watch?v=WhijmmePlU8[6]
- https://www.flocabulary.com/unit/symbolism/[7]

~ *Metaphor Mini Lesson*

Metaphors are used in writing to compare two different things. Unlike a simile that uses like or as, a metaphor simply indicates that something "is" something else. For instance, "The sun was an orange ball in the sky."

We use many metaphors for social media. One social medium is a "water cooler" because people typically stand around it and share news. It can also be the "spokes of a wheel," as the messages can all be distinct, but news can go around and around.

Students can view and discuss more details and examples of metaphors in the following:

- https://www.youtube.com/watch?v=xH5EgQS8ZIE[8]
- https://www.flocabulary.com/unit/similes-metaphors/[9]

~ *Idiom Mini Lesson*

Formal writing should not use idioms or slang. For instance, the idiom "it's raining cats and dogs" may be familiar from casual conversation, but it literally does not make sense, so avoid using it. Students can check out other samples of such expressions:

- https://www.ef.com/wwen/blog/language/20-english-idioms-that-everyone-should-know/[10]
- https://www.youtube.com/watch?v=jUT_WSavAC8[11]
- https://www.youtube.com/watch?v=KJS77wXttpI[12]

~ *Independent Clauses and Conjunctions Mini Lessons*

A clause is a complete sentence that has a subject and a predicate. The subject refers to the "what" or "who" of the sentence, and the predicate tells something about the subject. For example, "Jonas gave memories to Gabriel each night" is an independent clause with "Jonas" as the subject and "gave memories to Gabriel each night" as the predicate.

Conjunctions are words that join two independent clauses. For example, the word "and" joins two independent clauses in this extended version of the sentence: "Jonas gave memories to Gabriel each night, and he smiled back at him." Other conjunctions can be remembered by the acronym FANBOYS, which includes "for," "and," "nor," "but," "or," "yet," and "so." Students can view these videos to find out more about the use of conjunctions.

- https://www.youtube.com/watch?v=-catJZm_2TI[13]
- https://www.youtube.com/watch?v=8EJ8aSzuJnk[14]

~ Adverbial Clause Mini Lesson

An adverbial clause is a group of words that includes a verb which acts as an adverb. It is a dependent clause because it cannot be a complete thought (or independent clause) on its own. The clue to an adverbial clause is that it tells more about when, where, how, how much, or why something is happening. Clauses usually begin with "subordinating" conjunctions such as "because" and "when."

Adverbial clause starters abound. Students can make a list of subordinating conjunctions based on a review of grammar websites, including:

- https://www.englishgrammar101.com/module-10/clauses/lesson-4/adverb-clauses[15]
- https://www.grammar-monster.com/glossary/adverbial_clauses.htm[16]

The adverbial phrase "when the sun rises" in the sentence "We will escape when the sun rises" is a dependent clause supported by the independent clause "We will escape." Another example of an adverbial clause is underlined in the following example: "We will not have school tomorrow <u>because the forecast is for three feet of snow</u>." Adverbial clauses enable the writer to elaborate on a simple sentence.

- Students can use an Enriched-Language Chart to track two powerful nouns, two powerful verbs, two powerful adjectives, two adverbs, two adverbial phrases, two adjectival phrases, two metaphors, and one example of symbolism.

- Students can then revise the draft after first reading the article aloud and then listening to the text being read aloud.
- Students can discuss the draft in a writing conference with a peer or teacher using the interactive rubric (table 14.2).

Table 14.2. Sample Interactive Rubric for a Polished News Article

Interactive Rubric for Polished News Article		
Student Self-Score	*Quality of Writing* *(2) strong skill, (1) developing skill (still learning), (?) missing part*	*Teacher Score*
Substance: This piece of writing includes . . .		
	key details about the conflict or challenge	
	key details about the people involved in the story	
	key details about the setting	
	effective reference to symbolism	
	three examples of metaphors	
	at least three examples of clauses	
	does not use slang and idioms	
Organization: This piece of writing . . .		
	does not use run-on sentences, contractions, hyphens, dashes, or slang	
	demonstrates sequential flow of sentences	
	has clear and captivating introductory sentences for each paragraph	
	has clear and captivating concluding sentences for each paragraph	
	includes compelling and enriched nouns, verbs, adjectives, and adverbs	
	was read aloud by writer to a partner, which led to changes made to draft	
	was revised when writing was read aloud by a partner	
	is double-spaced and shows changes made to most sentences	
/30		/30
Comments:		

The teacher should conference with the student to determine whether the article has been revised to a proficient level. The next stage requires the student to record the final copy after ensuring that spelling and punctuation are correct and a creative title has been established

Presenting

The news article needs to be embedded in the class or newspaper for others to read. Digital copies of the newspaper can be distributed to other students, teachers, and parents at the school. Some school newspaper contexts could expand the readership of student work (e.g., paper forms of the newspaper can be displayed on bulletin boards).

STUDENT LEADERSHIP SPEECHES (GRADE 7)

Prompt

At the end of the school year, all grade 7 students at the William E. Doar, Jr. School for the Performing Arts in Washington, D.C., wrote speeches to apply for more than 15 leadership roles in their graduating year. Writing speeches encourages students to share their interest in taking specific leadership roles; this can be an inspiring way to enhance writing and speaking skills at the same time, as well as have student voices influence school culture.

Students prepared outlines and drafts, revised their speeches, and presented them to their classmates detailing their specific promises and how they planned to achieve them.

Each speech took three to five minutes to present, giving the audience ample time to consider the detailed evidence that each candidate presented. Students organized their speeches in five paragraphs with three detailed paragraphs. The introductory and closing paragraphs ranged between five and eight sentences in length, whereas the three detailed paragraphs were lengthier, usually totaling 10 or more sentences in length.

Providing a range of options for the length of each speech built in options for modification and differentiation. Some students were better suited to present in smaller groups, whereas others presented their speeches to the full class. Some students were confident enough to present to the whole school.

Many schools have few leadership roles such as president, vice president (VP), treasurer, and secretary, often determined by a popular vote. If all grade 7 students were given an opportunity to lead how this could shift a school culture?

Plan

Before a speech is spoken, it is written. The writing is different because it can blend expository writing with elements of script writing; notably, the presenter has much to add to the text. The time frame for the speech can determine how long each paragraph can be. Political speeches have much to share, so they tend to be long. The famous "I have a dream" speech by Dr. Martin Luther King Jr. was 55 minutes:

- https://www.youtube.com/watch?v=vP4iY1TtS3s[17]

In contrast, Eleanor Roosevelt's speech celebrating human rights was just over two minutes.

- https://www.youtube.com/watch?v=9yzakVOdh6k[18]

Political speeches need time to elaborate on their points. Learning about making speeches makes sense before making an outline. Just as a letter follows a distinct format, a speech has specific expectations for its introductory and concluding paragraphs.

The introduction needs to be captivating so the audience will tune in to what is being said. A speech can begin in different ways—with a compelling quote, or an alarming or surprising statistic. Some presenters use a stirring gesture to command attention. The following websites feature more ways to make a speech memorable:

- https://www.youtube.com/watch?v=XAaSZ64P8pA[19]
- https://www.youtube.com/watch?v=7tzentBmmUc[20]
- https://www.ypo.org/2015/04/7-memorable-ways-to-open-a-speech-or-presentation/[21]

An audience wants to hear original ideas. A known quote or joke is not a great speech starter. Students should discuss how to make "focused questions" so the audience can relate to the message. Sentence starters could include:

- Have you ever wondered?
- Did you know?

Students can also discuss how to make a story out of a message. Before completing the plan for the outline, it makes sense for students to listen to sample speeches. Students can listen to the news for snippets from politicians, but they can also review many examples featured on the internet.

- https://www.youtube.com/watch?v=9Ed8OeZcOBI[22]
- https://www.youtube.com/watch?v=gIU3HrCCT2k[23]

The more variety, the better. A sample framework for the introduction to the five-paragraph speech is detailed below.

Introduction (5–8 points)

- land/environment acknowledgment
- captivating intro idea
- the greeting
- info about student (family; how long at school)
- compelling questions
- list roles interested in

Students can create an outline for a five-paragraph speech beginning with the three detailed paragraphs that will focus on each leadership role choice separately.

The first detailed paragraph should emphasize interest in one student leadership role with evidence to back up qualifications (include at least 10 points). The second detailed paragraph should emphasize interest in a different student leadership role with evidence to back up qualifications (include at least 10 points). The third detailed paragraph should emphasize interest in a different student leadership role with evidence to back up qualifications (include at least 10 points).

The concluding paragraph should summarize the speech and leave the audience amused and inspired by the last words shared (five to eight points).

Such an outline would need many details and notes added before it can be ready to move to the first draft stage. Once the outline is completed, students can meet with the teacher to conference about the quality of the plan.

Producing the First Draft

- Students can begin by building sentences from the words in the outline for the three detailed paragraphs, ideally highlighting one leadership interest in each.
- Then they can write the more general introductory and concluding paragraphs.
- Students can then reorganize the paragraphs in order (introductory, followed by the first, second, and third detailed paragraphs, followed by the concluding paragraph).
- After the first draft has been written, students can self-assess their initial work and discuss further ideas during the conference with the teacher.

Polishing the Drafts

- Use track changes on the toolbar of the Word document to polish the speech.
- Each draft copy should be saved to provide evidence that the writing was revised throughout the process.
- Revisions should use more elaborate sentences with adjectival clauses.

At the polishing stage, the students can add literary devices as well as a variety of grammatical options to enhance the writing. In this sample activity, students can be encouraged to include allusions, transition words and phrases, elements of flashback, and varied clauses to cultivate more elaborate sentences.

~ Allusion Mini Lesson

Adding allusions can be an interesting way to polish a speech. An allusion is a literary device that links what is written or spoken to something familiar such as a politician's speech, a book, or television/film series. For instance, in Ray Bradbury's book *Fahrenheit 451*,[24] a line references the Cheshire cat in *Alice in Wonderland*:[25]

> "Montag stopped eating . . . he saw their Cheshire cat smiles burning through the walls of the house."

More examples are featured in the following websites:

- https://www.youtube.com/watch?v=vUMOmBxC3Cg[26]
- https://blog.prepscholar.com/allusion-examples[27]
- https://medium.com/the-shadow/did-you-catch-them-6-allusions-in-bidens-inaugural-address-b9ed5ec5ce92[28]

~ *Transition Words and Signposting Mini Lesson*

Transition words can link sentences together throughout a text. Transition words "are used to link words, phrases, or sentences. They help the reader to progress from one idea . . . to the next idea. Thus, they help to build up coherent relationships within the text."[29] Examples of transition words or phrases include "in the first place," "as a matter of fact," "in addition," "equally important," "thus," "by the same token," "then," "as well," "together with," "likewise," "similarly," "furthermore," "additionally," and "therefore."

Signposts in writing, however, occur as topic sentences that either introduce or link paragraphs to each other in a variety of ways. Signposts, according to MLA, "are words or phrases that help articulate the structure of a piece of writing and ensure that readers don't get lost. Signposting will flag the most important parts of an argument, signal transitions, and clarify the stakes of an argument."[30]

~ *Flashback Mini Lesson*

Flashbacks can be used in speeches to link the past with the present. According to literarydevices.com, a flashback is "a literary device wherein the author depicts the occurrence of specific events to the reader, which have taken place before the present time the narration is following, or events that have happened before the events that are currently unfolding in the story."[31]

The book *The Giver*[32] includes many episodes of flashback:

- I knew that there had been times in the past—terrible times—when people had destroyed others in haste, in fear, and had brought about their own destruction.
- Our people made that choice, the choice to go to Sameness. Before my time, before the previous time, back and back and back. We relinquished color when we relinquished sunshine and did away with difference.

Examples of the use of flashbacks can be found in many resources and websites, including

- https://www.youtube.com/watch?v=xLyDwslqxiY[33]

~ Adjective Clause Mini Lesson

An adjective clause is a group of words that includes a verb that acts as an adjective. It is a dependent clause because it cannot be a complete thought (or independent clause) on its own. The clue to an adjective clause is that it describes a noun. An example of an adjective clause is in the following sentence from *The Giver*: "He was awed by the surprises that lay beyond each curve of the road after a life of Sameness and predictability."

- Students should edit their drafts to ensure that the text includes enriched word use. The speech should use powerful verbs, nouns, adjectives, adverbs, phrases, and clauses.
- Students can then revise the draft after first reading the speech aloud and then listening to it being read aloud.
- Students can discuss the draft in a writing conference with a peer or teacher using the interactive rubric (table 14.3) to gather further feedback about the revised draft.

Table 14.3. Sample Interactive Rubric for a Polished Speech

Interactive Rubric for the Polished Speech		
Student Self-Score	*Quality of Writing* *(2) strong skill, (1) developing skill (still learning), (?) missing part*	*Teacher Score*
Substance: This piece of writing includes . . .		
	a land/environment acknowledgment in the introduction	
	a clearly laid out purpose to persuade or convince the audience of the message	
	details of three school problems, promises, and solutions	
	evidence to support speaker's capacity to take on a leadership role	
	interesting background about the writer	
	creative details	
	effective use of flashback	
	at least two examples of allusions	
	effective use of transition words	
	at least three sentences expanded using adjectival clauses	
	does not use slang and idioms	
Organization: This piece of writing . . .		
	does not use run-on sentences, contractions, hyphens, dashes, or slang	
	includes effective use of transition words	
	demonstrates sequential flow of sentences (ideas presented in a logical manner)	
	includes clear signposting in introductory sentences for each paragraph	
	has a captivating clincher and concluding paragraph calling the audience to action	
	includes compelling and enriched nouns, verbs, adjectives, and adverbs	
	was read aloud by writer to partner, which led to changes made to draft	
	was revised when writing was read aloud by a partner	
	is double-spaced and shows changes made to most sentences	
/30		/30
Comments:		

The teacher conferences with the student to provide feedback. When the drafts are ready to be finalized, each student records the final text, ensuring that spelling and punctuation are accurate in the hard copy.

Presenting

Clearly one of the most important actions a speaker takes is rehearsing the speech. Making time for partners to provide feedback about the spoken version of the speech prior to the presentation can be very helpful. Many websites feature tips for presenting speeches and criteria for speech contents, such as this site from the University of Texas:

- https://www.uiltexas.org/speech/extemp/criteria-for-evaluating-informative-speakers[34]

With technology, students can also record themselves while self-assessing their spoken delivery using a rubric such as the sample interactive speech rubric in table 14.4.

Students can also conference with peers about their writing and use alternative tools for appraising the quality of a speech, such as the tool featured on Wikihow[35]:

- https://www.wikihow.com/Evaluate-a-Speech

LETTERS TO THE EDITOR (GRADE 8)

Reading between the lines in a text is a meaning-making process. Letters to the editor are usually brief but in their brevity invite interpretation. The writer of such a letter should anticipate and ideally, lead the reader to fill the gaps with nods of agreement with the position presented. Although many may "like" the contribution, the expected opposing messages may be shared as well.

Ideal editing usually makes a larger number of words into a smaller, more precise collection of text. In writing an executive summary, and for business letters, it is imperative that students learn how to get to the point. To prepare for the rigor of writing research papers and essays in high school and college, it is important for grade 8 students to draft and revise

Table 14.4. Sample Interactive Speech Rubric

Interactive Speech Rubric		
Student Self-Score	*Quality of Writing* *(A) ample evidence, (S) some evidence, (NY) no evidence yet* *The speaker . . .*	*Teacher Score*
	waited for silence before starting speech	
	captured the attention of classmates and kept it throughout the speech	
	kept solid eye contact with the audience	
	demonstrated enthusiasm about the topic	
	stated the topic clearly	
	enunciated words clearly	
	demonstrated solid fluency (the speech did not feel interrupted by pauses)	
	used a strong and varied tone	
	spoke with respect for the audience	
	kept an interested body look throughout the presentation	
	used gestures to add variety and emphasis	
	demonstrated poise and confidence	
	moved from point to point smoothly (if note cards were used)	
	completed the speech within the time frame (3–5 minutes)	
	had rehearsed the speech on several occasions	
/20 points	Total Score: /40 points	/20 points
Comments:		

more lengthy pieces of work. So that more people can read the work, students also need to learn how to condense the message.

Different from a descriptive summary, a letter to the editor is a persuasive response to a concern, usually focused on one perspective or side of a story. Although current events are often viewed as audio or video snippets, sometimes students can read newspaper articles from hard or digital copies.

Letters to the editor can be interesting reads, different from news articles where journalists are responsible for writing an unbiased article. They do so by sharing both sides of a story. Editorial space is reserved for members of the public to write their responses to news stories, usually to persuade readers to consider one side or alternative perspectives. The following letters to the editor of the *New York Times*[36] in 2001 feature opposing views about standardized tests:

Sample 1:

May 31, 2001

Off the Testing Bandwagon

To the Editor:

Re "School Testing Bandwagon Spawns Web Coaching Sites" (May 24), about online test preparation and the questions it raises about how much emphasis should be placed on standardized tests:

Computerized test preparation may be more efficient than the old-fashioned kind, but that distinction threatens to distract us from the bigger picture. Every hour spent coaching students to raise their test scores is an hour not spent helping them to become critical, curious, creative thinkers. Schools across the United States are being transformed into giant test-prep centers, forcing out things like music and the arts and high-quality electives for older students.

This is not an argument against the use of computers. In fact, parents, teachers and students in many states are creating Web sites, and making other good use of technology, to organize a growing grass-roots rebellion that includes a boycott of the tests.

ALFIE KOHN, Belmont, Mass. The writer is the author of "The Schools Our Children Deserve," (Houghton Mifflin, 1999).

Sample 2:

To the Editor:

The article about online test preparation overlooked a big change in educational assessments. The newer—and better—assessments do not rely solely on multiple-choice questions. Rather, they also ask the student to read material and compose a short response. Many of these short responses are in fact mini-essays.

There are more variations of this "reading into writing" type of assessment. But however they are constructed, they cannot be scored by a machine, and they cannot be crammed for. These newer assessments (New York and New Jersey have good models) remove the onus of "teaching to the test."

SHEILA CROWELL, Montclair, N.J. The writer is the founding director of the Writers' Room Program in the Montclair Public Schools

Source: Crowell, S., (May 31, 2001). "Off the Testing Bandwagon." *New York Times*. https://www.nytimes.com/2001/05/31/technology/l-off-the-testing-bandwagon-574988.html

Both letters are brief; they clearly state their position and provide evidence to back it.

Writing letters to the editor is an authentic activity. When students select an issue about which they feel strongly, they can become more invested in the writing experience, more willing to polish and rework the text, emulating what writers do in the real world. Professional writers often engage in rigorous research to find evidence and details to support their position and be aware of opposing arguments.

Prompt

Students can plan, draft, revise, and submit letters to the editor about a variety of societal issues. The 17 United Nations (UN) Sustainable Goals[37] were drafted to help countries create action plans to support social justice on a wide range of global social fronts. Students can choose one issue from the list and write a letter to an editor of a local newspaper.

Plan

A sample framework for the three-paragraph letter follows. Students will need to research to find supportive evidence for their position.

Paragraph 1

- Introduction stressing one key position
- Reference to recent article in newspaper
- Clear statement of claim
- May include striking initial statistic to back up

Paragraph 2

- Continue with claim
- Emphasize at least three pieces of evidence to back up claim

Paragraph 3

- Include more points to support position
- May address weakness of counterclaim
- Conclude message

Sign-off, first name, grade.

The original article should accompany the draft outline when conferencing with the teacher. The student should be able to reference the original article to explain the intent of the letter to the editor. When the teacher agrees that the outline has enough compelling detail, the student will be permitted to move on to the drafting stage of the writing. Once the outline is completed, students can meet with the teacher to conference about the quality of the plan.

Producing the First Draft

- Students begin by building sentences from the words in the outline.
- After the first draft has been written, students can self-assess their initial work and discuss further ideas during a writing conference with the teacher.

Polishing the Drafts

The first draft of the letter to the editor should go through many polishing phases. Students can consider adding literary devices such as irony and foreshadowing.

~ *Irony Mini Lesson*

Using irony can be an interesting addition to a letter to an editor. Irony refers to the use of words that "express something other than and especially the opposite of the literal meaning. . . . The word *irony* has come to be applied to events that are merely curious or coincidental, and while some feel this is an incorrect use of the word, it is merely a new one."[38] Examples of irony are present when:

- *Fahrenheit 451*, an anticensorship novel, is one of the books most consistently banned in the United States.
- People claimed and/or believed that the *Titanic* was an "unsinkable" ship.
- Alexander Graham Bell invented the telephone but refused to keep one in his study.

More examples are featured in the following website:

- https://www.youtube.com/watch?v=IiR-bnCHIYo[39]

~ *Foreshadowing Mini Lesson*

Foreshadowing is "the use of details, description, and mood that will take on more meaning later in a written work."[40] Examples of the use of foreshadowing can be found in many resources and websites including:

- https://www.youtube.com/watch?v=P07O8cacBsk[41]
- https://www.youtube.com/watch?v=IiR-bnCHIYo

Students should edit their drafts to ensure that the text includes enriched word use. The letter to the editor should use powerful verbs, nouns, adjectives, adverbs, phrases, and clauses. Students can then revise the draft after first reading the text aloud and then listening to the text being read aloud. Students can use track changes on the toolbar of the Word document to provide evidence that the writing was revised throughout the process.

Students can also generate a feedback tool for self-assessment, based on reviewing qualities of an effective letter to the editor and samples of criteria used in other rubrics.

Presenting

When the work is ready to send to an editor of a media news outlet, it is important that the teacher has ensured that the students' parents support sharing the message publicly. Students can also share letters to the editor in the class or school in digital or paper form; they can also post the work on a communal bulletin board.

Taking the step to increase readership beyond the school would require a written confirmation from each parent, as the family can be associated with the ideas shared in the letter. Addressing one position can also lead to important discussions about censorship and how information is conveyed. During writing conferences with the teacher, students can gain deeper understanding of how content should be displayed in public forums. Addressing the question "What is fake news?" can be part of a more in-depth interdisciplinary research-based inquiry, as noted in chapter 4.

NOVEL WRITING: AN ENRICHING AND SUSTAINED WRITING EXPERIENCE

Writing a novel can be an exciting and memorable long-term project. Students can use dedicated time in grade 6 to develop a plan for a novel that would involve researching details to support the development of characters, setting, and plot. Students could interview experts to gather information from primary sources. Students may also plan to write a fiction or nonfiction text.

In grade 7 students could use "novel writing time" to generate the first written draft. Students may plan novels that are longer than others, which can accommodate for differentiated needs of each learner. Third-year students can revise the draft and finalize it to be published, ideally in a glue-bound book, with a copy for each student and at least one for the school library. A freshly bound copy in a student's graduating year makes a personal and memorable gift.

Middle school writers span grades 6 through 10. In the next chapter, examples of writing activities for grades 9 and 10 applications of purpose-based writing instruction will be featured as a progressive link to what students can experience in grades 6 through 8.

NOTES

1. First News Education. https://schools.firstnews.co.uk/blog/journalistic-writing/how-to-start-a-school-newspaper/.
2. Make My Newspaper. https://makemynewspaper.com/how-to-start-a-school-newspaper/.
3. Oglesby, A. (August 4, 2021). How to start a school newspaper. WikiHow. https://www.wikihow.com/Start-a-School-Newspaper.
4. Veroff, R. (January 31, 2018). Behind the scenes in the broadcast room. New York: *Lycee Magazine*. https://life.lfny.org/2018/01/31/behind-the-scenes-in-the-broadcast-room-2.
5. ELA Through Film. Learn symbolism using movies and TV. https://www.youtube.com/watch?v=Xc7Qt5sGPeg.
6. Constantine, C. Symbolism in film. https://www.youtube.com/watch?v=WhijmmePlU8.
7. Flocabulary. https://www.flocabulary.com/unit/symbolism/.
8. Easy Teaching. Metaphor and similes. https://www.youtube.com/watch?v=xH5EgQS8ZIE.
9. Flocabulary. https://www.flocabulary.com/unit/similes-metaphors/.
10. EF. https://www.ef.com/wwen/blog/language/20-english-idioms-that-everyone-should-know/.
11. Melissa. Grammar songs. https://www.youtube.com/watch?v=jUT_WSavAC8.
12. English in General. Learn idioms with TV series. https://www.youtube.com/watch?v=KJS77wXttpI.
13. BYU MCOM "FANBOYS: Coordinating conjunctions. https://www.youtube.com/watch?v=-catJZm_2TI.
14. MC Grammar. The FANBOYS song. https://www.youtube.com/watch?v=8EJ8aSzuJnk.
15. Nash, K. Adverb clauses. English Grammar 101. https://www.englishgrammar101.com/module-10/clauses/lesson-4/adverb-clauses.
16. Shrives, C. Adverbial clause. Grammar Monster. https://www.grammar-monster.com/glossary/adverbial_clauses.htm.
17. Rare Facts. I have a dream speech. https://www.youtube.com/watch?v=vP4iY1TtS3s.
18. FDR Library. Eleanor Roosevelt human rights speech. https://www.youtube.com/watch?v=9yzakVOdh6k.

19. LaCroix, D. How to write a speech opening: Example. https://www.youtube.com/watch?v=XAaSZ64P8pA.

20. Science of People. How to start a speech: The best (and worst) speech openers. https://www.youtube.com/watch?v=7tzentBmmUc.

21. YPO. (April 2, 2015). https://www.ypo.org/2015/04/7-memorable-ways-to-open-a-speech-or-presentation/.

22. Renstrom, J. TedX Talks. Science fiction: Teaching students how to save the world. https://www.youtube.com/watch?v=9Ed8OeZcOBI.

23. Trekkie Channel. Risk is our business. https://www.youtube.com/watch?v=gIU3HrCCT2k.

24. Bradbury, R. (1951). *Fahrenheit 451.* New York: Simon & Schuster.

25. Carroll, L. (1865). *Alice in Wonderland.* New York: Macmillan.

26. Chungdahm Learning. What is allusion? https://www.youtube.com/watch?v=vUMOmBxC3Cg.

27. Muniz, H. (December 3, 2019). https://blog.prepscholar.com/allusion-examples.

28. Us, K. (January 21, 2021). https://medium.com/the-shadow/did-you-catch-them-6-allusions-in-bidens-inaugural-address-b9ed5ec5ce92.

29. English Language Smart Words. https://www.smart-words.org/linking-words/transition-words.html.

30. Modern Language Association. https://style.mla.org/effective-signposting/.

31. Literary Devices. https://literary-devices.com/content/flashback/.

32. Lowry, L. (1993). *The Giver.* New York: Houghton Mifflin Harcourt.

33. Wilcox, B. Literary devices: Flashback. https://www.youtube.com/watch?v=xLyDwslqxiY.

34. University Interscholastic League. https://www.uiltexas.org/speech/extemp/criteria-for-evaluating-informative-speakers.

35. Munoz, P. (December 15, 2022). WikiHow. https://www.wikihow.com/Evaluate-a-Speech.

36. Kohn, A. (May 31, 2001). Off the testing bandwagon. *New York Times*. https://www.nytimes.com/2001/05/31/technology/letters-to-the-editor.html.

37. UN Sustainable Goals. https://sdgs.un.org/goals.

38. *Merriam-Webster*. https://www.merriam-webster.com/dictionary/irony#note-1.

39. Warner, C. What is verbal irony? TedEd. https://www.youtube.com/watch?v=IiR-bnCHIYo.

40. *Cambridge Dictionary*. https://dictionary.cambridge.org/us/dictionary/english/foreshadowing.

41. Vox Letters. Foreshadowing. https://www.youtube.com/watch?v=P07O8cacBsk.

15

MIDDLE SCHOOL WRITING IN A HIGH SCHOOL SETTING

PROFESSIONAL CONVERSATION STARTERS

1. Do you recall writing something in high school that you are proud of today? Discuss.
2. Provide examples of repetition or overlap of expectations between elementary and secondary writing instruction.
3. Which forms of writing in upper middle school (grades 9 and 10) do you think should be distinct from elementary and senior high writing experiences?

Like an elementary school includes part of a middle school—that is, the senior grade 6, 7, and 8 students—the high school also includes the other part of middle school—that is, the grades 9 and 10 students. This chapter will feature some ideas for upper middle school (grades 9 and 10).

SENIOR BUDDY BIOGRAPHY WRITING PROJECT

Prompt

Grade 9 students at the Jalen Rose Leadership Academy gathered information from seniors at the Oakpointe Senior Care and Rehab Centre in Detroit, Michigan, to write their biographies for English class and take part in a service-learning activity at the same time. Each student met with their senior buddy once a month for the school year. They played cards and board games and shared stories about their lives. Often the senior buddy offered advice along the way.

Plan/Outline

After creating a list of questions in English class, the students asked the seniors about their perceptions of Detroit over time. Students then transcribed their interviews to add to the points gathered in note form. Tape recorders allowed students to capture the exact wording of quotes, which added a rich dimension to stories within the published collection of senior biographies.

The transcripts were used to create an outline that was organized according to the different themes shared throughout the interviews. The teacher reviewed the outlines to ensure that students had enough material to write a biography. Students were encouraged to generate more questions for follow-up interviews for outlines that required more details. One page with at least three detailed paragraphs was the minimum requirement, although most biographies were three to five pages in length.

Feedback about each outline took the form of a series of conference questions that the teacher and novice biographer discussed during regularly scheduled English classes. These starter questions helped students come up with more questions to ask their senior buddies and shape their outline for their biographies:

- What did you discover about your senior buddy and his family?
- What details were shared about where the senior buddy had lived?
- What are the proudest moments in your senior buddy's life?
- Who does your senior buddy admire the most?
- What did your senior buddy recall about war?
- What powerful quotes did you get from your senior buddy?
- What creative and unplanned questions did you ask your senior buddy?

The outline ensured that students gathered rich quotes, addressed historical perceptions, and added good images of settings and family experiences. The students then carefully examined and grouped the themes based on information gathered to fit into separate coherent paragraphs. Once the details were sorted and grouped, the students then numbered each subtopic to help organize the biography in a logical order. In most cases, the stories were organized in a chronological pattern from past to present. The teacher then let each student know whether she was ready to begin writing the first draft of the biography.

Producing the First Draft

Organizing the first draft of each biography involved writing the detailed paragraphs about different themes first. Then the students were guided to write their introductory and concluding paragraphs.

Polishing the Drafts

In polishing the draft biographies, students were expected to revise their work to include analogies, euphemisms, quotations, and compound sentences using semicolons. They were also instructed to remove colloquialisms and clichés. This required a series of mini lessons to clarify what these terms meant.

~ *Analogy Mini Lesson*

Analogies compare two different things to describe and inspire the reader. According to literaryterms.net: "An analogy is a literary technique in which two unrelated objects are compared for their shared qualities . . . analogies are strong rhetorical devices used to make rational arguments and support ideas by showing connections and comparisons between dissimilar things."[1] Here are more examples of analogies:

- https://www.masterclass.com/articles/what-is-analogy#how-do-you-write-a-good-analogy[2]
- https://www.youtube.com/watch?v=Jo11LnWr6AA[3]
- https://www.youtube.com/watch?v=ZrBBylNNf6A[4]

~ *Quotations Mini Lesson*

High school is an ideal time to introduce quotations. When students are reading plays or conducting primary research, it is important to edit for correct quotation punctuation. Introducing speech into the context of written work can involve a complex arrangement of capitalization and other punctuation (commas, colons, periods, question marks, exclamation marks) with quotation marks around spoken words.

When quotations are used in sentences, they are linked to what is called "attribution," which is a sophisticated way of indicating who said what is being quoted. Writers use quotations to capture spoken words or words that have been published previously. Although it is possible for younger students to learn about quotations, it does not need to be added to punctuation and genre expectations already taught in elementary grades.

Various styles for accurately recording quotations can be found in reference guides (e.g., APA,[5] Chicago,[6] MLA,[7]) as well as websites dedicated specifically to teaching about quotations. Sample sites include:

- https://www.youtube.com/watch?v=V7LNkNcDMEY[8]
- https://www.youtube.com/watch?v=rFIIqPolFXo[9]
- https://www.englishclub.com/writing/punctuation-quotation-marks.htm[10]

~ *Semicolon Mini Lesson*

After students have mastered the understanding of independent clauses and use of conjunctions is a good time to introduce semicolons. Semicolons are often used in combination with connecting words, but they separate two independent clauses in a compound sentence.

The key to knowing whether a semicolon belongs in a text is being able to identify a subject and a predicate in two different independent clauses. Intuitively readers may anticipate a pause and place a comma rather than a semicolon in a compound sentence, but this would be a writing mistake. Website resources that further describe semicolons include:

- https://www.youtube.com/watch?v=th-zyfvwDdI[11]
- https://www.thepunctuationguide.com/semicolon.html[12]
- https://www.grammarbook.com/punctuation/semicolons.asp[13]
- https://www.youtube.com/watch?v=d-3nnht-b40[14]
- https://www.merriam-webster.com/words-at-play/a-guide-to-using-semicolons[15]

~ Euphemism Mini Lesson

Euphemisms are used to soften certain words or phrases. For instance, instead of saying in a sympathy note, "I'm sorry your grandfather died," a euphemism could be "I'm sorry for your loss" or "I'm sorry to hear of your grandfather's passing." At times, especially when the seniors spoke of the Vietnam War, an explanation of a euphemism was required as the biographies were going to be in the public domain. Examples of euphemisms can be found on the following websites:

- https://www.thoughtco.com/euphemism-words-term-1690680[16]
- https://www.grammar-monster.com/glossary/euphemism.htm[17]
- https://www.studiobinder.com/blog/what-is-a-euphemism-definition/[18]
- https://www.youtube.com/watch?v=6LFg_5zs7CY&t=15s[19]

~ Colloquialism Mini Lesson

Similar to slang, colloquialisms are part of casual communication. People may say, for example, they have "FOMO," short for "fear of missing out." Colloquialisms should only be used in settings where everyone has a shared understanding; otherwise, for new speakers of a language, such devices can take away from an inclusive community.

Further descriptions of colloquialism can be found on many websites, including:

- https://www.youtube.com/watch?v=duQwf2dIWo0[20]
- https://www.youtube.com/watch?v=ePKl1jZ9x0M

~ Cliché Mini Lesson

A cliché is a saying that lacks creativity. Clichés can be overused, and, therefore, leave the reader thinking that the writer has not put much thought into the work. "The word 'cliché' originated from the French sound of a printing plate, which prints the same thing over and over."[21] Other examples of clichés on the internet include:

- https://www.be-a-better-writer.com/cliches.html[22]
- https://www.masterclass.com/articles/writing-101-what-is-a-cliche-learn-when-to-use-cliches-in-writing-and-20-common-cliches-all-writers-should-avoid#quiz-0[23]

Students were expected to read their biographies aloud and listen to their work being read aloud to identify common errors such as wrong word endings and missing words. Students were instructed to review their draft work in relation to the interactive rubric for assessing their revision. This assessment tool is featured in table 15.1.

Table 15.1. Sample Interactive Rubric for the Polished Drafts of the Senior Biography

Interactive Rubric for the Polished Drafts of the Senior Biography		
Student Self-Score	*Quality of Writing* *(2) strong skill, (1) developing skill (still learning), (?) missing part*	*Teacher Score*
Substance: This piece of writing includes . . .		
	interesting details about the senior buddy	
	at least five examples of quotes from senior buddy	
	at least two creative examples of analogies	
	effective use of euphemisms	
	does not use slang, idioms, clichés, jargon, or colloquialisms	
Organization: This piece of writing . . .		
	ideas for each paragraph were organized in logical themes	
	does not use run-on sentences, contractions, hyphens, or dashes	
	includes at least three compound sentences using semicolons	
	includes effective use of transition words	
	demonstrates sequential flow of sentences (ideas presented in a logical manner)	
	has captivating introductory and concluding sentences	
	includes compelling and enriched nouns, verbs, adjectives, and adverbs	
	was read aloud by the writer to a partner, which led to changes made to draft	
	was revised when writing was read aloud by a partner	
	is double-spaced and shows changes made to most sentences	
/30		/30
Comments:		

The final copy of the biographies needed to be free of spelling errors. Using proper punctuation with quotations, using semicolons, and crafting creative titles were assessed on the final copy to make it ready for publication.

Presenting

The teacher collected the biographies into a book that was distributed to the school library, with copies provided for the seniors to share at the Oakpointe Senior Care and Rehab Centre. The seniors could view their own story while reading about others there. Seniors were provided with a copy of their biographies.

This authentic experience created lasting memories for both the students and seniors, making it much more than just an English assignment. Students learned to spend time with seniors, and gain insight into their wisdom, contributions, and struggles. School can compartmentalize students in unnatural age groupings that rarely, except for sports and assemblies, mix young people together. Learning that people can be primary sources of information, beyond the textbook, was also a powerful benefit of becoming biographers.

THE HIGH SCHOOL STUDENT HANDBOOK WRITING PROJECT

Students in a grade 10 class took part in writing a student handbook as an integrated inquiry project linking writing with graphic arts, technology, and survey analysis in mathematics. At first, the students examined student handbooks from other schools; then they gathered information from the existing family handbook that would be important to revise for a student audience.

In the next step, they created a survey to gather ideas from fellow classmates. With the draft ideas in hand, the students generated a draft table of contents as the outline for the first draft. Students broke into writing groups to draft different sections of the handbook. They then exchanged sections and revised the initially drafted manuscript.

Next, they chose fonts and graphics. Students wanted their handbooks to include captivating graphics. A group eager to design the cover encouraged all students to make a tile in art class that symbolized their idea of the school. These were photographed and arranged in an image of the school.

Students emulated what it is like to work on a magazine. They learned how to create questions and use the responses from electronic surveys. They became more aware of inclusive word usage and the need to avoid bias and sexism. Apart from working with others and publishing work that others would read, the student handbook makers identified ideas for school improvement. In a way, this project contributed to cultivating a more present and invested student culture.

Upper middle schools present many opportunities for students to write in more authentic ways. High schools with leadership and internship programs are ripe with meaningful experiences. Teachers have many engaging options, beyond responding to literature, to support student writing in middle school settings.

NOTES

1. Literary Terms. https://literaryterms.net/analogy/.
2. Master Class. What is analogy? https://www.masterclass.com/articles/what-is-analogy#how-do-you-write-a-good-analogy.
3. Mister Messenger. How to use examples, analogies, similes and metaphors when writing essays. https://www.youtube.com/watch?v=Jo11LnWr6AA.
4. Lincoln Learning Solutions. Analogies. https://www.youtube.com/watch?v=ZrBBylNNf6A.
5. American Psychological Association (APA). https://www.apa.org.
6. *Chicago Manual of Style*. https://www.chicagomanualofstyle.org/tools_citationguide.html
7. Modern Language Association (MLA). https://www.mla.org.
8. Howcast. How to use quotation marks. https://wlww.youtube.com/watch?v=V7LNkNcDMEY.
9. Miacademy Learning Channel. Quotation marks: Language skills for kids. https://www.youtube.com/watch?v=rFIIqPolFXo.
10. English Club. Quotation marks. https://www.englishclub.com/writing/punctuation-quotation-marks.htm.
11. Bryce, E. How to use a semicolon. https://www.youtube.com/watch?v=th-zyfvwDdI.
12. The Punctuation Guide. https://www.thepunctuationguide.com/semicolon.html.
13. Grammar Book. https://www.grammarbook.com/punctuation/semicolons.asp.
14. Green Learning Tools. How to use a semicolon. https://www.youtube.com/watch?v=d-3nnht-b40.

15. *Merriam-Webster*. https://www.merriam-webster.com/words-at-play/a-guide-to-using-semicolons.

16. Nordquist, R. ThoughtCo. https://www.thoughtco.com/euphemism-words-term-1690680.

17. Shrives, C. Grammar Monster. https://www.grammar-monster.com/glossary/euphemism.htm.

18. Deguzman, K. (June 20, 2021). Studio binder. https://www.studiobinder.com/blog/what-is-a-euphemism-definition/.

19. Lisa's Study Guide. Euphemism. https://www.youtube.com/watch?v=6LFg_5zs7CY&t=15s.

20. St. Paul's College. Colloquial language. https://www.youtube.com/watch?v=duQwf2dIWo0.

21. Literary Terms. https://literaryterms.net/cliche/.

22. Be a Better Writer. 681 cliches to avoid in your creative writing. https://www.be-a-better-writer.com/cliches.html.

23. Master Class. Writing 101: What is a cliché? https://www.masterclass.com/articles/writing-101-what-is-a-cliche-learn-when-to-use-cliches-in-writing-and-20-common-cliches-all-writers-should-avoid#quiz-0.

16

UPPER HIGH SCHOOL WRITING

PROFESSIONAL CONVERSATION STARTERS

1. Why should students enjoy writing before they enter the world of work or college?
2. Which distinct writing genres should be introduced in grades 11 and 12?
3. What would be advantages and disadvantages of creating a two-year course combining grades 11 and 12 English language arts (ELA)?

Ideally, by grade 11 students will have mastered the writing process and are ready to expand their writing portfolios to include concentrated work in a broader base of genres, including work that can be sustained for more than one school year. The extended essay requirement for the International Baccalaureate (IB)[1] program emulates a more realistic time frame for research. In their final two years, students in IB programs must choose an area or discipline of study and conduct research that fits a particular genre.

When the time line extends beyond the term or school year, it is possible to raise expectations for applying what they know and have learned, usually through a written report. How can schools restructure, or better yet, create structures that enable more deep-seated learning opportunities?

Writing in the high school senior grades should not be a remedial activity or continue to be a series of responses to literature.

Emphasizing argumentative writing addresses not only the quality of the substance but also an order that helps the audience understand how the evidence supports an idea or theory the author is presenting. It's not enough to produce technically accurate writing; to be meaningful, it needs to serve a purpose.

What other kinds of purpose-based (PB) writing experiences might be valuable for high school students to master?

Apart from writing poetry in multiple forms, including ballads, sonnets, and epic poems, many kinds of prose writing can cater to the high school student. A quality education means that all students should master many forms of writing. Before students enter college and the world of work, high schools should equip them with the skills to write through an argumentative and editorial lens and be comfortable writing and reading business letters, résumés, and portfolios; literature reviews and annotated bibliographies; research studies; articles; debates; scripts; blogs; journals; autobiographies; and consumer reports.

THE FORMAL BUSINESS LETTER

"There was something about the format of a letter—personal but structured, an invitation to dialogue, the anticipation of response that always got kids writing."[2] One of the most practical skills for all students to master is how to write a formal business letter. Students can review these websites to ensure that their formatting is correct:

- https://cs.appstate.edu/~egp/1410_archive/Word97/bl_eg_pics.html[3]
- https://www.indeed.com/career-advice/career-development/types-of-business-letters[4]
- https://www.wikihow.com/Write-a-Business-Letter[5]

It is important to use an accepted business letter format to demonstrate the formality of the letter. Using a standard format removes both the potential for distraction and the perception of carelessness. Formatting should not take away from the message.

What makes a strong business letter stand out is the message, one that is succinct and original at the same time. The goal of writing such a letter is to persuade the reader that the writer or her ideas are worthy of consideration for college entry, recruitment, or a career. Students involved in leadership and co-curricular activities can have an advantage over others because they have more experiences with and for supporting others. Candidates who demonstrate a degree of selflessness can be attractive to some readers.

RÉSUMÉ AND PORTFOLIO WRITING

The cover letter for an application or job should be written in the form of a standard business letter. In certain cases, however, more creative careers are influenced by original formats. At Disney, a cast member was hired after putting his cover letter and résumé on a basketball! But for the most part, students need to learn how to write cover letters that accompany a portfolio and/or a résumé. Although cover letters generally are prose writing, résumés tend to be an organized set of bullet points with details. What distinguishes one cover letter and résumé from another is the originality of the ideas organized on each page.

A portfolio can be brought to interviews to provide evidence of the experiences shared in bullet and image form. Portfolios can be a collection of materials, including letters, photos, articles, schoolwork, and awards. It takes time to generate and update such important communications; it makes sense for schools to dedicate many weeks, if not a month, for students to draft, revise, and craft such an important document.

LITERATURE REVIEW AND ANNOTATED BIBLIOGRAPHIES

Students who have completed literature reviews and annotated bibliographies as part of their high school experience are better prepared for college than students who have not. Not only is it helpful to learn how to gather deep and broad material about a topic, but it demonstrates critical and creative thinking skills. Students will have annotated the references by assigning a value to the source based on, for instance, the succinctness, readability levels, links to other significant research, level of current or dated research, and use of helpful examples.

RESEARCH WRITING

The chapter on interdisciplinary writing (chapter 4) had numerous examples of inquiry-based or project-based writing. Depending on the discipline, research writing can vary in format and structure. When students in IB programs write their two-year "extended essay" as part of their graduation requirements, they must choose a discipline area for study. The formats provide a framework similar to the patterns in related arts and science (e.g., sociology, science, fine arts) areas of concentration.

Students can learn how to write using qualitative and quantitative research, as well as coordinate projects that examine and analyze both kinds of data. Students who take part in action research published locally or in reviewed journals can contribute to solving real-world problems, locally, nationally, or globally. How each stage of research is conveyed using writing is just as important as each stage of writing that expresses the research findings.

Students often submit first drafts of essays and research, but if they plan to use their research skills in the future to apply for jobs and research grants, for instance, they need to learn how to revisit and edit their work with persistence and persuasive rigor. Depending on the kind of research, specific protocols require precise written work. Teachers must provide time for students to complete rigorous research, as well as the comprehensive editing required to prepare and present quality work.

ARTICLE WRITING

Research writing often leads to submitting an article for publication in a magazine or journal. These articles can require writing an abstract as a condensed summary of the research. In this way, article writing can be both lengthy (depending on the number of pages or words for the article) and abridged (in an abstract version). Different journals have different formatting requirements, so students would need to review the expectations carefully when polishing texts for submission.

WRITING IN RESPONSE TO READING

In the most common form of writing in high school, students are assigned tasks that align with reading expectations in the curriculum. Often students respond to readings by comparing story elements in two different books with similar themes, settings, or characters. Some assignments invoke a piece of writing that compares stories by the same author. When students are expected to move beyond the comparisons, such as create a rating scheme for categorizing and reviewing books, then the writing activity can facilitate higher levels of thinking.

In an ELA classroom, writing opportunities tend to be limited to responses to readings. A team of teachers planning a carefully designed curriculum should be aware of such an imbalance and work to make a better balance of writing experiences available for students. Even though government documents list debate, script, poetry blog writing, biographical writing, review writing, or multiauthor text writing as options, schools or districts do not seem to make a concerted effort to ensure that students are exposed to each of these authentic modes of written expression in rigorous and deliberate ways. Further, emphasis does not appear to be strong on writing in other subject areas such as science and social studies where reports, projects, and essay writing are common practice.

DEBATE WRITING

Taking part in debates is not a requirement in school, yet planning, writing, and presenting positions is a powerful and authentic way to learn argumentative writing. Schools can, for example, make debating a regular part of an English class throughout a school year. Although initial exposure may not make students into expert debaters, it can give all students an equal opportunity that could lead to participation in extracurricular debate clubs or competitions, or make them more prepared for legal, political, and leadership roles in varied professions.

SCRIPT WRITING

Given the increasing interest students and society have in entertainment, script writing can be a practical, creative, and meaningful context for learning. It's not enough for students to only read plays. They can learn how to create storyboards for film or television applications, which can require critical thinking on many levels.

Preparing texts for real audiences is authentic. It enables students to apply quotations and more complex punctuation, as well as linking text with movement and gestures. Planning scripts for documentaries can be a powerful medium for sharing research findings.

BLOG WRITING

Writing blogs may be an informal writing activity, but public viewing of the text makes it formal in many ways. Blogging is a relevant 21st-century skill in a world where multiple voices can have opportunities to be heard. Schools and classes can set up blogs to encourage and inspire students and teachers to share their ideas.

JOURNAL WRITING

Many schools encourage journal writing, often to promote reflective writing that is personal, private, and not privy to formal writing conventions. It may be assumed that the more students write, the more their writing will improve; however, it is not known what blend of formal and informal writing is best for students.

Journaling can be a haven in that students' words and sentence construction can be off limits in judging the quality of the work. In Calkins's 600-page guide *The Art of Teaching Writing*, students are encouraged to record what they wonder about in their "writer's notebooks."[6] It is important for students to learn the difference between recording ideas for their eyes only and recording a response to questions for assignments in different subject areas for grading purposes.

Although students can use a journal to capture first or ongoing impressions, it typically is a nongraded text. In other cases, teachers can assess the quality of discussions or arguments within "dialogic journals" when students share their ideas with each other or with the teacher. To support a solid communication flow between writers sharing dialogic journals, teachers need to provide clear directions to ensure safe communication. Teachers may introduce the idea of such multiauthor texts in "telegram journals," modeling ways to respectfully link ideas between different writers.

Many students apply the practice of journaling when they text or e-mail responses to friends daily; they may also add commentary to social media sites. Although schools address digital literacy and the need for personal safeguards, young people have many opportunities to access texts and write texts without adult intervention. Journaling experiences have a place in school-wide writing; but given the variety of writing genres for students to explore and master, journal writing should not be considered the sole path to a comprehensive development of their writing lives.

AUTOBIOGRAPHICAL WRITING

Students can work on finding their personal voice through informal writing, but they can also find their voice in autobiographical work that is formal in nature. Students are experts about their own lives, and they should be highly encouraged to write their own stories. Dedicating time for students to think about capstone events in their lives can also help them develop résumés and school applications. Students should not have to write their stories and applications outside of school hours but should be encouraged to bring their experiences as contexts for written expression in the classroom.

WRITING REVIEWS

Students can read and write reviews about many topics—for example, music, film, restaurants, and vacation homes. The tone of a review can reflect well on the writer, or not. Like any piece of writing, reviews need to be planned, drafted, edited, and presented in a style that reflects the student, now and in the future, as anything digital can have a lengthy life span.

Applying Literary Devices

High school students should not only identify but explore using more sophisticated literary devices. In addition to using analogies and euphemisms while avoiding clichés and colloquialisms, certain forms of writing can be more suitable contexts for using juxtaposition, paradox, motif, and oxymorons.

~ Juxtaposition Mini Lesson

Writers use juxtaposition to emphasize a striking comparison or contrast between things. According to Literary Devices: "Writers create juxtaposition by placing two entities side by side to create dramatic or ironic contrast. This allows the reader to discern how the paired entities are similar or different."[7] An example of juxtaposition is when Dickens describes the *Tale of Two Cities*,[8] drawing attention to the marked differences in how people live in the same community. Other examples of juxtaposition can be found in the following links:

- https://blog.reedsy.com/literary-devices/#25__juxtaposition[9]
- https://literarydevices.com/juxtaposition/[10]

~ Paradox Mini Lesson

According to Literary Devices: "A paradox is a statement that appears at first to be contradictory, but upon reflection then makes sense. This literary device is commonly used to engage a reader to discover an underlying logic in a seemingly self-contradictory statement or phrase. As a result, paradox allows readers to understand concepts in a different and even non-traditional way."[11] Further explanations of the paradox can be found on the following websites:

- https://literarydevices.net/paradox/[12]
- https://literaryterms.net/when-and-how-to-write-a-paradox/[13]

~ Motif Mini Lesson

A motif, as defined by Literary Devices, "is a recurring narrative element with symbolic significance. If you spot a symbol, concept, or plot structure that surfaces repeatedly in the text, you're probably dealing with a motif. They must be related to the central idea of the work, and they always end up reinforcing the author's overall message."[14] Any arrangement of words that can add a dimension of critical thinking, such as the use of motif and other symbolic devices, usually strengthens the writing. Other examples of motif can be found on websites including:

- https://blog.reedsy.com/what-is-a-motif/[15]

Developing an Editorial Lens

High school students have much to gain by developing an editorial lens. When editors view a piece of prose for a newspaper, article, or book, they can be distracted from the message when they stumble over common writing errors. Teachers who explicitly teach students how to avoid such mistakes play a key role in supporting quality writing. High school students need to learn how to see their writing through an editorial lens so they can avoid run-on sentences and use of mixed tenses, as well as limited and repeated word choices.

~ *Run-on Sentence Mini Lesson*

High school students should no longer write simple sentences such as "The book was interesting." Without understanding dependent and independent clauses, it is possible for sentences to be too cumbersome and grammatically incorrect. It's OK to have some simple sentences with only one verb; however, sentences should be lengthier to clarify ideas further. Run-on sentences make it difficult for the reader to keep track of the message. If a sentence has more than three verbs, it is possible that the writer has embedded a "run-on" sentence.

Many websites provide examples and ideas for revising run-on sentences. Sample websites listed below are popular options for students interested in improving patterns of weak writing:

- https://grammar.yourdictionary.com/sentences/run-on-sentences.html[16]
- https://www.grammarly.com/blog/run-on-sentence-basics/[17]

~ *Tenses and Third-Person Mini Lesson*

High school students need to review their written work to be sure that the tenses are consistent. Many publishers encourage writers to submit work in the past tense and in third person (removing the narrative "I," "we," or reference to second-person words such as "our" or "us"). Students need to learn the difference between formal narrative and expository writing, and journal writing, which is more casual.

~Word Usage Mini Lesson

Using extraneous or excess words is a common faux pas in writing. Students need to learn how to edit their writing to make sentences smaller and more concise. Deliberately reshaping sentences can make the difference between a drab piece of writing and a compelling one.

Repeated words in a paragraph or sentences must be addressed in the polishing stage of writing. When names need to be repeated, it is important for students to apply the "every other pronoun rule" to break up the monotony of hearing a name repeated over and over in a paragraph. Students should go through each sentence with a keen eye for repetition and a thesaurus for revisions. Such habits can do much to reduce unwanted distractions in a piece of writing.

What separates strong writers from writers who need to improve? Weaker writing often includes the use of absolute words, such as "best," "only," "all," "every," and "always." Writers should try to eliminate them when they creep into their work. Even teachers can be caught using absolutes on report cards. How often do statements such as "Joe always completes his work in a timely manner" appear as written comments on formal reports?

Absolutes make statements that do not stand the test of time. It is doubtful that Joe always completes his work in a timely manner, nor will Jane be the best forever.

Simple words such as "little," "pretty," and "got" need to be removed from any formal writing; students need time to build in and feature more elaborate vocabulary during the editing stages of writing.

The editorial lens begins before high school and continues when students move to further education, the world of work, and in roles as parents. The purpose-based (PB) approach to writing for high school graduates should emphasize both argumentative and editorial lenses as part of the need for a comprehensive process to master the art and craft of writing.

To be prepared for the demands of high school and college writing, students need to be aware of their strengths and weaknesses. In addition to keeping a portfolio of writings throughout their school experience, students can benefit from developing their own assessment tools, conferencing with teachers and peers, and reflecting on the nagging flaws that can affect the quality of their work.

Writing should be a social process. It should not be a lonely endeavor, undercover. Students need opportunities to write on their own and with others. Students are not born great writers; they have been helped along the way, especially if they are not wired to learn via osmosis from reading.

Writers can be grouped in one of three categories: those who learn by "winging it" (somewhat disengaged writers), those who learn by rigorous review (strong writers), and those who learn by osmosis (avid reader writers). It is possible that strong readers could have difficulty editing their own work, relying on the less than adequate "Does this sound right?"

Rather than students using websites as interventions, or worse yet to correct their writing for them, it makes sense for high school teachers to make writing lessons explicit, so students can further develop. In the world of work, you would not expect your employees to use writing support sites to check their writing, but this is now becoming more commonplace.

After at least 12 years of ELA, graduates should not require technology or tutorial aids to edit their writing. But it makes sense that when students are exposed to everything at the same time, many will give up trying to grasp them all. If, however, the curriculum emphasizes how to remove a few common errors at a time, then it is possible to gradually build the student's editorial lens in a progressive and meaningful fashion.

Rather than expecting a high school English teacher to review and teach about all writing flaws, which can be hit and miss in ensuring that all students avoid them, there should be an understanding of what most students should master in elementary school. Teams of ELA teachers that span K through 12 can develop comprehensive curriculum; in doing so, trust can be established as elementary and high school teachers agree upon what concepts can be mastered, and when.

By developing realistic expectations, students and teachers can ensure that writing capacity can improve in a progressive, organized fashion. In this way, teachers can spend more time helping students master new concepts and less time randomly repeating similar lessons. With a fresh focus in each grade, and a trust that students have mastered the curriculum from the prior grade, students might become strong writers.

NOTES

1. International Baccalaureate Organization (IBO). https://www.ibo.org.
2. Aguilar, E. Motivating students: Writing for an audience. http://www.edutopia.org/blog/motivating-student-writers-audience-elena-aguilar.

3. Appalachian State University. Business letter format. https://cs.appstate.edu/~egp/1410_archive/Word97/bl_eg_pics.html.

4. Indeed Editorial Team. 15 types of business letters and the purpose of each. https://www.indeed.com/career-advice/career-development/types-of-business-letters.

5. O'Brien, S., & Rusciano, A. Writing a business letter: A step-by-step formatting guide. WikiHow. https://www.wikihow.com/Write-a-Business-Letter.

6. Calkins, L. (1986). *The art of teaching writing.* Portsmouth, NH: Heinemann.

7. Literary Devices. https://literarydevices.net/juxtaposition/.

8. Dickens, C. (1859). A *Tale of Two Cities.* New York: Cosmopolitan Book Corp.

9. Reedsy Blog. https://blog.reedsy.com/literary-devices/#25__juxtaposition.

10. Literary Devices. https://literarydevices.com/juxtaposition/.

11. Literary Devices. https://literarydevices.net/paradox/.

12. https://literarydevices.net/paradox/.

13. Literary Terms. https://literaryterms.net/when-and-how-to-write-a-paradox/.

14. Literary Devices. https://literarydevices.net/motif/.

15. Reedsy Blog. https://blog.reedsy.com/what-is-a-motif/.

16. Gunner, J. Run-on sentences: What they are and how to fix them. Your Dictionary. https://grammar.yourdictionary.com/sentences/run-on-sentences.html.

17. Calonia, J. How to fix and prevent run-on sentences. Grammarly Blog. https://www.grammarly.com/blog/run-on-sentence-basics/.

Part IV

DEEP DIVE INTO WRITING FORCES

17

DIFFERENTIATING WRITING INSTRUCTION

PROFESSIONAL CONVERSATION STARTERS

1. How does your school differentiate expectations for written instruction?
2. All students should have access to gifted or extended learning options. Discuss.
3. How can differentiated programming support new language learners?

Differentiating writing instruction can be as specific as customizing expectations for each student and/or implementing standard guidelines developed for students who require English language learner (ELL) and special education supports. Many set policies are legal requirements as outlined in an individual education program (IEP), which include accommodations and modifications for remedial support and extension programming for students identified as "gifted."

Whether or not students are distinguished as requiring ELL or special education services, differentiating curriculum to meet all students where they are is beneficial. Students are varied; they were not born on the same day, nor are they the same sex, nor do they have the same capacity to demonstrate mastery of literacy at the same time or learning in a context with the same teaching conditions.

Students need time and often, personalized experiences to develop a solid foundation in writing. Assuming that all middle school students are ready to write an essay is naive. Some students need more time to think deeply about their writing to apply their understandings.

~ *From Prose to Poetry Mini Lesson Extension*

It is possible to create poems from existing prose. This is another way for students to launch into poetry writing. By removing smaller words and keeping mainly the nouns, verbs, and some descriptive words, any paragraph can be reformulated in a poetic form. Students can also transform their own writing into "found poems." Grade 3 student Chris, who wrote an e-pal letter, chose to take part in an extension activity where she fused key ideas from her letter into a poem that she titled "Not Again."

Not Again (a poetic rendition)

Awaken some mornings
feeling Dad's hurried haste
scent of bread,
ignored in toaster
creeps up wooden stairs,
through brass keyhole
under my door
eyes closed
sleep interrupted
clock reads 6:57
unpleasant smell
knocks on my nose
sniffing burnt toast
words NOT AGAIN
screeching in my head.

Dunning and Stafford[1] introduced the idea of "found poetry," which is created when students collect a list of words from a text and then add in a few words to compose a poem. More information on found poems is featured on the National Council of Teachers of English (NCTE) and the Read, Write and Think websites:

- https://cdn.ncte.org/nctefiles/resources/books/sample/18488chap1.pdf[2]
- https://www.readwritethink.org/classroom-resources/lesson-plans/poetry-prose[3]

Samples of other extension activity, for older students, could include:

How would students revise Eleanor Roosevelt's speech about the United Nations, knowing what is known today?

- https://www.fdrlibrary.org/documents/356632/390886/Eleanor+Roosevelt+Transcript+of+Speech+on+Human+Rights+1951.pdf/7c4b27f5-0512-46f0-8119-8b57f201caa9[4]

Apply to participate in the Toastmaster's Youth Leadership Program.[5] This workshop consists of eight one- to two-hour sessions that enable young people under the age of 18 to develop their communication and leadership skills through practical experiences. The program is presented during or after school, or on weekends. In the workshop, young people learn valuable skills, including the following:

- Evaluating their own speaking ability
- Preparing and giving speeches
- Giving impromptu talks
- Controlling their voice, vocabulary, and gestures
- Giving constructive feedback and more[6]

Some educators may view such experiences as reserved for students in gifted programs, but all students should have the opportunity to extend their learning. When students extend their learning experiences to grapple with and employ more complex concepts typically introduced at higher grade levels, such contexts can fall into "gifted" programming.

When primary students write and read much more complex texts than their peers, it is important for the teacher to respond to their individual needs, whether or not they are identified by the system. The teacher should not allow exceptional students to raise expectations for all students

Figure 17.1. Sample of Grade 1 Extended Writing

in the class. A grade 1 student, for example, composed a question and a statement response when asked to write about an "invisible thing," as revealed in figure 17.1. Although she demonstrated work expected to be mastered by grade 2, all students in the class should not be expected to master such an extension by the end of grade 1.

Extension opportunities can support and motivate students who demonstrate work at the next grade level. It can be easy for teachers to view such work as a new ceiling for all students in a grade, assigning higher grades to students who work at the next grade level and lower grades to students who master the standards of their own grade level. It is important for teachers to identify which work is at grade level and which is at the next level to be clear about expectations, not making "extended work" the goal for all students in a class.

While focusing on the writing of second-grade children, Dutro and Haberl examined their experiences living at the United States-Mexico border. They found that children reveal "keen insights into their political and personal worlds."[7] As long as students are engaged, many forms of writing can be media for thinking and enrichment. Stretching expectations by providing "extensions" that all students can access, not just for those identified as "gifted," is worth considering.

Students who benefit from gifted experiences beyond what is expected for all students should not be ranked in comparison with others. Their curriculum extensions should be customized and challenging. Although the teacher may use extensions to support gifted programming, all students should have opportunities for enrichment.

Differentiation includes everything that can be done to enhance learning. Teachers who organize experiences around varied learning styles and develop multiple intelligences are also differentiating their programs. The goal in quality teaching and learning is not to find out what students do not know; rather, the goal is to find a way for students to demonstrate what they do know.

Differentiation is not just working with students where they are; it is reducing the gap between what they know and what they need to know to succeed in college, work, and life. A "one-size-fits-all" approach to teaching and learning may seem like a simple solution to today's education challenges, but school is a complex organization. Applying differentiated options provides students with learning experiences that fit their learning styles as well as providing opportunities to develop multi-intelligences.

In an ideal "differentiated" classroom, students who have not mastered writing a paragraph should not be asked to write more than one paragraph. When a swimmer demonstrates poor technique in the backstroke, the coach does not have the individual swim fifty more lengths. When students are asked to write multiple paragraphs and essays before they are ready, this can instill poor writing habits. Just as the coach would pull swimmers out of the water to provide specific feedback for improving their strokes, a teacher needs to stop writers and point out where they can improve their writing. This can empower young writers and ultimately increase their confidence.

Writing samples gathered and analyzed before the school year begins can provide the teacher with information about individual student writing skills; in this way, instruction can be designed to meet differentiated needs. This means that all students could be assigned the same task of writing a biography, but the volume of writing could vary. Expecting writers who need more support to write five paragraphs before they have mastered one or three paragraphs will only deepen poor writing habits.

Students need to demonstrate excellence on a smaller scale first. Ideally, a teacher will aim, by the end of the course, to increase the critical mass of students writing the expected volume at grade level. Given the concerns that professors in higher education have with respect to the quality of writing, it is naive to assume that everyone leaves high school English classes ready for college writing expectations.

A biographical writing task might be one paragraph, three paragraphs, five paragraphs, or more than 100 pages. This book provides general age and grade guidelines, but students should be able to work at what they need to learn next. By coordinating a kindergarten to college focus electronically, students could easily experience individualized programming in all subject areas, removing the arbitrary walls that accompany conventional grades in schooling.

Many students are handed a "one-size-fits-all" writing program, regardless of where their skills fit on a continuum. When 120 grade 9 students were tested on a diagnostic test for entry into a Detroit charter high school, their reading, language, and writing skills ranged from grade 3 to grade 9, with a critical mass at the lower end of the spectrum.

Less than 15% of the incoming students were ready for grade-level programming, so it was critical that a differentiated program be in place to move students forward from their point of entry. Ignoring the skill sets that need to be mastered in grades 3 through 8 did not help students succeed and master grade 9 understandings or feel confident moving forward.

The context for learning can play a significant role in differentiating writing instruction. Flores examined how "culturally and linguistically diverse youth" engaged in "writing and performance literacies" in the Youth Writing Collective, which was set up as a creative writing summer program. The findings from her research support out-of-school writing experiences as they can "inspire classroom teachers to improve writing instruction in school."[8]

After-school programs often spawn education innovation. Dave Eggers's[9] pirate-themed tutoring program (826 Valencia) in San Francisco evolved as tutors and students fine-tuned the prompts and authentic purpose of the program. This creative story called "Once upon a School" is worth the half hour invested in this link:

- https://www.youtube.com/watch?v=FaSF1gPBKrA&t=27s[10]

826 Valencia removed the divide between writing professionals and novice writers while allowing imaginations to let go of a fixed view of learning spaces; the program revealed many incredible treasures for enhancing written instruction.

New English language learners can benefit from differentiated programming to master the expectations that their classmates may have mastered in previous years. Being an ELL student should not be a barrier to writing. Williams and Lowrance-Faulhaber claimed that "bilingual children had a wider range of linguistic resources, including language-specific and cross-language strategies."[11]

Grade 2 students in a U.S. multilingual school collaboratively composed writing in an e-book on a daily basis. Students were engaged when they had the opportunity to co-construct ideas "that honored and acknowledged their own and peers' heritage languages." As a result of this research, Rowe highly recommends that educators "provide opportunities for students to connect their school and peer worlds to their heritage language and backgrounds."[12]

In working with English language learners, photography and drawing opportunities reveal their comprehension and the messages they share. Picture books, created by students with learning challenges, elementary school ELL students, and adult ELL students, reveal examples of the rich interplay of photography and comprehension.

The use of images as a cue and a clue for developing language is well documented across a variety of fields and within quality learning environments. All students in grades 1 through 4 in a school in Dubai[13] took part in the same differentiated assignment. They were asked to draw and describe an imaginary thing. In each class they linked their own experiences and shared their senses as imaginary things to augment their stories. Figure 17.2 illustrates samples of grades 1, 2, and 4 ELL image writing. The ELL teacher wrote the grade 1 and 2 student descriptions of the image and their senses, and the grade 4 writing was shared as a first draft.

Progressively, the grade 1 sample featured an elaborate image, with the teacher doing all the physical writing of the message. By grade 2, the student created labels for his image, and by grade 4 the teacher was no longer scribing for the student without labeling to scaffold the message. Images can be a significant support for writing.

Writing about a birthday party, a grade 3 student whose first language is Hebrew shared the following in image, labels, and writing in figure 17.3.

In New Jersey, Maryellen Moffitt and Hope Blecher used live improvisation and then illustrations to scaffold writing steps from sharing the pen to holding the pencil. Their work featured an audience of gifted and talented students and teachers, and English as a second language teachers in collaboration with English language learners, the students. Their years of classroom experience, as documented in *See It, Be It, Write It*,[14] support the use of images to scaffold the transference of ideas and the development of written language for those challenged by having the words on the tip of the tongues and fingertips.

Grade 1 ELL Sample Image Writing

"I am in Thailand with my family. I can see elephants and waterfalls. The tour guide told me that I can feed the animals, but it's time to go back home."

"I can hear the sound of the waterfalls. I can smell flowers. I am so excited."

Grade 2 ELL Sample Image Writing

"I went to a mountain with my family. I saw lava getting out from the ground. I was so afraid so I decided to go back home."

"I can hear thunder. I could smell charcoal. I was afraid."

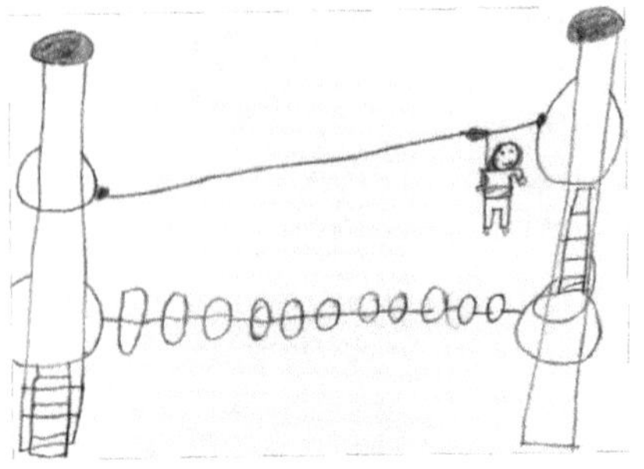

Grade 4 ELL Sample Image Writing

"I go to the park with my friends. I see a rabbit. It so cute and they smell of the flower is soo beiutful and I play a zilizip."

Figure 17.2. Sample of Grades 1, 2, and 4 ELL Image Writing

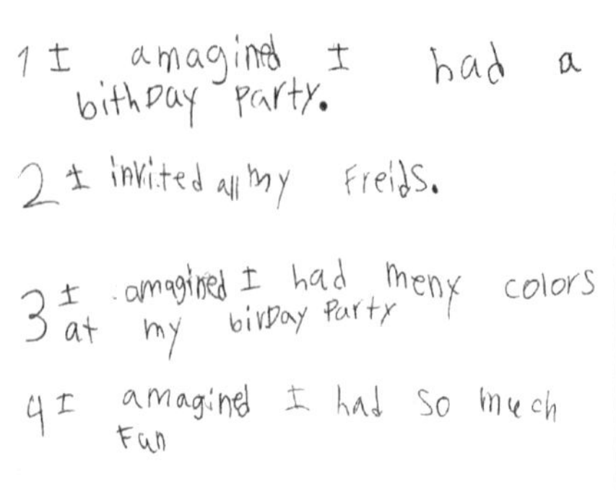

Figure 17.3. Grade 3 ESL Student Writing and Image

Pictures, whether drawn by students or found in print or digital resources, are the basis of storyboards and graphic novels. In comic books and graphic novels, images carry the storyboards. Every picture tells a story and aids the reader in understanding what is happening. Hope Blecher's presentations connect the use of picture word walls with Vygotsky's zone of proximal development (ZPD).[15] She emphasizes how teachers can incorporate pictures onto word walls that can be shared with parents and educators.

For students learning a new language, images serve as a scaffold. The teacher who adds pictures to the word wall is opening windows and doors for the student who doesn't yet have the word but can recognize the pictured item. This is akin to the well-known rebus in *Highlights Magazine*[16] and the use of images in the *Geronimo Stilton* book series.[17] Examples, demonstrations, free-form activities, and using a variety of materials such as pencils, paint, ink, and pixels can transform writing into mixed forms of expression and verse. The blend of the visual markings on the page can influence the organization of written expression in outlines and prose, ready for revising, editing, revisiting, and reading.

Blecher was prompted to cultivate written expression when connecting a daily comic strip to a book and an experience. Hope used this three-pronged engagement when she read a *Peanuts* comic[18] that featured a bemoaning Peppermint Patty missing out on trick-or-treating to try to glimpse the Great Pumpkin. Charlie Brown offered her his rock, all he gleaned from his Halloween hunting. Hope linked the text to Byrd Baylor's book *Everybody Needs a Rock*[19] as she physically touched and turned over a smooth rock in her hands. Such a multisensory approach to the literal and figurative meaning of the images and the text helped to shape ideas for writing.

Blecher used Baylor's book as well as Peter Reynolds's book *The Dot*[20] as texts to support the transformation of students into authors, illustrators, and narrators. After a read-aloud and the opportunity to reread the books in small groups, students were asked to create their own versions of the stories. They used a photo of their own hand holding a rock—their own "dot"—which prompted creation of a deluge of wonderful drawings. After the students created their stories using bookcreator.com, they shared the following reflections:

- "You gave us a safe place."
- "I didn't have to talk first."

- "Look at this picture, it is a story."
- "This is fun and comfortable."
- "Look mom, this is my book."

With a smile and tears of accomplishments, all shared a flood of more elaborate and newly charged language. The students felt seen and heard.

Imagine how students feel when they can draw a picture on a blank sheet of paper. In one class, a primary student drew a cup and saucer. Above the saucer were three wiggly lines. When asked to label the picture, the young child froze. The teacher paused, smiled, and uttered the word "Hot." With less than a timed breath, the child said, "Yes, Nestlé," then, "Ah, hot chocolate," and then, "Hot cocoa." Selected oral prompts can help open the writing process. Building trust with each young writer can lead to a year's worth of drawings, expanded vocabulary, comprehension, and collaboration.

Differentiation involves all communication with all senses; a good writing program does not stop at the walls of the classroom. Writing needs to fit into the big academic picture so that all kinds of learners can exhibit what they know and, in doing so, be confident about their written expression. Supporting capable, confident student writers who can share and read each other's work is a quality goal of a strong academic program, where writing is worthy of being read.

NOTES

1. Dunning, S., & Stafford, W. (1992). *Getting the knack: 20 poetry writing exercises.* Urbana, IL: National Council of Teachers of English.

2. National Council of Teachers of English (NCTE). Found and headline poems. https://cdn.ncte.org/nctefiles/resources/books/sample/18488chap1.pdf.

3. Read, Write and Think. Poetry from prose. https://www.readwritethink.org/classroom-resources/lesson-plans/poetry-prose.

4. United Nations Eleanor Roosevelt Transcript of Speech on Human Rights. (1951). https://www.fdrlibrary.org/documents/356632/390886/Eleanor+Roosevelt+Transcript+of+Speech+on+Human+Rights+1951.pdf/7c4b27f5-0512-46f0-8119-8b57f201caa9.

5. Toastmasters Youth Service Leadership Program. https://www.toastmasters.org/education/youth-leadership-program.

6. https://www.toastmasters.org/education/youth-leadership-program.

7. Dutro, E., & Haberl, E. (2018). Blurring material and rhetorical walls: Children writing the border/lands in a second-grade classroom. *Journal of Literacy Research, 50*, 167–189.

8. Flores, T. (2018). Breaking silence and amplifying voices: Youths writing and performing their worlds. *Journal of Adolescent & Adult Literacy, 61*, 653–661. https://ila.onlinelibrary.wiley.com/doi/abs/10.1002/jaal.733.

9. Eggers, D. (2008). Dave Eggers: 2008 TED prize wish: Once upon a school. https://www.youtube.com/watch?v=FaSF1gPBKrA&t=27s.

10. https://www.youtube.com/watch?v=FaSF1gPBKrA&t=27s.

11. Williams, C., & Lowrance-Faulhaber, E. (2018). Writing in young bilingual children: Review of research. *Journal of Second Language Writing, 42*, 58–69.

12. Rowe, L. W. (2019). Constructing language ideologies in a multilingual, second-grade classroom: A case study of two emergent bilingual students' language-use during ebook composing. *Linguistics and Education, 52*, 1–12.

13. Selected student writings from Al Mizhar School in Dubai, United Arab Emirates. (November 4, 2022).

14. Blecher-Sass, H. S., & Moffitt, M. (2010). *See it, be it, write it.* Minneapolis: Free Spirit Publishers.

15. Vygotsky, L. *Zone of proximal development* (ZPD).

16. *Highlights Magazine.* https://en.wikipedia.org/wiki/Highlights_for_Children.

17. *Geronimo Stilton* book series. https://en.wikipedia.org/wiki/Geronimo_Stilton.

18. *Peanuts* cartoon. (November 1, 2022).

19. Baylor, B. *Everybody needs a rock.* https://blogs.scientificamerican.com/rosetta-stones/a-perfect-book-for-hooking-kids-on-rocks/.

20. Reynolds, P. (2003). *The dot.* Candlewick Press. https://www.thedotcentral.com.

18

FEEDBACK AND ASSESSMENT OF WRITING

PROFESSIONAL CONVERSATION STARTERS

1. How do you know whether the way students are taught writing at your school or in your district is having a positive impact on their writing?
2. How do you define assessment, feedback, grading, and evaluation?
3. How can assessment practices support learning?

It is time to move away from ranking systems in schools. All students need to learn how to write well, period.

Recognizing that learning something of value is complex, and that a narrow focus only on standards cannot suffice, Spear claimed, "we need to shift away from traditional report cards that offer rank order descriptions of student achievement within different subject areas"[1] to the use of comprehensive portfolios to document learning.

Writing is a comprehensive process. As such, the assessment tools used to provide feedback should not only evolve but be newly invented to support confident, capable young writers. This chapter discusses issues of assessment, but examples are shared throughout this resource, as assessment and feedback should never be considered separate from curriculum. They are integral parts of a comprehensive design for teaching and learning.

For some educators, assessment is synonymous with testing, but here this is not the case. Assessment includes feedback throughout a process and in a summative way at the end with a product. Assessment also includes grading and evaluating work for purposes of reporting or certification. Relying on testing as a narrow form of assessment may seem like a simple solution, but when the goal is learning, convenience is not an option.

Teaching writing is about teaching the habits of professional writers. It is recommended that students move from novice (i.e., make changes to the paper draft) to apprentice practice (i.e., make track changes using computer functions) before they instinctively can make quality or expert changes instantaneously.

Building in explicit steps to learn how to revise written work in a systematic way can move a novice writer to master the skill of writing like an expert writer. To be ready for college writing, students need to know their strengths and weaknesses. Being aware of typical mistakes can help the writer minimize them.

Students can learn to appropriate practices of strong writers during conferences with their teacher or peers. Some experts insist that behaviors should not be part of student assessment; however, it could be argued that good habits of authors do contribute to their writing capacity.

Table 18.1, used in concert with other rubrics, can provide students with feedback about their writing behaviors.

Table 18.1. Sample Quality Behaviors of Writers

Quality Behaviors of Writers		
Student Self-Score	*Quality of Writing* *(A) ample evidence, (B) some evidence, (?) did not see evidence* *The writer . . .*	*Teacher Score*
	asked questions to clarify expectations	
	invested time in the outlining part of the task	
	took risks with original and abstract ideas	
	persisted with the editing part of the task	
	completed work in a timely and professional manner	
Comments:		

By making habits of strong writers transparent, in combination with helping students identify their mistakes, teachers can provide specific support for writing in a variety of genres from fiction to research papers. Feedback tools that support the growth of writing in action can guide writing mastery for different age levels and forms. Interactive rubric samples have been embedded throughout this book to provide distinct contexts for feedback. Such examples also affirm the interdependence of assessment and curriculum.

Typically, assessment tools focus on the product rather than the process. It is important, therefore, to develop rubrics that can support the growth of writing in action. Rubrics are rarely applied to draft work or for purposes of self-evaluation to help the writer before making a piece of work public. By making an "editing" rubric transparent, students can then return to their revised draft and aided by self-assessment, think about next steps.

Students can evaluate their work by determining whether their writing has "ample" (A) evidence, "some" (S) evidence, or no evidence of the designated writing criteria. Fewer distinguishing choices for assessment bring clarity for students and teachers, but just because choices are fewer does not mean the assessment is less rigorous.

It could be argued that adding more layers of assessment—such as a host of engineered options in between including letter grades with plusses and minuses (F, D–, D, D+, C–, C, C+, B–, B, B+, A–, A, and A+)—or number systems beyond three contributes to making scores less accurate and efficient. The odds that different reviewers will arrive at the same assessment decrease relative to the number of qualifiers. When different reviewers have four or more options, regardless of the samples provided, the likelihood they will all arrive at the same score is limited.

Peha suggests that "criteria are more valuable to the students than the teacher . . . The only way for criteria to be truly helpful to students is if they know how to apply these criteria accurately to their own work."[2] The discussion between the teacher and student relative to the criteria in the context of the student's written work can be invaluable.

There is little research on what students do with assessment; however, there are many findings about declining student engagement, generally beginning in grade 5. Although it is probable that stronger student writers will submit assignments and pay attention to what distinguishes each percentage or ranking, some students do not bother to self-assess or simply hand in something just to get it over with.

Without evidence from qualitative research that pays attention to how students use assessment tools, educators may never discover whether students see the value in the complexity of a grading system, or simply go through the motions with an attitude of "whatever." The sample tools designed for various phases of the writing process were meant to clear away the weeds so the jargon and degrees of weakness do not cloud the expectations or the clarity and fairness of the assessment.

So, what might be considered fair in grading? And how might educators determine whether a tool is fair? The process of "moderation" can field test assessment tools. When three reviewers assess a single piece of student writing, they should arrive at the same grade or score. When they do not, the results can be challenged. The solution is not to average the scores. Users must trust the assessment, and when more options exist, subjectivity creeps in and calls into question the integrity of the tool and those who dare not challenge the system that promotes it.

Graham, McKeown, Kiuhara, and Harris analyzed 115 studies on writing intervention: "Both typically developing students (grade 4) and struggling writers (grades 2–6) benefited when they were taught how to apply self-regulation procedures, such as goal setting and self-assessment, to help them manage the writing strategies they were taught."[3] When students draft something, spell check it, and hand it in, they tend to wait passively for someone else to assess the work. Generating rubrics that help guide self-regulation possibly can advance learning in writing and all subject areas.

Graham noted that effective writing instruction and assessment require time.[4] Noting that different teachers assign grades in different ways, Peha asserts that "grades are arbitrary. . . . Even when criteria are used, the interpretation of the criteria and the final translation into a letter or number is highly subjective."[5] Further reflection highlights his frustration that grading took so much precedence over learning:

> I would spend hours correcting and recording scores into a grade book, and then at the end of each quarter I would somehow try to come up with grades that represented what my students had learned . . . I realize now that it was all pretty much a waste of time because none of it—not the planning, or the correcting, or the grading, or even the narratives (written comments on report cards) has anything to do with what my students needed to learn or what I needed to do to help them.[6]

Peha suggests that "no teacher should have to spend hour after frustrating hour recording information, processing data, and filling out forms that don't help them teach, don't help their students learn, or don't help parents and other adults support children effectively."[7]

It takes extensive time for a teacher to unpack and communicate what is meant by criteria that could fall between "not yet," developing, and strong parameters of a piece of writing. When elaborate descriptions overlap one another, the time expected to assess, rather than teach, can be interpreted as time wasted.

Many teachers find ready-made assessment tools in the form of rubrics on websites and in textbooks; many of those commercially designed are too wordy and far too subjective to engage genuine student participation. Wordy rubrics can cloud teaching and learning. If such tools were simplified to guide the improvement of writing and provide more accurate feedback, they could be much more effective.

Part of the role of curriculum designers is to make determinations about assessment. For some educators, assessment that matters is about the scores on standardized tests. For others, assessment includes evidence of and for learning gathered from teachers and students. Establishing routines for collecting writing samples at the beginning and end of the term or school year is a way for teachers and students to compare the pieces to determine if what happened in between (the teaching choices) contributed to improvement.

Ideally the writing task would be the same, and both pieces of writing (before and after) would be viewed through the rubric lens. Three findings can emerge:

1. The writing shows improvement.
2. The writing does not demonstrate any change.
3. The end-of-year writing is weaker than the piece shared at the beginning of the school year.

Examining all the writing samples (from outlines to drafts to the final product) can indicate student, class, school, or district trends. If most students show solid improvement, then it makes sense for the teachers to continue on a similar path. If the student work demonstrates weaker skills or no change at all, then the curriculum should be modified. Teachers of English at one high school used the following two-level template (table 18.2) to begin discussions about their students' writing skills throughout the school year.

Table 18.2. Writing Sample Comparison Chart

Initial Writing Sample			*End-of-Year/ Semester Writing Sample*	
Not Yet Mastered	*Strong*	*Criteria*	*Not Yet Mastered*	*Strong*
		use of details		
		rich vocabulary		
		phrasing		
		effective use of complex sentences		
		use of similes		
		use of parallel structure		
		no sentence fragments		
		accurate use of punctuation		
		powerful starter sentence		
		powerful concluding sentence		
Comments:				

After documenting the patterns from each student, teachers discussed the following questions:

- If there were changes, what do you think caused them?
- What changes to your curriculum materials will you recommend after viewing the samples?

Each writing sample in draft, edited, and final form should be kept as part of a formal student portfolio. This record would show long-term writing development. Such internal measures can be compared with the reading and literacy scores from standardized tests. Given that writing can strengthen thinking, a positive correlation between writing strength and increased test scores might follow.

Too often a rubric for a history essay is established in isolation of language arts writing expectations for a certain grade. Student writing can be augmented when educators look for ways to assess the application of writing in other subjects and, more authentically, to develop projects together. Social studies and science teachers might have more insight into how students come to know what they know by asking students to hand in each stage of work, thus sharing the growth of ideas and their thinking along the way.

Many state or provincial documents list and group detailed expectations, but what tends to be missing are examples of how outcomes can be organized within project-based work so that the mastery of key "learning" is not lost. It is important to develop precise assessment tools so that rigorous expectations are met, documented, and passed on from teacher to teacher as students move from grade to grade. Developing a culture for generating quality writing for all students is not easy.

Who should design feedback tools? Teachers, and not far behind, students should be at the forefront of creating assessment tools, provided their license to design is "grounded in a solid understanding of current progressive practices in school assessment." Further, Smith claims, "Teachers who have the freedom and autonomy to generate assessment tools and reporting systems have distinct opportunities to choose what their expertise determines is the most appropriate metric for providing feedback to students and parents."[8]

Teachers and teacher leaders can design writing curriculum and accompanying assessment tools initially in the form of checklists to break down qualities of good outlines, drafts, and final copies. Interactive rubrics, like checklists, are easy to use, but they enable students to think about the quality of their work relative to specific expectations. Interactive rubrics provide more support for clarifying whether "some" or "more" criteria are present in the work.

Viewing the transformation of a piece of writing from words and images to prose gives the teacher a bird's-eye view of learning. By examining the process, teachers are no longer burdened with checking for plagiarism. When students craft their work, they are not tempted to cut and paste material that others have written. It should be easy to see how students have moved their writing from point form to revised draft to final copy.

Finally, writing happens over sustained time; it cannot be demonstrated properly in a timed exam setting. Just as authors do not draft ideas, craft sentences, mobilize paragraphs, and edit their work in an afternoon, no one should make judgments about student writing in such a stressful artificial setting. Adding an essay question so standardized tests can pose open-ended questions to create a balance has not been vetted seriously.

Writing cannot be seriously addressed in a standardized testing format, but if the time dedicated to practice tests and reading comprehension tests were reduced, students would have much more time to master writing in many more genres than most do today.

Fischetti's question "Why should schools invest in testing systems that tell us what we already know?" emerged from the claim that "High school as we've known it has been dominated by high stakes, high-pressure exams that have outlived their usefulness. If we can reliably predict the results, we don't need the tests."[9] Based on the increase in early offers and acceptances in many universities, he argued:

> Our research shows you can reliably predict a student's year 12 results by year 11. This also suggests we don't need a battery of stressful exams to work out if a student is suited for tertiary education. This gives us the opportunity to radically rethink how the final years of school are structured.[10]

Given that such predictions are reliable, he adds, "it's time to replace stressful exams with more meaningful education." And, "There is an enormous opportunity here to reallocate resources and create a modern, meaningful school experience that excites young people."[11]

Standardized tests make it difficult to breathe in a classroom. With too little time, teachers have little room to create inspiring learning experiences. Imagine what could happen if schools were bold enough to remove such clutter. Students would have time to write and edit authentic work. More time dedicated to developing habits of strong writers means that schools would be investing in stronger, more capable thinkers and citizens.

NOTES

1. Spear, T. (2019). *Education reimagined: The schools our children need.* New London, NH: Eaglecliff Publishing.
2. Peha, S. (1995–2003). Assessing writers assessing writing. https://www.ttms.org/PDFs/09%20Writing%20Assessment%20v001%20(Full).pdf.
3. Graham, S., McKeown, D., Kiuhara, S., & Harris, K. H. (2012). A meta-analysis of writing instruction for students in the elementary grades. *Journal of Educational Psychology, 104*(4), 879–896, esp. 891.
4. Graham, S. (2008). *Effective writing instruction for all students. Renaissance learning.* Nashville, TN: Vanderbilt University Press.

5. Peha (1995–2003).
6. Peha (1995–2003).
7. Peha (1995–2003).
8. Smith, B. (2022). *Assessment tools and systems*. Lanham, MD: Rowman & Littlefield.
9. Fischetti, J. (September 19, 2022). We can predict final school marks in year 11. *The Conversation.* https://theconversation.com/we-can-predict-final-school-marks-in-year-11-its-time-to-replace-stressful-exams-with-more-meaningful-education-190071.
10. Fischetti (September 19, 2022).
11. Fischetti (September 19, 2022).

19

HANDHELD DEVICES

PROFESSIONAL CONVERSATION STARTERS

1. What do you think should be in a 21st-century pencil case?
2. Technology is not the only path to innovation in schools. Discuss.
3. How can schools embrace new resources that support teaching and learning in classrooms?

At first glance, one might think this chapter is about cell phones, but many classroom resources are ones that students can hold and hold meaning at the same time. Of course, an iPad is handheld, but so is a book and an outline for a piece of writing. Thoughtfully selected resources can support student writing.

At the end of the summer, school personnel post a supply list of materials each student needs to bring to school for the new school year. Teachers and school leaders use many other resources. Some will explore the possibilities of new devices; some hold onto materials and approaches like trusted friends, key accessories in their teaching and learning toolkit.

The marble composition lined notebook in the United States or the Hilroy in Canada are staples on most back-to-school lists. Even though young people may have high hopes of filling the pages with brilliant work, the motivation is usually short-lived.

How many teachers read the words on the pages of these handheld devices? How many students keep these notes as reference for future study? How many parents question throwing away unfinished notebooks, year after year? Even though young people seem more inspired to write and share ideas using graphic organizers, teachers still feel the conventional tug to use notebooks. Why?

Perhaps educators think students who keep legible notes will be better prepared to be successful in school, at work, and in their daily lives? If this is true, then where is the evidence that students with neat and complete notebooks have soared to great heights in school and beyond? Or maybe they think notebook writing is preparing them for future drudgery.

Although uniform practice prepares students for more uniform practice, using notebooks can be viewed as a hangover from an industrial model of education. Perhaps educators believe that students need to put ideas in their own words, as well as make as many complete sentences as possible?

Does research support the belief that a neat notebook filled with a massive collection of sentences is a gateway to mastering the craft of writing? If such a claim were true, let us see the school notebooks of esteemed writers. If the notebook was a precursor to their writing prowess, then where are their testimonials acknowledging the role of the notebook in their success?

Everything we do in school needs an authentic purpose. Writing becomes merely a mock exercise when the eventual destiny of the notebook is a garbage can. Recycled or not, a notebook can symbolize busy work and for many who struggle to write, an annoying source of frustration.

Recall that feeling of starting anew, that sensation that each notebook is a fresh start, a mistake-free source of pride. Opening that first page and pressing down the cover may set the stage for a blossoming work of art for some, but many students may simply be over it. Usually, by page 3 the romance with the notebook fades, as sloppiness seeps in and gives way to more elaborate doodling.

David Booth from OISE-UT once said that many kids are building tunnels under teachers, thereby learning outside conventional classrooms. They are writing in the form of texting, they are finding solutions to problems online, and they are communicating often without words by using Instagram. It is doubtful that student success—or not—can be traced back to the marble composition or the Hilroy[1] notebook.

Yet the makers of supply lists continue to require not just one but multiple packs of notebooks at the start of the school year. Maybe it is time to look more closely at the contents of the back-to-school supply lists and ask why.

Anything that is simply thrown out cannot be a symbol of value. Examining what students keep at the end of a school year may reveal much about how to prompt future writing of an authentic kind. How would a notebook stack up against artwork, cherished projects, letters to and from experts, résumés, sports medals, journals, Shutterfly[2] photo books, Book Creator ebooks, or student-made videos?

It is time to include 21st-century artifacts that elicit pride at the same time as house evidence of learning. How to help young people see themselves as writers of reference books for further study is much more meaningful than replicating study notes. Writing must be more than taking notes. After all, anything thrown away is not worthy of one's best effort.

On the other hand, a notebook, as a place that embellished design plans, to-do lists with messy evidence of thinking: now that's a different story. Ritchhart and Perkins suggest that "papers, logs, computers, conversation, and various means of recording and keeping track of ideas and thoughts free the mind up to engage in new and deeper thinking."[3] Although students may not need such a notebook for every subject, the notebook can have alternative functions, especially if it captures evidence of critical and creative thinking. When students use the evidence collected, and readers decipher the treasures of original thought, then such paper tools can be valuable for both students and teachers.

A notebook can be part of a portfolio in an inquiry, much like an outline serves a final copy of a written work. The transformation from ideas to a meaning-making construct gives the learner and the teacher more appreciation for the relationship between product and process. Just as the notebook cannot be the only source for thinking, neither can the use of a computer be relied upon as a paperless solution to manifesting thinking and innovation. Applying understanding through a design process should not be limited to one tool. Not all that one learns can be housed in folders and files of e-portfolios; however, the robust options technology can provide should not be overlooked.

The 21st-century pencil case requires students to have pens, pencils, notebooks, paper, whiteboards (and working markers), as well as computers, printers (both 2- and 3-D), and a healthy variety of resources in print and electronic forms. How educators enable the blending of such materials cannot be bound by a fixed blueprint. Rather, teachers need the autonomy to create and design the learning environment that includes creating artifacts and selecting and implementing learning tools. Ultimately, students will learn how to analyze the effectiveness and trustworthiness of the items in their pencil case as well.

The idea of a paperless school may be supported by environmental and financial arguments, but such decisions are not grounded in educational research and theory. Technology should not limit the tools for thinking. In the real world, robotics designers use a combination of whiteboards and computers to generate new possibilities. A scientist in a lab still uses beakers and graduated cylinders along with iPads, notebooks, and other devices to record observations. Storyboards may be created electronically, but revisions often are edited by hand on paper.

The capacity of writers and their joy of writing must take on new meaning when writers can use so many different kinds of tools and software to communicate their ideas. According to Beach:

> With today's computers and mobile devices, illustration is far easier to include as a part of a communication with the advent of mobile telephone cameras, clip art, and similar options. Word processing and spreadsheet programs allow the creation of elaborate charts, tables, and graphs that may be included in texts, while slide show programs feature illustrative material as the dominant form for communication.[4]

Further, being able to link 2- and 3-D images with text and the power to send files of texts electrically can make collaborative effects much more streamlined.

Even though the internet is a medium that spreads false claims, it also provides access to a depth and breadth of information, making virtual libraries a reality for researchers. Those who did not experience what it was like to research, write manuals, or submit novels in paper form, for instance, may take for granted the ease of writing in a post-typewriter age.

Technology has been a time-saver, but it has also created a scavenger hunt culture; with so much to browse and scan, it can take literally years to gather and determine which literature best supports an argument or recommendation for action. The challenge for innovation must shift to helping students and teachers model critical and creative thinking and action.

Without technology, it would be difficult for students to run their own radio station as they do at the Lyons Township High School[5] near Chicago.

Other schools use AzuraCast,[6] an open-source, self-hosted internet radio management solution. Rimes suggests that "everyone can be a content creator" when schools can "host with any hosting provider, or locally on internal resources with the help of your district's Technology Department."[7] He added that most podcasts today seem to fall into the "talk radio format" and would only require loose ideas of segments, interviews, and so forth. It would be easy to expand a student- or school-run radio station by playing recorded band and choir performances, reruns of radio broadcasts from basketball and football games, or even encourage students to produce spoken word poetry.[8]

Technology provides and will continue to design a full range of handheld devices and software to support students. Tech-savvy teachers may use Padlet[9] to gather feedback from all classmates instantaneously, the Socrative©[10] app to collect virtual exit tickets, or Mindweister[11] to support mind-mapping activity. We have no shortage of software with built-in frameworks to support the organization of ideas.

Many websites feature prompts for writing and publishing options such as Fan Fiction,[12] Quote TV,[13] Wattpad,[14] Goodreads,[15] and Tumblr.[16] In the Sims Writer's Hangout,[17] students gather feedback from the fan community about their stories that weave text with images they created within the video game. Lammers described the experience in his ethnographic study of the interactions in the Hangout.[18]

Based on research in four British schools using Story Engine,[19] Connolly and Burn confirm that a digital writing tool can complement learning when combined with a school's writing program.[20] Websites that support digital storyboarding include the following:

- storyboardthat.com[21]
- www.boords.com[22]
- pixton.com[23]
- kedt.pbslearningmedia.org/tools/storyboard[24]

Apart from learning how to import written work to different kinds of software programs, students in ideal schools can have their work featured in school-wide publication forums, in electronic or printed formats. Too often the written work used with technology is not vetted through a systematic writing process. With so many technology steps to building a website or creating an iMovie, it can be so cumbersome that a writer only has time to submit one draft of a storyboard or written complement.

Writing professionals spend months or years revising to get their work just right. Not to be mistaken for perfection, getting something just right often means making it worthy of the time invested, a sense that the work has been afforded the deepest thought possible. A piece of writing, therefore, does not have an absolute end; it can always be rewritten or adapted for another place and time.

The authenticity of the video narrative increases student motivation to create interesting, accurately written texts for broadcasts. Encouraging students to create original narratives based on personal interests and popular media is a great way to get students to use literacy in a new and genuine way. Creating these narratives can help struggling students build accuracy in their written language and language fluency, as well as confidence in their writing ability. Confidence is at the heart of digital tools with a human touch such as ReadM.app that evolved from the vision of a software engineer frustrated with the reading and writing approach that teachers of his three immigrant and ELL children used.

Technology can provide an engaging avenue for exhibiting student ideas; although it seems to save time, it can require more time to edit to improve all aspects of its application. Apart from integrating technology in an authentic way within courses or projects, exhibiting the writing piece is augmented in authentic ways when digital tools make the message accessible to others.

Students can be much more engaged when they are aware that their efforts to craft written content will be featured as a link or reference for others to use or quote for their work in the future. It is becoming increasingly evident that separating media literacy from writing is no longer a realistic way to address the complexities of communication in digital forums.

The value placed on images is often much more profound than on the written word. When Facebook first came on the scene, it blended words and images, but with the surge in popularity of Instagram and Snapchat, for instance, technology more than ever should not be ignored. According to Unsworth: "In order to understand the role of print in the digital age, it is essential to have a solid grasp of the growing integrative relationship of print and graphics."[25]

Beach suggests, "Technology enables us to employ many more visual addenda to texts than ever before, so attention is needed to teaching learners how to appropriately select and use such elements."[26] Using hypertext to link writing beyond the reference list to the original source is a powerful tool for helping readers delineate the reliability of content. According to Dagostino and Casatelli: "The Web's hypertext offers destinations for further reading on related topics, and data visualization combines facts and figures in a snapshot of digestible information."[27]

As a description, digital writing and reading are perhaps more precise than media literacy, which can seem like an add on to an ELA curriculum bound by traditional handheld materials. Media in a progressive ELA curriculum must be viewed in an interdependent context, not separate from reading and writing. As Dagostino and Casatelli note, "Digital writing is an evolving art, and teachers need to challenge their students to enhance their writing with video, audio, embedded links and graphics, and to adapt it for specific audiences, situations and purposes."[28] They suggest that teachers "may need to revise their conception of literacy and text, as students learn how to read and write with hypertexts, graphs, charts, pictorial models and even virtual realities."[29]

If technology can support learning, what are the barriers to its implementation in any classroom? To the claim that schools can't afford devices for all students, decision makers in education can consider the following:

1. Repurposing budgets to allow for the purchase of one device per two students—perpetuating both individual and more collaborative work that enables the sound pedagogical practice of negotiating the text and material on the screen
2. Repurposing budgets to allow for the purchase of technology for each student
3. Establishing a bring your own device (BYOD) policy

BYOD rarely gets off the ground because the equity argument brings the idea to a full stop. Even though young people in all demographic areas use technology, the concern that all may not have access makes the practice difficult to defend. BYOD may be more prevalent in independent schools where parents pay tuition, but this makes it even more important for public schools to make the modern-day pencil case (with technological devices) available for all. The challenge is not so much whether students can use technology as a tool for learning, but how school leaders can make it happen.

A 2018 survey of fewer than 1,000 teenagers revealed that 95% owned or had access to a smartphone and 88% had a desktop or laptop computer, with 45% indicating that they were always online.[30] Whether 3 or 93% of the school population can bring their devices, how can the school provide access, beyond sharing a library computer lab, for those who cannot afford technology?

Although technology is a necessary tool, it is not the curriculum. Assuming that technology corners the market on innovation is a false claim. Incredible new digital options can seem dazzling; however, it is important to recognize that innovation can happen in many forms—creating models for utility patents, displaying new gymnastics skills, articulating a fine art or the work of a master chef in action.

Innovation is not synonymous with technology; however, in many cases technology can help the process of innovating substantially. For instance, 40 years ago, no one had the option to cut and paste a text. A mistake on a page in a thesis meant the full page had to be retyped, with fingers crossed that another mistake was not made in the revision.

Teaching and learning can be enhanced by the clever use of handheld devices to support individual students in individual classrooms. Students can grow as young writers when they use digital and other creative tools. To be meaningful, such tools need to help learners hold on to their memory-making writing experiences.

NOTES

1. Hilroy. https://www.123ink.ca/p-366550-740-11174-hilroy-multi-size-exercise-notebook-8-38-x-10-787-mm-ruling-40-pages-assorted-colours.
2. Shutterfly. www.shutterfly.com.
3. Ritchhart, R., & Perkins, D. N. (2005). Learning to think: The challenges of teaching thinking. In K. J. Holyoak & R. G. Morrison (Eds.), *The Cambridge handbook of thinking and reasoning* (pp. 775–802). Cambridge: Cambridge University Press.
4. Beach, J. D. (2017). *Bridging old and new communication modes: A theory to transform literacy education practice*. New York: St. John's University, 301.
5. Lyons Township High School.
6. AzuraCast. https://www.azuracast.com.
7. Rimes, B. (February 21, 2022). Where are the K–12 student-run radio stations? *Tech Savvy Educator*. https://www.techsavvyed.net/archives/4354/.
8. Rimes (February 21, 2022).
9. Padlet. https://padlet.com.

10. Socrative©. https://www.socrative.com.

11. Mindweister. https://www.mindmeister.com/?utm_source=google&utm_medium=cpc&utm_campaign=US_en_Brand_brand&utm_content=homepage&gclid=Cj0KCQiAgribBhDkARIsAASA5buMmz68BYjARRKb3DWteQ6SHAh_vKVykY6A0gwp0Xw7JxdnEhgPJyAaAmWREALw_wcB.

12. Fan Fiction. https://www.fanfiction.net; Bippert, K. Fan fiction to support struggling writers. In J. Pilgrim, (Ed.). *Tale yearbook*. https://files.eric.ed.gov/fulltext/EJ1305137.pdf.

13. Quote TV. https://www.quotev.com/quizzes/c/TV.

14. Wattpad. https://www.wattpad.com.

15. Goodreads. https://www.goodreads.com.

16. Tumblr. https://www.tumblr.com/tagged/fanfic.

17. Sims Writer's Hangout. https://www.flickr.com/groups/sims2/.

18. Lammers, J. C. (2016). The Hangout was serious business: Leveraging participation in an online space to design Sims fanfiction. *Research in the Teaching of English, 50*(3), 309–332. http://www.ncte.org/journals/rte.

19. Story Engine. https://storyenginedeck.com.

20. Connolly, S., & Burn, A. (2019). The Story Engine: Offering an online platform for making "unofficial" creative writing work. *Literacy, 53*, 30–38.

21. storyboardthat.com.

22. www.boords.com.

23. www.pixton.com.

24. kedt.pbslearningmedia.org/tools/storyboard.

25. Unsworth, L. (2008). Negotiating multimodal text. In J. Coiro, C. Lankshear, M. Knobel, & D. J. Leu (Eds.), *Handbook of research on new literacies* (pp. 377–406). New York: Routledge, 384.

26. Beach (2017).

27. Dagostino, L., & Casatelli, C. (2017). Content creation for a new generation: A guide for digital writing. *NERA Journal, 52*(1), 99.

28. Dagostino & Casatelli (2017), 94.

29. Dagostino & Casatelli (2017).

30. https://www.pewresearch.org/internet/2018/05/31/teens-social-media-technology-2018/; Anderson, M., & Jiang, J. (May 2018). *Teens, social media and technology 2018.* https://www.pewresearch.org/internet/2018/05/31/teens-social-media-technology-2018/.

20

PARENT ROLE IN STUDENT WRITING

PROFESSIONAL CONVERSATION STARTERS

1. Should parents take part in editing their child's work?
2. What constructive roles do you think parents can play in their child's learning?

Parents should not view writing as a mystery, and all parents can be supported to help their children improve their writing skills. When the expectations are transparent—that is, when teacher, student, and parent are aware of the criteria and the process for crafting a piece of writing— then no one must guess at what needs to happen.

Workshops can help parents understand how they can support their children at different ages. Making the grading or scoring schemes explicit can, in a way, help students take the teacher home with them. If the school supports a process and common language for teaching writing, then students and parents need not adjust to different stylistic changes each year.

Parents do not have to edit their child's work or get someone with a college degree to do so. Students do not need to ponder or be tempted to plagiarize. Cutting and pasting from the Web can be a dishonest solution to mounting assignments.

Imagine a professional learning activity where all the teachers plan a series of parent workshops on how the school teaches writing and what parents can do at home to support and extend the process. Parents can support the following activities at home:

- Write thank-you letters to family members
- Write blogs
- Write Amazon reviews
- Write in a diary
- Journal about vacation

While engaging activities exist that encourage authentic writing, students may come to see them as busywork, especially if the writing process does not match what they have been working on in class. More importantly, the notion of writing more without careful review can have the opposite effect—that is, build weak writing habits.

Students need to write less but analyze their contributions more. Enlist parents as oral readers and active listeners of their child's writing. Parents of younger children can help them embrace words and sentences—not just answering questions but building questions. Rushing to writing paragraphs and sentences can do more harm than good.

Many parents can benefit from writing workshops. They can feel more empowered to help their children at home; at the same time, some might improve their own writing and possibilities for employment. Rather than tell parents what the school is doing, educators can teach parents a common language of writing to enlist their support at the same time.

Encourage parents to participate as co-learners in project-based activities that include writing to express understanding. At the Middleburg Community Charter School[1] in Virginia, parents took part in Leo Projects once a quarter with their children. Families presented artifacts in response to open-ended challenges including the following:

- If you could create your own planet, what would it be like?
- Interview community members, create postcards, and design your own community stamp.
- How can you generate a creative family tree?

Each student-and-parent team had to prepare a presentation that involved anticipating what viewers of the artifact might want to know more about. Although they did not present speeches, they did need to think through how they would present their creations.

During the Leo Nights, students had the opportunity to view the family projects while the parents remained at their tables to present the projects. After an hour, the roles were reversed—the students had their opportunity to share their work with all the parents, who also had a chance to view the body of work prepared for the whole school community. It was similar to a science fair, except that students and parents were accepted as cocreators. Both signed off on the work.

The curriculum at this multigrade school was based on a blend of interdisciplinary work and a conventional emphasis on subjects. Less homework was assigned, which freed families to work together on their Leo Projects and read more for pleasure. Parents were permitted to be supports; rather than following the traditional lead of a teacher's homework pages, parents and children could set goals together to read, think, write, research, and design their creative projects.

The Leo Projects had more than 95% family participation on the four evenings in the first year of this new school. Each quarter the quality of the work improved, as students and parents took pride in their work, celebrated creativity, and reaped the benefits of a passionate and engaged school culture.

Parents can be more invested in schools, and schools can control the narrative of their involvement. Some working parents find it difficult to be the "tutor" at home, and some parents do not feel confident teaching their children after hours. Other parents "helicopter in" to create architecturally award-winning projects, taking on the role of ghost writers who contribute to the child's habitual learning by relying on others to do their thinking for them.

In such scenarios, the novice has nowhere to go. When parents take the reins on the work, usually in a rush to finish, little time is available to discuss or co-construct anything. Students miss the opportunity to appropriate more complex language and understandings, as they would, for example, in an internship.

Fewer assignments along with targeted parent-student projects could support a more productive social learning situation. As well, fewer tasks would give students more time in class to conference with their teachers to formulate deep understandings.

A quick browse of articles responding to the question "Should parents help with homework?" reveals an easy consensus: No. Yet the practice continues in a separate silo from the classroom. Even students in college email essays home for revising and proofing. Often the line is blurred when it comes to assessment. Is the professor grading the student or the parent? And should professors answer calls from parents challenging the grades?

Alfie Kohn's book *The Homework Myth*[2] thoroughly explains why requiring homework for elementary school students is a flawed practice in the first place. No research indicates that homework contributes to or enhances learning. So why is it happening? Parents assume it is helpful and trust the teachers who require it. The existence of homework, in many ways, sets the table for parental overreach. Without homework, the issue of parents doing their child's work is eliminated.

Comparing homework to administering cod liver oil, Kohn notes, "after spending the day at school, they [students] must then complete more academic assignments at home. The predictable results: stress and conflict, frustration, and exhaustion."[3] Kohn suggests that schools

> need principals who question the slogans that pass for arguments: that homework creates a link between school and family (as if there weren't more constructive ways to make that connection!), or that it "reinforces" what students were taught in class (a word that denotes the repetition of rote behaviors, not the development of understanding), or that it teaches children self-discipline and responsibility (a claim for which absolutely no evidence exists).[4]

If six plus hours a day are not enough for teachers and students to get through the curriculum, then the volume of material in the curriculum needs to change. The home should not be a helipad to rescue the school from overloaded expectations. Just as students who write thick descriptions are not necessarily better writers, schools that need to turn pages sideways to shove more content into a curriculum "framework" are not providing a more rigorous education.

When parents are expected to use after-school time to plow through assignments in multiple subject areas, the system is not working. Having parents support young writers is one thing, but parents should not artificially extend the school day as tutors. Parents need room and time to be effective supporters so that all students can have meaningful interactive opportunities to cocreate written works.

NOTES

1. Middleburg Community Charter School.
2. Kohn, A. https://www.alfiekohn.org/homework-myth.
3. https://www.alfiekohn.org/homework-myth.
4. Kohn, A. https://www.alfiekohn.org/article/rethinking-homework/.

21

CHALLENGES TO CHANGING WRITING INSTRUCTION

PROFESSIONAL CONVERSATION STARTERS

1. Does the writing curriculum at the school level accommodate for ongoing rigorous peer-reviewed research and experience at the grassroots level of learning?
2. Has your school developed a common language for teaching writing?
3. Do your teachers emulate the practices of published writers?
4. Does your school have a vertical team of curriculum designers for English language arts (ELA)?
5. Does your school have a distinct writing curriculum for each grade?
6. Do your teachers customize and share writing rubrics with one another?
7. Are the rubrics your school uses interactive?
   - Do students use them to self-assess their work?
   - How do you know students use them?
   - How do you know students read and understand each part of the rubrics they use?
8. Is writing assessed formally at the outlining, drafting, and editing stages of the work?

9. Is written work authentic in that it is viewed by an audience other than the teacher and parent?
10. Have you surveyed students to find out which writing tasks they like more than others?
11. Do students have opportunities to coauthor written work?
12. Do students have rigorous writing expectations for outlining, drafting, and editing in interdisciplinary projects and in other subject areas?
13. Do school administrators model writing for students and staff?

If the answer to many of these questions is "No" or "I'm not sure," then what might be getting in the way of making quality writing experiences happen?

Numerous barriers in schools today limit progress in how writing is taught to students around the globe. If those responsible for education can read more, write more, and think more about better solutions to the rising problems of student and teacher apathy, low student achievement, and increased discipline problems, they have much potential to change education.

Writing is a constructive practice that can help students break through barriers to become the authors of their understandings. Rather than teachers relying on a "test what is known" approach, students can show teachers and others, through writing, what and how they have come to know.

Referring to inquiry-based learning, Shope notes: "When you are preparing for a journey, you own the journey. Once you've started the journey, the journey owns you."[1] Writing for an inquiry project can be engaging; when students own the writing, it can be a powerful learning tool for growth.

Helping students learn and feel confident about crafting ideas using various writing forms typically has been the key responsibility of the English teacher. With so many genres to explore within ELA and so many writing forms in other subject areas, it can be a challenge for a single teacher in one academic year to ensure that all students achieve writing mastery in so many different areas.

Looking beyond the arbitrary school year may be helpful in designing a curriculum that can address such an extensive scope. Coordinating curriculum in three-year cycles, for instance, might be more beneficial than cramming too much into one year. By spreading out what is emphasized when, students can have less repetition, less superficial exposure, and more opportunity for deep learning that inspires good writing practices.

For informed practices to "stick," educators must be aware of the forces holding back progress. Five key forces have been identified as handcuffing the development of strong student writers:

1. Obsessive emphasis and value placed on standardized test measures as single measures of school and student success
2. Assumptions about informed "best" practices in teaching and learning not grounded in classroom research
3. Overreliance on textbooks as curriculum
4. Lack of support for teacher leaders and teacher researchers
5. Reduced cooperative education and other authentic experiences for students to write about

OBSESSIVE EMPHASIS ON STANDARDIZED TESTS

Writing takes a backseat to reading in many schools, as reading comprehension assessment is commonplace on standardized tests. Further, students are subjected to far too much test preparation curriculum for which they read samples of disconnected passages followed by answering a series of disconnected multiple-choice questions. In those classrooms, selecting the response deemed most correct replaces much of "prime-time" teaching.

To prepare students for standardized tests, responding to literary text is the chosen emphasis for writing. Assessing what is handed in during a timed writing period removes the practice of comprehensive editing; test designers and examiners are virtually assessing a first draft. This is problematic when time limits reduce the opportunity for students to demonstrate their capacity to edit their initial responses. For students deliberately taught to make changes to their texts, then cautioned to limit "rub-out rates" on a test, this does not make sense.

A whole industry exists in which people examine tests and frown upon changes. It seems inconceivable that students are encouraged to make changes to their original texts during classroom instruction, then not be permitted to make changes in a testing situation. As more standardized tests include more written contributions, the changes to texts should be rewarded as testimony to a student thinking through problems with more precision.

In such scenarios, the disconnect is between what is taught and what is tested. This gap increases anxiety and the affective filter of some students, thus inhibiting their abilities to show what they know. Further, educators and parents who pay for a public education need to understand that students should be discouraged from thinking that a first draft of anything is good enough.

ASSUMPTIONS ABOUT BEST PRACTICE

Many assumptions drive how students are taught and what they learn. A curriculum can be built with an emphasis on regurgitating knowledge that others define, or it can use current knowledge others define to help students think about making new meaning and generating new ideas.

It is assumed that the more students can absorb content, the better prepared they will be to solve tomorrow's problems. The notion of trial and error is not "trial and perfection" for a reason. In the real world, experts learn from mistakes. Using curriculum designed for students to be mistake-free is narrow and assumes that the knowledge we know now is all we will ever know or need to know.

Can educators be sure that the person who discovers the cure for cancer or the individual who can reverse the hole in the ozone layer was best prepared for making that discovery based on a right answer-focused curriculum? Schools that embed inquiry-based programming, where students move from novice to expert levels of understanding, should be more accessible for all young people. The extended essay, a cornerstone of the International Baccalaureate (IB) program, was designed to give students that edge before they enter college.

OVERRELIANCE ON TEXTBOOKS AS CURRICULUM

Educators often ask the question "What curriculum do you use?" Some may respond with the name of a textbook series; others may refer to government standards, and some may indicate they have designed a curriculum customized by informed practice in the context of their classroom.

Textbooks are resources that support a curriculum. Just as the Common Core State Standards in the United States guide curriculum development, other books, online articles, and websites can also support a curriculum. A quality curriculum should be constructed by schools to meet the direct needs of their community, not made made up of shortcuts or recipe books that can replace a quality education.

Teachers must be involved in curriculum development as they ultimately must own what they prepare for their students. It is assumed that handing out scripted lessons will lead to improved teaching and learning. It makes sense that a science and technology-based school would be informed by STEM. In an arts school, the notion of STEAM makes good sense, to promote the links between the arts and STEM; there is no point in denying students the benefits of thinking and developing multiple forms of intelligence.

Some schools adhere to a writing process that a text promotes; many texts, however, promote the idea that the more you write, the better you get. In the real world, you may compose multiple emails a day; given the volume of such communications, it is important to build in time for editing. Writing daily without revision basically promotes communicating via first drafts, which ultimately can lead to breakdowns in communication and escalating misunderstandings.

Writing curricula often ask students to respond to texts, fictional prose, and poetry—not the kind of writing people in the workforce do regularly. Although more emphasis is placed on writing in response to informational text, often it is in isolation. Busy work, when unedited or filtered, cements weak or mediocre student writing habits.

Project-based learning provides an authentic context for gathering and analyzing varied texts. But such approaches often are separate from texts so that, for the most part, they just organize and house content. It is rare for a writing curriculum to limit the number of assignments, but this is exactly what colleges do. Rarely do professors assign more than three papers a term; most assign one or two, so they can build in time to review the work with their students.

When the time comes to compose a report or create a piece of writing, ample time is needed to draft, craft, and revise written work. When high schools, for instance, coordinate assignments around the "less is more" principle—that is, limit the number of essays to, let's say, one per semester or term (across all subject areas)—then they can raise the bar on written expectations and thus prepare students better for what lies ahead in higher education.

LACK OF SUPPORT FOR TEACHER LEADERS AND TEACHER RESEARCHERS

What could possibly be wrong with a school filled with teacher leaders? Teachers have so much to do already, why would they want to add leadership and research responsibilities to their load? Teachers are the first to know that they do not have enough time to cover all the curriculum. Often when asked to explain how they choose what to prepare, many teachers simply sigh and say, "I pick and choose."

The teacher leaders/researchers in a school can do more than select what they deem is essential. They can play a key role in aligning essential expectations to reduce duplication and ensure against gaps. Teacher leaders also have the know-how and confidence to develop project-based assignments that build in authentic experiences to enhance student and teacher engagement. The pacing guide designed by the teacher leader/researcher should be purposeful and deliberate; nothing should be random about what students learn.

The traditional leadership structures in schools tend to formalize an administration focused on the basic operations of the school. Building a critical mass of talented teacher leaders committed to designing a quality writing curriculum sets the stage for exceptional programming. Teacher leaders can conduct action research aimed at improving writing instruction in the context of their own classrooms. A traditional "read more pages and books program" will not cut it.

REDUCTION IN COOPERATIVE EDUCATION AND OTHER AUTHENTIC EXPERIENCES FOR STUDENTS TO WRITE ABOUT

To prepare young writers for college and everyday life, teachers need to collaborate using expert ideas to craft school-wide strategies that fuel the development of writing talent. Much more can be done to help students improve and finely craft their writing. To prepare young writers for college and a more interconnected global life, educators need to agree that "everyone has the capacity to write, writing can be taught, and teachers can help students become better writers."[2] By restructuring schools in ways that encourage authentic, meaningful writing, educators can contribute to an engaging school-wide culture, shrinking the prolific boredom that shapes many schools today.

Sheninger suggests that "schooling and education are more in line with what adults want in the classroom, school and district as opposed to what's best for students."[3] It may be possible to do both, but all stakeholders need to embrace change. Later, in his book *Uncommon Learning*, he adds:

> Our education system has become so efficient in sustaining a century-old model because it is easy and safe. The resulting conformity has resulted in a sterilization of learning among our students as they see so little value in the cookie-cutter learning exercises they are forced to go through each day. The bottom line is that they are bored.[4]

According to Kennedy: "Good writing occurs because a writer passionately desires to say something."[5] How we teach writing, which processes we implement, how much writing we ask students to craft on their own and with others, and how authentic the audience is for a piece of written work are ways educators can adapt and create more engagement to support the writing lives of students. Each challenge can be an opportunity for growth.

Teachers often find themselves at the crossroads of divergent educational norms. A curriculum that ensures that students learn to write well, in a variety of ways, appears to be at the heart of ongoing study and commercial resource development. When community members, particularly teachers, and to some extent students, take an active role in planning the overall school curriculum for writing instruction, this can lead to an enriched writing culture.

Participants who invest in making meaning of curriculum engage in thinking and construction beyond the walls of a classroom. Any process that requires the review of stages of writing transformation can improve students' capacities for not just writing but thinking.

Supervisors at the graduate level must review dozens of drafts to support novice researchers as they write and prepare their final dissertations. The supervisor and the graduate student are both keenly aware that precision does not come easily. It requires crafting, recrafting, and rephrasing much of the original text.

Writing is rewriting; drafting is drafting. Why should students have to wait until graduate school to gain this kind of insight, feedback, and support? Transforming writing must begin at the early stages. No longer should language arts teachers rely on the single strategy of immersing writers through reading, when what they are reading written by real-world writers, for the most part, went through rigorous editorial review.

Educators need to deliberately teach, assess, and honor all parts of the writing process in all subject areas. No question, it is much easier for a teacher to only grade the finished product. However, the staff at more informed schools recognize that having a common writing process that transcends language arts classes to all classes is important. Ideally, the writing process would be synthesized with an inquiry approach, thus supporting a deliberate focus on critical and creative thinking with writing as a central skill in the overall goal of generating future innovators.

Coaches and academic leaders are central to implementing the changes needed for quality writing experiences in schools and teacher education programs at the college and university level. Preservice ELA programs for new teachers should be where research meets practice; that is, novice teachers working with expert teachers. It can be where teacher researchers have an opportunity to implement new practices during their practicums and extend the professional learning to their associate teachers' classrooms.

Mitton-Kükner and Orr's three-year study of literacy practices of preservice teachers discovered that they were "aware of the importance of integrating literacy into content-area teaching, but believe it takes too much time."[6] They also found that six factors relating to time influenced their lessons considerably: "scheduling, cooperating teacher expectations, loss of teaching days, curriculum, student responses to instruction, use of classroom time."[7] Such evidence also reveals what the associate teacher experiences in the school context. The way many schools are structured does not permit deep learning.

Rick Wormeli, author of *Fair Isn't Always Equal*, sums up the need to let challenges become the goals for improving education.

> So many times in schools, we take the politically expedient path instead of the mature climb. The path of least resistance wins, and students can't help but be diminished in our race towards complacency. It's ossifying. Climbing always reveals more, however, it strengthens our convictions and gets oxygen to the brain. From such perspectives, we can see the farthest and choose the most efficient course. With such provisioning, classroom instruction is revitalized, students learn well.[8]

By overcoming challenges to support a school culture of writers, it is possible to revitalize the system one student, one teacher, and one district at a time.

NOTES

1. Shope, R. E., III. (2006). Teaching science for conceptual change: Toward a proposed taxonomy of diagnostic teaching strategies to gauge students' personal science conceptions. University of Southern California ProQuest Dissertations Publishing, 165.

2. Writing Group of NCTE. (November 9, 2017). Everyone has the capacity to write. https://ncte.org/blog/2017/11/everyone-capacity-write-2/.

3. Sheninger, E. C. (2016). *Uncommon learning: Creating schools that work for kids.* Thousand Oaks, CA: Corwin, 19.

4. Sheninger (2016), 189.

5. Kennedy, X. J. (November 1984). Presentation at the National Council of Teachers of English annual conference, Detroit.

6. Mitton-Kükner, J., & Murray Orr, A. (2018). A multi-year study of preservice teachers' literacy practices in the content areas: Time epistemologies and indicators of stasis and growth. *Pedagogies: An International Journal, 13*, 19–35.

7. Mitton-Kükner & Murray Orr (2018).

8. Wormeli, R. (2021). How much does a great school cost? In Barbara A. Smith, *School economies and school values* (Lanham, MD: Rowman & Littlefield), 132.

CONCLUSION

From Student to Writer

The intent of this book was not to make universal claims about what should be the template for school-wide writing. Rather, the writers wanted educators to resist the ease of teaching writing in a rut that can repeat disengaging student experiences. The following assumptions can fuel interesting debate and conversation.

- KISS. Keep it simple, stupid.
- The more students write, the better they will get.
- Reflecting on writing mistakes is not necessary.
- A curriculum map means that the curriculum is aligned.
- Lowering scores for lateness will help improve writing.
- All writing needs to be in sentence or paragraph form.
- Teachers cannot evaluate point form work. (It must be in prose.)
- Students should learn to read and write multiple genres at the same time.
- Students do not need to make changes to most sentences in the editing phase.
- The use of a thesaurus and dictionary on the computer are good enough for revisions.
- Teachers and students do not need to integrate parts of speech with writing.

- Understanding how to identify and change clauses cannot improve writing.
- Students can craft 5 to 10 quality pieces of writing in a term.
- Teachers (or parents) should not edit student writing; students must always edit on their own.
- Students should be able to write a polished piece of work during a fixed time frame for an exam.
- Students do not like reading their writing aloud so teachers should not ask them to read their work aloud.
- Writing answers to questions at the end of chapters in a novel study is a good way to improve writing skills.
- Even if students cannot write one paragraph well, they should still learn to write multiple paragraphs and essays.
- Teachers already look over student outlines and drafts. Students should not need to hand them in with the assignment.

Even if some of the aforementioned assumptions were true, many professors are concerned about the quality of writers arriving on college campuses. It makes sense that if writing were mastered in the first 12 years of education, colleges would not need to provide the remedial programming that is so widespread today.

The tipping point for teachers of writing can happen when they change the teaching and learning conditions in place or adjust them to enhance innovative thinking and actions. The purpose-based (PB) writing process represents one example of how a new approach can make room for more authentic, collaborative, coordinated, and empowered writing experiences for all students. The new assessment structures shared throughout this book are aligned with the PB writing process so they can support students as guides and tools for self-reflection.

How to unravel the mysteries of writing will continue to be a source of debate. It is difficult to motivate young people to write when they are unsure of what the reader expects. It is impossible to anticipate every need of every reader, but it is possible to learn how to remove distractions in writing. Creative ideas may be lost when a reader trips over careless mistakes that a novice writer makes. By reviewing writing from students in PK through college and insisting that they make editorial changes that extend far beyond spell check, students and teachers can understand the following:

- Everyone can improve a piece of writing.
- Writing is large before it is small.
- Writing fewer pieces well is much better than writing many draft pieces.

WHY NOT LET WRITING TAKE THE LEAD?

It is rare for students to experience a progressive PK through 12 writing program. A purpose-based (PB) model is meant to encourage teachers and students to work with a common language of instruction. What separates this approach from others is that it stresses fewer writing tasks with rigorous layers of examination. It builds on the notion that real writers rarely have more than one project at a time, and they can spend months at a time reworking and revising their work.

Most English teachers recognize the value of editing and are concerned that many students do not engage in the process beyond spell check, but how much time and deliberate attention to revision can they dedicate to writing activities in school?

Write to Be Read was written to show how a single writing project can be sustained for several months or a term so that students can master writing in a task that emulates habits of expert writers. Unless someone is writing to meet a newspaper deadline, many writers in the real world do not write something new every day, every week, or every month.

Apprenticing students in the world of writing goes against the grain of writing something new every day. This is where the ideas in this book deviate from the present path, which relies on the assumption that more writing leads to developing strong writers. By having fewer writing assignments, students have time to invest in outlining, drafting, and editing their work, not simply "getting it over with."

In Lidvall's thesis, she claims that "traditional 8 1/2 x 11-inch pages bound together are not the way that real books are formatted, and bound together pages may prove to be inadequate."[1] Some schools are equipped with spiral binding machines that teachers use to give a sense of authenticity to published works. Lidvall hints at the idea that professional writers do not aspire to present their work in this way; rather they publish online, or when the printed page is used, she recommends emulating the glue-bound book. Perhaps it is time to move the present system of writing from spiral binding to more sustainable binding, writing that lasts and is worthy of being read by others.

School should not exist as a side dish to life. It can be a feast for young learners if we can find a way to make it more appealing. Not all students enjoy writing. It can be argued that students who read more and receive higher grades are more engaged in writing. Those who have earned success, who find the current system worked for them, might resist letting more folks into the club of increased understanding. But all students should master writing. The current curriculum to teach writing is only working for some students.

Teacher education programs can lead or follow when it comes to supporting innovative programs in writing or any area of study in their preparation curricula. Ideally, departments of education at the state, province, or national levels are committed to school improvement that is grounded in peer-reviewed educational research. When colleges and universities and governmental agencies recognize that improvement can only happen with change, and that change is supported by new directions in education, then the system will be ready and committed to adapting and creating new opportunities for teaching and learning.

In Bomer et al.'s analysis of 82 peer-reviewed studies that focused on preservice teacher preparation for teaching writing, they argued for "transparency of competing discourses that surround writing and writing pedagogy within teacher education." They recommended "emphasizing reflection on writing experiences, examining student work, bringing an asset-based view of student writers, and building communities of writers in preservice teacher programs."[2] There is little point, however, in developing reflective and innovative practitioners if the curriculum emphasizes adopting a specific writing process. Both new and seasoned teachers need to be encouraged to design curriculum based on their teaching and learning experiences.

Many solid options exist for teaching writing, but they lose their potency when they must be applied rigidly in the classroom. If a book such as *Write to Be Read* can find a broader audience, hopefully less predictable messages about education will find their way to the bookshelves. Future educators can have more choices to create a system beyond memorizing the past. Writing can be a constructive, innovative process, especially when the purpose is authentic. That authenticity is seen and felt not only by students but also by teachers. It has been said that differentiation involves taking risks. In the example in chapter 17, Hope was able to undertake such a gently guided instructional path because she was trusted, seen, and heard by Ghazala Nomani and Carol Cochi of the BCTA Adult Education Center. The teacher's impact and approach are intertwined with student engagement and learning.

At the end of the day, teachers can ask themselves, "Did I inspire my students to do better?" Even young writers in a class exhibit distinct strengths; however, they can miss key features that could enhance their writing. The teacher can help students see the worth of their writing and ways to improve their work. Further, how could writing and critical thinking be enhanced before a student arrives in college? What gaps could be addressed deliberately before a student is immersed in undergraduate experiences in preparation for the world of work?

After decades of piloting the ideas shared in this resource, it became clear that students need deliberate ways to enhance their writing with the tools and know-how to find their own mistakes. Without an organized PK through college writing curriculum, careless writing practices will continue to undermine students' capacity and distract the reader from seeing the creativity within. Students should not have to reach college before they realize that they are writing deficient.

Comparing students and schools using a slice of data may be the work of academic leaders who have taken a shortcut around peer-reviewed research. Using data to rank students and schools is a narrow, limited practice. Peer-reviewed journals are not what the public read. To promote a culture where more parents and taxpayers understand informed practice, we need scaffolded writing so parents can be more aware of educational choices and options.

Using a PB writing process should reduce the need for the editorial support currently provided while revealing a systematic option for students to enhance their own writing. Even avid readers can improve their writing, especially when using a transparent lens to assess their work. College professors should not have to read poorly crafted papers, nor should universities have to mandate remedial writing courses.

An education that ranks highly what is memorized about the past will not serve students as well as an institution focused on building generations of critical, creative thinkers—students with the capacity to handle the challenges that lie ahead. Teachers can identify specific patterns that demonstrate how writing can play a role in supporting the development of thinking cultures, within both staff and students, and in the broader school community.

Ideally, if more engaging and meaningful opportunities are commonplace in their school experiences, students and staff should come to see themselves as writers with ideas worthy of being read by others.

* * *

Until the lion learns how to write, every story will glorify the hunter.

—African proverb

In many ways teachers are hunters, often telling the story of students through their voices. Many of the original ideas for teaching writing in *Write to Be Read* emerged from looking for fresh ways to gain more traction for the goal of improving more student writers. The current approaches to teaching writing tend to keep the bell curve in place, with an "exceptional" few at the top, a few at the bottom giving up, and a large chunk in the middle churning out substandard work, making it difficult for young voices to respond in meaningful ways. Our students can learn to hunt and be inspired as writers. They can then tell their stories of glory, or not, about their school lives.

NOTES

1. Lidvall, C. D. (Spring 2008). *Get real: Instructional implications for authentic writing activities*. PhD dissertation, Vanderbilt University, Nashville, Tennessee.
2. Bomer, R., Land, C. L., Rubin, J. C., & Van Dike, L. M. (2019). Constructs of teaching writing in research about literacy teacher education. *Journal of Literacy Research, 51*, 196–213.

REFERENCES

681 cliches to avoid in your creative writing. Be a Better Writer. https://www.be-a-better-writer.com/cliches.html.

A7 Learning. Plural S and possessive S. YouTube, November 3, 2020. https://www.youtube.com/watch?v=KFdTz6GlUeg.

Abrams, M. H. A glossary of literary terms, seventh edition. WordPress. https://mthoyibi.files.wordpress.com/2011/05/a-glossary-of-literary-terms-7th-ed_m-h-abrams-1999.pdf.

Abrams, M. H. On reading poems aloud. YouTube, April 16, 2009. https://www.youtube.com/watch?v=d1Ofwljw4Y0.

Abrams, M. H., & Harpham, G. G. (1999). A glossary of literary terms, eleventh edition. Cornell University. https://static.s123-cdn.com/uploads/3433317/normal_606f55ccdaf2b.pdf.

Aguilar, E. Motivating students: Writing for an audience. Edutopia, February 18, 2011. http://www.edutopia.org/blog/motivating-student-writers-audience-elena-aguilar.

Anderson, L. W., & Krathwohl, D. R. (2001). *A taxonomy for learning, teaching, and assessing: A revision of Bloom's taxonomy of educational objectives.* New York: Longman.

Anderson, M., & Jiang, J. (May 2018). Teens, social media, and technology 2018. Pew Research Center, May 31, 2018. https://www.pewresearch.org/internet/2018/05/31/teens-social-media-technology-2018/.

Atwell, N. (2015). *In the middle: A lifetime of learning about writing, reading, and adolescents.* Portsmouth, NH: Heinemann.

Bakhtin, M. (1986). The problem of speech genres. In *Speech genres and other late essays* (pp. 60–102). Austin: University of Texas Press.

Barnes, D. (1976). *From communication to curriculum.* Thousand Oaks, CA: Sage.

Barnes, D. (2008). *Exploratory talk for learning.* Thousand Oaks, CA: Sage.

Bauer, M. Onomatopoeia. YouTube, March 26, 2012. https://www.youtube.com/watch?v=f1b5kCvVBo8.

Beach, J. D. (2017). *Bridging old and new communication modes: A theory to transform literacy education practice*. New York: St. John's University Press.

Behizadeh, N. (January 2014). Adolescent perspectives on authentic writing instruction. *Journal of Language and Literacy Education, 10*(1), 27–44.

Behizadeh, N. (2018). Teaching writing: What actually is authentic and meaningful writing? Best Delegate. https://bestdelegate.com/model-un-made-easy-how-to-write-a-resolution/.

Bippert, K. (2017). Fan fiction to support struggling writers. In J. Pilgrim (Ed.), *Tale yearbook*. https://files.eric.ed.gov/fulltext/EJ1305137.pdf.

Blecher-Sass, H. S., & Moffitt, M. (2010). *See it, be it, write it*. Minneapolis, MN: Free Spirit Publishers.

Bloom, B. S. (1956). *Taxonomy of educational objective handbook: The cognitive domain*. New York: David McKay.

Bomer, R., Land, C. L., Rubin, J. C., & Van Dike, L. M. (2019). Constructs of teaching writing in research about literacy teacher education. *Journal of Literacy Research, 51*, 196–213.

Booth, D. (2008). *It's critical: Classroom strategies for deepening and extending comprehension*. Portsmouth, NH: Heinemann.

Booth, D. (2011). *Caught in the middle: Reading and writing in the transition years*. Portsmouth, NH: Heinemann.

Booth, D. (2014). *Exploding the reading*. Portsmouth, NH: Stenhouse.

Booth, D., & Thornley-Hall, C. (1991). *Classroom talk*. Portsmouth, NH: Heinemann.

Bradbury, R. (1951). *Fahrenheit 451*. New York: Simon & Schuster.

Britton, J. N. (1970). *Language and learning*. Coral Gables: University of Miami Press.

Britton, J. N. (1993). *Language and learning*. Portsmouth, NH: Heinemann.

Bruner, J. (1960). *The process of education*. Cambridge, MA: Harvard University Press.

Bryce, E. How to use a semicolon. YouTube, July 6, 2015. https://www.youtube.com/watch?v=th-zyfvwDdI.

BYU MCOM. FANBOYS: Coordinating conjunctions. YouTube, May 4, 2015. https://www.youtube.com/watch?v=-catJZm_2TI.

Calkins, L. (1986). *The art of teaching writing*. Portsmouth, NH: Heinemann.

Calonia, J. How to fix and prevent run-on sentences. Grammarly. https://www.grammarly.com/blog/run-on-sentence-basics/.

Carroll, L. (1865). *Alice in wonderland*. New York: Macmillan.

Christie, C. P. The sky is busy. In Annie Ross, Brandon Bob, Eve Chuang, Steve Davis, and Robert Pictou, *Tea and Bannock stories: First nations community of poetic voices* (p. 35). Social Sciences and Humanities Council of Canada. https://www.sfu.ca/lovemotherearth/02poetry/tea_and_bannock.pdf.

Chungdahm Learning. What is allusion? YouTube, March 31, 2015. https://www.youtube.com/watch?v=vUMOmBxC3Cg.

Common core state standards (ELA literacy grade 5). California Department of Education. http://www.corestandards.org/ELA-Literacy/W/5/.

Common core state standards (ELA literacy grade 11/12). California Department of Education. http://www.corestandards.org/ELA-Literacy/WHST/11-12/.

Connolly, S., & Burn, A. (2019). The Story Engine: Offering an online platform for making "unofficial" creative writing work. *Literacy, 53*, 30–38.

Constantine, C. Symbolism in film. YouTube, May 10, 2010. https://www.youtube.com/watch?v=WhijmmePlU8.

Costa, A., & Kallick, B. (2000). *Habits of mind*. Alexandria, VA: Association for Supervision and Curriculum Development.

Crowell, S. (May 31, 2001). Off the testing bandwagon. *New York Times*. https://www.nytimes.com/2001/05/31/technology/l-off-the-testing-bandwagon-574988.html.

Dagostino, L., & Casatelli, C. (2017). Content creation for a new generation: A guide for digital writing. *NERA Journal, 52*(1), 93–102.

Deguzman, K. (June 20, 2021). What is a euphemism? Definition examples for all writers. Studio Binder. https://www.studiobinder.com/blog/what-is-a-euphemism-definition/.

Dewey, J. (1915/2015). *The school and society and the child and the curriculum.* Chicago: University of Chicago Press.

Dickens, C. (1859). *A tale of two cities.* New York: Cosmopolitan Book Corp.

Disney, W., in D. Heaton. (August 30, 2021). https://tomorrowsociety.com/disneyland-will-never-completed/.

Disney. "Colors of the Wind" in *Pocahontas*. https://youtu.be/O9MvdMqKvpUt.

Doctors are prescribing a daily dose of the outdoors. (April 21, 2017). CBS News Chicago. https://www.cbsnews.com/chicago/news/doctors-prescription-outdoors-health/.

Dombey/UKLA. (2013). *Teaching writing: What the evidence says UKLA argues for an evidence-informed approach to teaching and testing young children's writing.* London: UKLA.

DuFour, R. (2004). What is a "professional learning community"? *Educational Leadership, 61*, 6–11.

Duke, N. K., & Hall, L. A. (2006/2007). Authentic literacy activities for developing comprehension and writing. *Reading Teacher, 60*(4), 344–355.

Dunning, S., & Stafford, W. (1992). *Getting the knack: 20 poetry writing exercises.* Urbana, IL: National Council of Teachers of English.

Dutro, E., & Haberl, E. (2018). Blurring material and rhetorical walls: Children writing the border/lands in a second-grade classroom. *Journal of Literacy Research, 50*, 167–189.

Easy Teaching. Metaphor and similes. https://www.youtube.com/watch?v=xH5EgQS8ZIE.

Education Endowment Fund (EFF). (2014). *Using self-regulation to improve writing.* London.

EF. https://www.ef.com/wwen/blog/language/20-english-idioms-that-everyone-should-know/.

Eggers, D. (2008). Dave Eggers: 2008 TED prize wish: Once upon a school. https://www.youtube.com/watch?v=FaSF1gPBKrA&t=27s.

Eisner, E. (1985). *Beyond creating: The place for art in America's schools*. Los Angeles: Getty Center for Education in the Arts, 69.

ELA Through Film. Learn symbolism using movies and TV. https://www.youtube.com/watch?v=Xc7Qt5sGPeg.

Eliot, T. S. (1910). *The love song of J. Alfred Prufrock*. Bartleby. http://www.bartleby.com/198/1.html.

Ellis, M. (August 17, 2021). 28 common literacy devices to know. https://www.grammarly.com/blog/literary-devices/.

Emig, J. (1971). *The composing processes of twelfth graders: A reassessment*. Urbana IL: National Council of Teachers of English.

English Club. https://www.englishclub.com/esl-games/grammar/adjectives.htm.

English Club. Quotation marks. https://www.englishclub.com/writing/punctuation-quotation-marks.htm.

English in General. Learn idioms with TV series. https://www.youtube.com/watch?v=KJS77wXttpI.

English Language Smart Words. https://www.smart-words.org/linking-words/transition-words.html.

FDR Library. Eleanor Roosevelt Human Rights Speech. https://www.youtube.com/watch?v=9yzakVOdh6k.

Fifteen types of business letters and the purpose of each. Indeed. https://www.indeed.com/career-advice/career-development/types-of-business-letters.

First News Education. https://schools.firstnews.co.uk/blog/journalistic-writing/how-to-start-a-school-newspaper/.

Fischetti, J. (September 19, 2022). We can predict final school marks in year 11. *The Conversation*. https://theconversation.com/we-can-predict-final-school-marks-in-year-11-its-time-to-replace-stressful-exams-with-more-meaningful-education-190071.

Flores, T. (2018). Breaking silence and amplifying voices: Youths writing and performing their worlds. *Journal of Adolescent & Adult Literacy*, 61, 653–661. https://ila.onlinelibrary.wiley.com/doi/abs/10.1002/jaal.733.

Forest School Teacher Institute (FSTI). forestteacher.org.

Foreshadowing Lesson. https://www.youtube.com/watch?v=MuA9RUfjf5c.

Fratt, L. (2002). Less is more: Trimming the overstuffed curriculum. http://www.project2061.org/publications/articles/articles/da.htm?txtRef=https%3A%2F%2Fwww.google.com&txtURIOld=%2Fresearch%2Farticles%2Fda.htm.

Gadd, M. (2014). *What is critical in the effective teaching of writing? A study of the classroom practice of some year 5–8 teachers in the New Zealand context*. Unpublished doctoral thesis, Auckland: University of Auckland.

Gardner, H. (1997). http://www.edutopia.org/multiple-intelligences-howard-gardner-video#graph5.

Gardner, P., & Kuzich, S. (2017). Green writing: The influence of natural spaces on primary students' poetic writing in the UK and Australia. *Cambridge Journal of Education, 48*, 427–443. https://www.tandfonline.com/doi/abs/10.1080/0305764X.2017.

Gere, A. R., Limlamai, N., Wilson, E., MacDougall Saylor, K., & Pugh, R. (2019). Writing and conceptual learning in science: An analysis of assignments. *Written Communication, 36*, 99–135.

Gilbert, J., & Graham, S. (2010). Teaching writing to elementary students in grades 4–6: A national survey. *Elementary School Journal, 110*, 494–518.

Gladwell, M. (2010). *What the dog saw and other adventures*. New York: Little, Brown.

Goodreads. https://help.goodreads.com/s/article/How-do-I-write-a-book-review-on-Goodreads-1553870933519.

Goouch, K., Cremin, T., & Lambirth, A. (2009). *Writing is primary: Final research report*. London: Esmee Fairbairn Foundation.

Graham, S. (2008). *Effective writing instruction for all students. Renaissance learning.* Nashville, TN: Vanderbilt University.

Graham, S., Gillespie, A., & McKeown, D. (June 29, 2012). Writing, importance, development, instruction. *Reading and Writing, 26*, 1–15.

Graham, S., McKeown, D., Kiuhara, S., & Harris, K. H. (2012). A meta-analysis of writing instruction for students in the elementary grades. *Journal of Educational Psychology, 104*(4), 879–896, esp. 891.

Graham, S., & Perin, D. (2007). *Writing next: Effective strategies to improve writing of adolescents in middle and high schools*. New York: Carnegie Corporation of New York.

Grammaropolis. Adverb song. https://www.youtube.com/watch?v=kKw1j7sZni0.

Graves, D. H. (1994). *A fresh look at writing.* Portsmouth, NH: Heinemann.

Graves, D. H., & Kittle, P. (2005). *Inside writing: How to teach the details of craft.* Portsmouth, NH: Heinemann.

Green Learning Tools. How to use a semicolon. https://www.youtube.com/watch?v=d-3nnht-b40.

Greenblatt, S., & Abrams, M. H. (2006). *The Norton anthology of English literature* (eighth edition). New York: Norton.

Gunner, J. Run-on sentences: What they are and how to fix them. *Your Dictionary*. https://grammar.yourdictionary.com/sentences/run-on-sentences.html.

Gusteau. *Ratatouille* (movie).

Hasson, U. (2016). This is your brain on communication. Ted Talk. https://www.ted.com/talks/uri_hasson_this_is_your_brain_on_communication?language=en.

Hillocks, G. (2010). Teaching argument for critical thinking and writing: An introduction. *English Journal, 99*(6), 24–32.

Hilroy (notebook). https://www.123ink.ca/p-366550-740-11174-hilroy-multi-size-exercise-notebook-8-38-x-10-787-mm-ruling-40-pages-assorted-colours.

Howcast. How to use quotation marks. https://wlww.youtube.com/watch?v=V7LNkNcDMEY.

Huber, Raymond. Bee myths & folktales. https://www.raymondhuber.co.nz/honey-bees-ebook-life-cycle-honey-stings-crisis-myths/bee-mythology/.

Hunter, D. (March 24, 2015). A perfect book for hooking kids on rocks. *Scientific American*. https://blogs.scientificamerican.com/rosetta-stones/a-perfect-book-for-hooking-kids-on-rocks/.

Jackel, M. (June 5, 2008). Wisdom of the multi-ages: Students learn by teaching. Edutopia. https://www.edutopia.org/multiage-classroom-looping-peer-mentoring.

James, T. (August 8, 2019). Doctors in Oregon are writing prescriptions to get outside. *That Oregon Life*. https://thatoregonlife.com/2019/08/doctors-in-oregon-are-writing-prescriptions-to-get-outside/.

Kelly, G. A. (1955). *The psychology of personal constructs. Vol. 1, A theory of personality. Vol. 2, Clinical diagnosis and psychotherapy.* New York: Norton.

Kennedy, X. J. (November 1984). Presentation at the National Council of Teachers of English annual conference, Detroit.

Kewin, S. Writing prompts 101. *Daily Writing Tips*. http://www.dailywritingtips.com/writing-prompts-101.

Khan, S. https://www.khanacademy.org/humanities/grammar/parts-of-speech-the-preposition-and-the-conjunction/types-of-prepositions-and-phrases/v/prepositional-phrases.

Kiger Lee, B., Enciso, P., & Austin Theatre Alliance. (2017). The big glamorous monster (or Lady Gaga's adventures at sea): Improving student writing through dramatic approaches in schools. *Journal of Literacy Research, 49*, 157–180.

Kittelstad, K. 7 awesome adjective games. https://grammar.yourdictionary.com/parts-of-speech/adjectives/adjective-games.html.

Kohn, A. (2006). *The homework myth: Why our kids get too much of a bad thing*. Philadelphia: Da Capo Lifelong Books. https://www.alfiekohn.org/homework-myth.

Kohn, A. (January/February 2007). Rethinking homework. https://www.alfiekohn.org/article/rethinking-homework/.

LaCroix, D. How to write a speech opening: Example. https://www.youtube.com/watch?v=XAaSZ64P8pA.

Lain, S. (2017). Poetry is not out of the box. *NERA Journal, 52*(1).

Lammers, J. C. (2016). The Hangout was serious business: Leveraging participation in an online space to design Sims fanfiction. *Research in the Teaching of English, 50*(3), 309–332. http://www.ncte.org/journals/rte.

Lane, B. (2003). *Reviser's toolbox*. New York: Discovery Writing Press.

Langer, J. A. *Envisioning literature: Literary understanding and literature instruction*. New York: Teachers College Press.

Langer, J. A., & Applebee, A. N. (1987). *How writing shapes thinking: A study of teaching and learning*. Urbana, IL: National Council of Teachers of English.

Lawrence, D. H. https://www.poetryfoundation.org/poems/148471/snake-5bec57d7bfa17.

Learn English. How to start a sentence in English with an adverb. https://www.youtube.com/watch?v=Io0dCPwFPTo.

Lemke, J. L. (March 2010). Lessons from Whyville: A hermeneutics for our mixed reality. In *Games and Culture*. Thousand Oaks, CA: Sage.

Lemke, J. L. (March 31, 2010). After schools what comes next? Jay Lemke Online. http://www.jaylemke.com/imported-20110501025959/tag/school-reform.

Lidvall, C. D. (Spring 2008). Get real: Instructional implications for authentic writing activities capstone experience. Nashville, TN: Vanderbilt University's Peabody College of Education. https://ir.vanderbilt.edu/bitstream/handle/1803/789/CarlyLidvallCapstone.pdf?sequence=1&isAllowed=y.

Lincoln Learning Solutions. Analogies. https://www.youtube.com/watch?v=ZrBBylNNf6A.

Lisa's Study Guide. Euphemism. https://www.youtube.com/watch?v=6LFg_5zs7CY&t=15s.

Literary Terms. https://literaryterms.net/when-and-how-to-write-a-paradox/.

Lowry, L. (1993). *The giver*. New York: Houghton Mifflin Harcourt.

Magnifico, A. M., Woodard, R., & McCarthey, S. (2019). Teachers as co-authors of student writing: How teachers' initiating texts influence response and revision in an online space. *Computers and Composition, 52*, 107–131.

Make My Newspaper. https://makemynewspaper.com/how-to-start-a-school-newspaper/.
Mansky, J. (November 22, 2010). Abrams explains the neglected "fourth dimension" of a poem: "Oral activity" in its reading. *Cornell Chronicle.*
Marciano, J. E., & Warren, C. A. (2019). Writing toward change across youth participatory action research projects. *Journal of Adolescent & Adult Literacy, 62*, 485–494.
Mason, C. Simply Charlotte Mason. https://simplycharlottemason.com/blog/nature-study-in-a-nutshell/.
Master Class. (September 7, 2021). 22 essential literary devices and how to use them in your writing. https://www.masterclass.com/articles/22-essential-literary-devices.
Master Class. What is analogy? https://www.masterclass.com/articles/what-is-analogy#how-do-you-write-a-good-analogy.
Master Class. Writing 101: What is a cliché? https://www.masterclass.com/articles/writing-101-what-is-a-cliche-learn-when-to-use-cliches-in-writing-and-20-common-cliches-all-writers-should-avoid#quiz-0.
Maus. https://en.wikipedia.org/wiki/Maus.
McAdie, P., & Leithwood, K. (2005). Less is more: Teaching for deep understanding. *Voice: Elementary Teachers Federation of Ontario (ETFO), 7*(2), 17–20.
McClure, L. When to use apostrophes. https://www.youtube.com/watch?v=My6oGvkHnfY.
MC Grammar. The adverb song. https://www.youtube.com/watch?v=cfenLGAYDeg.
MC Grammar. The FANBOYS song. https://www.youtube.com/watch?v=8EJ8aSzuJnk.
McQuitty, V. (2012). Emerging possibilities: A complex account of learning to teach writing. *Research in the Teaching of English, 46*, 358–389.
Melissa. Grammar songs. https://www.youtube.com/watch?v=jUT_WSavAC8.
Miacademy Learning Channel. Quotation marks: Language skills for kids. https://www.youtube.com/watch?v=rFIIqPolFXo.
Mindweister. https://www.mindmeister.com/?utm_source=google&utm_medium=cpc&utm_campaign=US_en_Brand_brand&utm_content=homepage&gclid=Cj0KCQiAgribBhDkARIsAASA5buMmz68BYjARRKb3DWteQ6SHAh_vKVykY6A0gwp0Xw7JxdnEhgPJyAaAmWREALw_wcB.
Mister Messenger. How to use examples, analogies, similes and metaphors when writing essays. https://www.youtube.com/watch?v=Jo11LnWr6AA.
Mitton-Kükner, J., & Murray Orr, A. (2018). A multi-year study of pre-service teachers' literacy practices in the content areas: Time epistemologies and indicators of stasis and growth. *Pedagogies: An International Journal, 13*, 19–35.
Model United Nations. https://bestdelegate.com/model-un-made-easy-how-to-write-a-resolution/.
Muniz, H. (December 3, 2019). https://blog.prepscholar.com/allusion-examples.
Munoz, P. (December 15, 2022). WikiHow. https://www.wikihow.com/Evaluate-a-Speech.
Mythical Factory. The Curupira. YouTube, July 15, 2018. https://www.youtube.com/watch?v=ahSm_Bk2HQE.
NAAEE. Press release: Educators across the nation are invited to go outside for 5/NAAEE. https://naaee.org/news/newsroom/press-release-educators-across-nation#:~:text=The%20NAAEE%20Affiliate%20Network%20invites%20educators%20of%20all,5%20minutes%20a%20day%20outside%20with%20their%20students.

Nash, K. Adverb clauses. English grammar 101. https://www.englishgrammar101.com/module-10/clauses/lesson-4/adverb-clauses.

National Council of Teachers of English (NCTE) Writing Group. (November 9, 2017). Everyone has the capacity to write. https://ncte.org/blog/2017/11/everyone-capacity-write-2/.

National Council of Teachers of English (NCTE). Found and headline poems. https://cdn.ncte.org/nctefiles/resources/books/sample/18488chap1.pdf.

National Reading and Writing Project (NRWP). https://readingandwritingproject.org.

Naylor, S., & Keogh, B. (1999). Constructivism in classroom: Theory into practice. *Journal of Science Teacher Education, 10*(2), 93–106.

Nordquist, R. ThoughtCo. https://www.thoughtco.com/euphemism-words-term-1690680.

O'Brien, S., & Rusciano, A. Writing a business letter: A step-by-step formatting guide. WikiHow. https://www.wikihow.com/Write-a-Business-Letter.

Oglesby, A. (August 4, 2021). How to start a school newspaper. WikiHow. https://www.wikihow.com/Start-a-School-Newspaper.

Patron, M. Crefeld School in Philadelphia. https://www.binghamsplace.com/less-is-more.html.

Paulick, J. H., Myers, J., Quinn, A., Couch, L., & Dunkerly-Bean, J. (Winter/Spring 2019). Examining practice: Examining elementary writing methods instruction. *Teaching/Writing: The Journal of Writing Teacher Education, 6*(1), 55–75.

Peha, S. (1995–2003). Assessing writers assessing writing. https://www.ttms.org/PDFs/09%20Writing%20Assessment%20v001%20(Full).pdf.

Piaget, J. (1952). *The origins of intelligence in children.* New York: International Universities Press.

Pixar. *Finding Nemo.* https://en.wikipedia.org/wiki/Finding_Nemo.

Purcell-Gates, V., Duke, N. K., & Martineau, J. A. (2007). Learning to read and write genre-specific text: Roles of authentic experience and explicit teaching. *Reading Research Quarterly, 42*(1), 8–45. https://doi.org/10.1598/RRQ.42.1.1.

Purdue University. Visual patterning. Purdue OWL®—Purdue University. https://owl.purdue.edu/owl/subject_specific_writing/creative_writing/pattern_and_variation_visual/index.html.

Rare Facts. I have a dream speech. https://www.youtube.com/watch?v=vP4iY1TtS3s.

Read, Write and Think. Poetry from prose. https://www.readwritethink.org/classroom-resources/lesson-plans/poetry-prose.

Renstrom, J. TedX Talks. Science fiction: Teaching students how to save the world. https://www.youtube.com/watch?v=9Ed8OeZcOBI.

Rimes, B. (February 21, 2022). Where are the K–12 student-run radio stations? *Tech Savvy Educator.* https://www.techsavvyed.net/archives/4354.

Ritchhart, R., & Perkins, D. N. (2005). Learning to think: The challenges of teaching thinking. In K. J. Holyoak & R. G. Morrison (Eds.), *The Cambridge handbook of thinking and reasoning* (pp. 775–802). Cambridge: Cambridge University Press.

Roberts, E. (March 9, 2022). LinkedIn contribution.

Rosenshine, B. (2012). Principles of instruction: Research-based strategies that all teachers should know. *American Educator, 36*(1).

Rowe, L. W. (2019). Constructing language ideologies in a multilingual, second-grade classroom: A case study of two emergent bilingual students' language-use during ebook composing. *Linguistics and Education, 52*, 1–12.

Rubin, R., Abrego, M. H., & Sutterby, J. A. (2015). What are the best strategies for streamlining your curriculum? Teach Thought. http://www.teachthought.com/uncategorized/less-is-more-4-strategies-to-streamline-your-curriculum/.

Science of People. How to start a speech: The best (and worst) speech openers. https://www.youtube.com/watch?v=7tzentBmmUc.

Selected Student Writings from Al Mizhar School in Dubai, United Arab Emirates. (November 4, 2022).

Dr. Seuss. *The Lorax*. (1971). https://en.wikipedia.org/wiki/The_Lorax.

Shaw, C. G. (1947). *It looked like spilt milk*. New York: HarperCollins.

Sheninger, E. C. (2016). *Uncommon learning: Creating schools that work for kids*. Thousand Oaks, CA: Corwin.

Shepard, L. S. (2008). A brief history of accountability testing, 1965–2007. In K. E. Ryan & L. S. Shepard (Eds.), *The future of test-based educational accountability* (pp. 25–46). New York: Routledge.

Shope, R. E., III. (2006). Teaching science for conceptual change: Toward a proposed taxonomy of diagnostic teaching strategies to gauge students' personal science conceptions. University of Southern California ProQuest Dissertations Publishing.

Shrives, C. Adverbial clause. Grammar Monster. https://www.grammar-monster.com/glossary/adverbial_clauses.htm.

Shrives, C. Grammar Monster. https://www.grammar-monster.com/glossary/euphemism.htm.

Silverstein, S. (1964). *The giving tree*. New York: Harper & Row.

Smagorinsky, P. (2009). The culture of Vygotsky. *Reading Research Quarterly, 44*, 85–95.

Smagorinsky, P. (2011). Vygotsky's stage theory: The psychology of art and the actor under the direction of Perezhivanie. *Mind, Culture, and Activity, 18*(4), 319–341. https://doi.org/10.1080/10749039.2010.518300.

Smith, B. J. (2021). *How much does a great school cost? School economies and school values*. Lanham, MD: Rowman & Littlefield, 132.

Smith, B. J. (2022). *Assessment tools and systems: Meaningful feedback approaches to promote critical and creative thinking*. Lanham, MD: Rowman & Littlefield.

Spandel, V. (2013). *Creating writers: Six traits, process, workshop, and literature*. Boston: Allyn & Bacon.

Spear, T. (2019). *Education reimagined: The schools our children need*. New London, NH: Eaglecliff.

Stowell, D. Prepositions and prepositional phrases. https://www.youtube.com/watch?v=brxQFHE3b6Q.

St. Paul's College. Colloquial language. https://www.youtube.com/watch?v=duQwf2dIWo0.

Studio Binder. https://www.studiobinder.com/blog/what-is-assonance-definition/ (review of alliteration).

The Tech Savvy Educator. https://www.techsavvyed.net/archives/4354.

Thoreau, H. D. (2012). *Walden*. Princeton, NJ: Princeton University Press.

Toastmasters Youth Service Leadership Program. https://www.toastmasters.org/education/youth-leadership-program.

The Touring Teacher. Assonance examples for kids. https://www.youtube.com/watch?v=5dLGAjMGhZs.

Trekkie Channel. Risk is our business. https://www.youtube.com/watch?v=gIU3HrCCT2k.

Tremmel, R. (2001). Seeking a balanced discipline: Writing teacher education in first-year composition and English education. *English Education, 34*(1), 6–30.

United Nations Eleanor Roosevelt Transcript of Speech on Human Rights. (1951). https://www.fdrlibrary.org/documents/356632/390886/Eleanor+Roosevelt+Transcript+of+Speech+on+Human+Rights+1951.pdf/7c4b27f5-0512-46f0-8119-8b57f201caa9.

University of Dayton. The GEMnasium: A test lab for transdisciplinary learning. https://www.youtube.com/watch?v=uns65hnH7-A.

Unsworth, L. (2008). Negotiating multimodal text. In J. Coiro, C. Lankshear, M. Knobel, & D. J. Leu (Eds.), *Handbook of research on new literacies* (pp. 377–406). New York: Routledge, 384.

Urquhart, K. M. (May 2, 2017). 5 honeybee myths, legends & folklore. https://www.hobbyfarms.com/5-honeybee-myths-legends-folklore/.

Us, K. (January 21, 2021). https://medium.com/the-shadow/did-you-catch-them-6-allusions-in-bidens-inaugural-address-b9ed5ec5ce92.

VanDerHeide, J. (2018). Classroom talk as writing instruction for learning to make writing moves in literary arguments. *Reading Research Quarterly, 53*, 323–344.

Veroff, R. (January 31, 2018). Behind the scenes in the broadcast room. New York: Lycee Magazine. https://life.lfny.org/2018/01/31/behind-the-scenes-in-the-broadcast-room-2.

Vico, G. https://en.wikipedia.org/wiki/Giambattista_Vico.

Vox Letters. Foreshadowing. https://www.youtube.com/watch?v=P07O8cacBsk.

Vygotsky, L. (1978). *Mind in society*. London: MIT Press.

Vygotsky, L. (1986). *Thought and language.* London: MIT Press.

Walden University. The benefits of reading aloud to your students. https://www.waldenu.edu/online-bachelors-programs/bs-in-elementary-education/resource/the-benefits-of-reading-aloud-to-your-students.

Warner, C. What is verbal irony? TedEd. https://www.youtube.com/watch?v=IiR-bnCHIYo.

White, E. B. (1952). *Charlotte's web*. New York: HarperTrophy.

Whitney, A. E. (July 2017). Keeping it real: Valuing authenticity in the writing classroom. *English Journal, 106*(6).

Wilcox, B. Literary devices: Flashback. https://www.youtube.com/watch?v=xLyDwslqxiY.

Williams, C., & Lowrance-Faulhaber, E. (2018). Writing in young bilingual children: Review of research. *Journal of Second Language Writing, 42*, 58–69.

Wood, D. (2002). *A quiet place.* New York: Simon & Schuster.

Wood Ray, K., & Laminack, L. (2001). *The writing workshop: Working through the hard parts (and they're all hard parts)*. Urbana, IL: National Council of Teachers of English.

Wormeli, R. (2021). How much does a great school cost? In B. Smith (Ed.), *School economies and school value* (p. 132). Lanham, MD: Rowman & Littlefield.

Wray, D., Beard, R., Raban, B., Hall, N., Bloom, W., Robinson, A., Potter, F., Sands, H., & Yates, I. (1988). *Developing children's writing.* Leamington Spa: Scholastic.

YPO. (April 2, 2015). https://www.ypo.org/2015/04/7-memorable-ways-to-open-a-speech-or-presentation/.

ABOUT THE AUTHORS

Barbara J. Smith, PhD, is a passionate educator who promotes critical and creative thinking in the design of schools and school curriculum.

Hope Blecher, EdD, is an interdisciplinary expert who encourages and inspires educators and schools to engage students in deep learning both inside and outside the traditional school classroom.

Milton Keynes UK
Ingram Content Group UK Ltd.
UKHW011113201123
432908UK00007B/1075

9 781475 873078